After Literacy

Studies in the Postmodern Theory of Education

Joe L. Kincheloe and Shirley R. Steinberg
General Editors

Vol. 184

PETER LANG
New York • Washington, D.C./Baltimore • Bern
Frankfurt am Main • Berlin • Brussels • Vienna • Oxford

John Willinsky

After Literacy

Essays

PETER LANG
New York • Washington, D.C./Baltimore • Bern
Frankfurt am Main • Berlin • Brussels • Vienna • Oxford

LIBRARY OF CONGRESS CATALOGING-IN-PUBLICATION DATA

Willinsky, John.
After literacy: essays / John Willinsky.
p. cm. — (Counterpoints; vol. 184)
Collection of unpublished and previously unpublished essays, articles; the eight previously published essays were originally published 1986/87–2000.
Includes bibliographical references and index.
Contents: Introduction: after literacy—Postmodern literacy: a primer—Qualities of student-adult electronic communications—The paradox of text in the culture of literacy—Curriculum after culture, race, nation—The educational politics of identity and category—Cutting English on the bias: five lexicographers in pursuit of the new—Learning the language of difference: the dictionary of high school—Wittgenstein's dictionary—L'essai d'Edgar Z. Friedenberg—Up the down escalator—The Parker vacumatic and the diaspora—Why Allan isn't my friend anymore.
1. Language and education. 2. Literacy. 3. Lexicography.
I. Title. II. Counterpoints (New York, N.Y.); vol. 184.
P40.8 .W55   306.44—dc21   2001029735
ISBN 0-8204-5242-4
ISSN 1058-1634

DIE DEUTSCHE BIBLIOTHEK-CIP-EINHEITSAUFNAHME

Willinsky, John:
After literacy: essays / John Willinsky.
–New York; Washington, D.C./Baltimore; Bern;
Frankfurt am Main; Berlin; Brussels; Vienna; Oxford: Lang.
(Counterpoints; Vol. 184)
ISBN 0-8204-5242-4

Use of quotation from *Wittgenstein's Nephew* by Thomas Bernhard, copyrighted 1988; reprinted by permission of Alfred A. Knopf, Inc.

Cover photo: *Reading the Suffregette* © Hulton-Deutsch Collection/CORBIS
Cover design by Joni Holst

© 2001 Peter Lang Publishing, Inc., New York

All rights reserved.
Reprint or reproduction, even partially, in all forms such as microfilm, xerography, microfiche, microcard, and offset strictly prohibited.

In memory of
Edgar Z. Friedenberg
1920–2000

Table of Contents

Acknowledgments — xi

Part One: Current — 1

1 / Introduction: After Literacy — 3
This collection of published and previously unpublished essays pursues the forms of literacy that come after the literacy that overcomes illiteracy. Their scope and intent are introduced within current concerns over the schools' responsibilities for producing literate students and sustaining a literate society.

2 / Postmodern Literacy: A Primer — 13
In which a fictional account of a student's project on coyotes is used to develop ten practical principles of a postmodern literacy that might guide not only how we teach the young to read and write but how we teach them to think about reading and writing.

3 / Qualities of Student-Adult Electronic Communication: Immediate, Pedagogical, Aberrant — 41
When a high school class enters into email correspondence with employees of a high-tech firm, it can demonstrate how this medium transcends traditional conventions of print and communication and why this extended literate engagement with the world should give us pause.

Part Two: Cultural — 57

4 / The Paradox of Text in the Culture of Literacy — 59
This reconsideration of the divide between oral and literate cultural traditions explores the continuing intellectual

contribution of the spoken word by drawing a lesson, complete with classroom implications, from the Passover Haggadah's celebration of intellectual interruption and interpretation-without-end.

5 / Curriculum after Culture, Race, Nation — 83
That the study of culture was originally introduced into anthropology a century ago as a way of curtailing the discipline's racism serves as a lesson for new strategies that would let students in on how the concepts of culture, race, and nation have long been used to divide up the world in ways that are by no means to everyone's advantage.

6 / The Educational Politics of Identity and Category — 121
Following on themes raised in the previous chapter, an education is proposed in the categories by which we live and the concepts in which our identities are rooted. Inspired by the work of Simone Weil, this rooted reading of difference is brought to bear on Charles Taylor's and Arthur Schlesinger's opposing takes on multiculturalism.

Part Three: Authoritative — 143

7 / Cutting English on the Bias: Five Lexicographers in Pursuit of the New — 145
Based on visits to major English-language dictionary publishers, the question of how new words find their way into the dictionary becomes a way of revealing the very human art and science of authorizing the language, which otherwise remains hidden in the Wizard-of-Oz-like creation of the dictionary.

8 / Learning the Language of Difference: The Dictionary in the High School — 171
The dictionary's critical role in defining sexuality and sexual difference for high school students is considered by examining how the leading dictionaries used in high schools sustain a number of gendered inequities that once prevailed within the traditions of the language and are ready to be superseded.

9 / Wittgenstein's Dictionary — 187

The development of Wittgenstein's philosophy of language, in which he finally arrives at the idea that meaning is a function of a word's use, is used to temper the sometimes overbearing authority of the dictionary by revealing that it can only offer a reading of how others have worked these words in the past.

Part Four: Personal — 221

10 / L'Essai d'Edgar Z. Friedenberg — 223

This man's abilities as a writer shaped his scholarly contribution far more so than his research studies, as his work amounted to a long and artful essay that cultivated an impassioned caring for life and liberty, in the face of a diminished, if more orderly, semblance of them both.

11 / Up the Down Escalator — 239

The epistemological effectiveness of the academic conferences is assessed from the fictional perspective of a slightly jaded conference participant, caught up in the exasperating enormity of fragmentation and personal ennui felt amid the massive performance of the known and the learned that is the conference.

12 / The Parker Vacumatic and the Diaspora — 253

The overlapping and parallel stories of Jewish and Chinese families on their way to the promised land of the New World are told through the engravings on a Parker fountain pen. The distances crossed, and created in that crossing, speak to how differences have long been written and are still open to rewriting.

13 / Why Allan Isn't My Friend Anymore — 279

This brief autobiographical essay explores how the very idea of literature came between two lifelong students of literacy's great artform, bringing into focus the question of what can be reasonably asked of literacy as a way of living out the power of the word.

Index — 289

Acknowledgments

I know that I cannot adequately thank Shirley Steinberg and Joe Kincheloe, the two indefatigable scholars and series editors who have done so much to advance critical themes and communities in the study of education. Their much appreciated support for this book, as well as for other resonant projects we've undertaken together, always has a good beat and you can dance to it. Given the years that the work in this book represents, I also have the pleasure of recalling and thanking again current, continuing, and former contributors to my research and writing, including Debbie Begoray, Carl Braun, Peter Chin, Lon Dubinsky, Vivian Forssman, Ricki Goldman-Segall, Jim Greenlaw, Anne Hawson, Sandra Hoenle, Lorri Neilsen, Miriam Orkar, Mike Paterson, Janice Penner, Ross Penner, David Piper, Gary Raspberry, Anne White, and Tammy Zambo.

I also want to take the occasion of this collection to acknowledge and honor the contribution of Edgar Z. Friedenberg, not only to my work but far more widely, as he has added to how people understand "the dignity of youth and other atavisms" (to invoke that quality of incisive wit marking his work, and in this case the title of his essay collection). Several years ago, I had the pleasure of serving as his first "successful" doctoral student, when he accepted me, with only two years of full-time university study to my name, into a short-lived program from which no one had yet graduated. Such are the turning points that a life is sometimes offered, and I thank him for it.

The Social Sciences and Humanities Research Council of Canada, the Wm. Allen Chair in Education at Seattle University, and the Peter Wall Institute for Advanced Studies at the University of British Columbia have generously supported aspects of the work represented here. The eight essays in this collection which have been previously published are reprinted here with the kind permission of their original publishers: "Postmodern Literacy: A Primer" appeared in *Interchange*, 22/4 (1991);

"Immediacy, Intimacy, Aberration: E-mail between Worlds" appeared as "Qualities of Student-Adult Electronic Communication: Immediate, Pedagogical, Aberrant" in the *International Journal of Educational Telecommunications* 6/1 (2000); "The Paradox of Text in the Culture of Literacy" appeared in *Interchange*, 18/1-2 (1987); "Curriculum after Culture, Race, Nation" appeared in *Discourse: Studies in the Cultural Politics of Education*, 20/1 (1999); "The Educational Politics of Identity and Category" appeared in *Interchange*, 29/4 (1998); "Cutting English on the Bias: Five Lexicographers in Pursuit of the New" appeared in *American Speech*, 63/1 (1988); "Learning the Language of Difference: The Dictionary in the High School" appeared in *English Education*, 19/3 (1987); and "L'Essai d'Edgar Z. Friedenberg" appeared in the *Dalhousie Review*, 66/4 (1986–87).

PART ONE

CURRENT

Chapter 1

Introduction: After Literacy

The essays gathered here represent work that I've done over the last decade and a half, with some previously published in journals and others set aside as the book they were intended for took on new directions. They speak to aspects of literacy, language and learning, that came out of my work with teachers and students and student-teachers. They address what seemed to me to be notable gaps in all that was said and written about literacy, from the influence of postmodernism on literacy education to the impact of new communication technologies on students' literate reach; from the authority of the dictionary to the identity issues of culture and history, family and friendship. These essays represent my ongoing efforts at working out what it is that we know—and what it is that we care about—when it comes to an education in reading and writing.

My educational aim with these essays, it seems to me now, is simple enough: We need to be students of literacy, to attend to how writing and reading works on us and our comprehension of the world, and we need to understand how this knowledge roughly defines the scope of what we might owe the young when we teach them to read and write. At issue are the hopes, the promises and pleasures, that come of working language's possibilities.

You will notice that the topics that I cover fall outside of what might be considered the normal range of "literacy" topics. They are about the personal, professional, and public framing of the world in language, rather than students' decoding abilities and related pedagogical concerns. These essays do not deal directly, then, with what may seem to be the obvious—perhaps the only—question that a professor of literacy should be addressing, namely, what is the best method for ensuring that all children learn to read and write. Not only the answer but the question itself goes missing in what follows. There is nothing here, for example, on letter-sound correspondences or the cognitive processing of complex text.

If this admission has not led you to immediately put the book down in disappointment, I would ask you to stay with this failing for a moment. My work takes a different tack on literacy, one that runs against its common hold on our educational imaginations. It is true that "literacy" has always been a decidedly educational concept, but that "always" has really not been a very long period of time. The word *literacy* was first used in print, as I've had reason to point out before, by the *New England Journal of Education* in 1883 (according to the *Oxford English Dictionary*) to identify Massachusetts' success in fighting the scourge of illiteracy. This concern for something called literacy comes with the initiation of public education in the industrialized world during the latter half of the 19th century. Literacy is about the institutional eradication of illiteracy among the general population. Literacy's end, it is important to note here, is all about ending illiteracy. We are all born illiterate into this world, and the schools alone, we imagine, hold the path to our literate salvation. Eradicating illiteracy is literacy's goal, and that goal is assessed today with increasing frequency and seeming precision through standardized reading tests.

These test results have focused literacy efforts on improving children's mental capacities, namely, in enhancing their capacity for letter-recognition, word decoding, and sentence comprehension. In the great and nearly century-long debate over how best to teach reading, the phonics-first approach appears to be triumphing over whole-language methods in this era of high-stakes testing. To put it all too simply, the phonics program is intensely focused on overcoming the initial state of original illiteracy, offering greater chances of a child's coming through the test with a better bill of health. Whole-language programs are, perhaps, too far gone on the shared pleasures of the literate state.[1]

I make this claim having devoted a good deal of my research and teaching to the whole-language approach, drawn by what I saw as the romance of the book, over the tedium of the worksheet; and still I tend to support, in my work with teachers and in my research, what is whole in language—whole in its literary expression, whole in its social practices, whole in its larger system of meanings, whole in its definition of the world.[2] But without renouncing this interest in what is whole about language, I have come to respect the highly structured programs that use phonics and other strategies to tackle the reading-score gap between white and black Americans that has been increasing over the last decade (after having narrowed in the 1980s). These programs range from the highly focused schools, such as the Knowledge is Power Program (KIPP) in New

York, which use what I would term a charismatic concentration on academic achievement to increase student results, to the California state system that has adopted a phonics-first policy, as well as reducing class size and cancelling bilingual programs.[3] Given that it is not yet clear exactly what within these programs makes a critical difference, we should all closely follow these sources of hope and inspiration with great interest. The success of these programs has not only posed a healthy challenge to my own educational tendencies. They also speak to the benefits of fostering an educational atmosphere of democratic pluralism, in which one resists promoting ideological consistency in favor of the play and testing of ideas and ideals.

It may well be that determining the best way of teaching the young to read in some universal sense pushes against what the social sciences can ascertain in any helpful way, judging by recent research disputes over relatively small differences in students' ability to decode nonsense syllables.[4] Certainly, the essays in this book do not claim to throw much additional light on these controversies of early literacy. If they are not about what is most likely to improve reading test scores, they are decidedly aimed at the next question: What is it that we would score with these scores? What do we and the students know *of* literacy, and how it works?

The goal in hockey, we used to say in Canada, is *the goal* in hockey. The goal in reading and writing, we too rarely hear education officials say, is not the reading and writing test score. The test score is but a measure of the steps taken toward the goal. The goal of reading and writing, on the other hand, is not so easily identified. It is certainly not a given—not in the workplace, not in the home, not in any one life. Thus, it is very much worth thinking about the purposes and possibilities, the ends to which this literacy has been, can be, and should be turned.

What these essays each try to identify and name are possible goals of this work with written language. Each of them attempts to connect educational issues with the larger history of literate practices and with the ends to which this education in language might well be directed, as those goals are suggested by, for example, the reading the Haggadah at the Passover seder or the spelling of a name on the barrel of a pen. They dare to approach, if only falteringly, the history and mystery of what reading and writing can mean for people. They seek literacy's wonder and fascination, possibility and hope. They are concerned with both the political and the literary sense of literacy's power as they attempt to deepen the wonder of the word, historically and philosophically, rather than resolve it. They go after the workings of language and why that working of language matters. They are about the forms of literacy that come *after* the literacy that is meant to defeat illiteracy.

Rather than reflecting my earlier efforts on behalf of whole language, with its focus on early literacy, the political and historical interests reflected in these essays, if not their literary and philosophical themes, position them within easy reach of two contemporary pedagogical initiatives that go by the name "critical language awareness" and "critical literacy."[5] These critical approaches do take up the literacy education that follows the period which the phonics-versus-whole-language debate concerns. Their rigorous attention to the linguistic and rhetorical elements of literacy takes the breath out of Diane Ravitch's recent charges of antiintellectualism among progressive educators.[6] The work represented here is not of the critical language awareness and critical literacy schools, per se, but is closely enough associated in aspiration and intent to make a comparison speak to shortcomings in both what I do and what they do. After all, it has long been the scholar's habit to dismiss in passing those who have chosen to reside elsewhere while presuming to improve, in some detail, those with whom the scholar has, finally, chosen to sit.

The essays that follow take up specific issues, from the conceptualization of culture to literature's relation to life, all of which have a bearing on what we learn about language. They are critical, in the manner of the critical-literacy and language-awareness initiatives, of the educational "practices and processes of exclusion and inclusion," as Allan Luke names the critical-literacy focal point for "teaching students from the most at-risk groups."[7] Yet my work contributes nothing to critical literacy's program of "direct instruction in the workings of mainstream texts," which Luke points out does much to placate "conservative parents and communities." If my work offers little in the way of "a sophisticated technical language for talking about text" (lexicon, syntax-cohesive ties, discourses, propositional structures) that is featured in critical literacy and language awareness, they do afford their own form of direct instruction in the play of ideas fostered by, among others, Franz Boas, Edgar Z. Friedenberg, Simone Weil, and Ludwig Wittgenstein, while arguing that these are ideas worth sharing with those we would presume to educate in the language.

In reflecting on how these essays might contribute to the critical literacy and language awareness that Luke, Norman Fairclough, and others would foster, I propose that they augment their efforts to equip students with a "tool-kit" of literate resources that will enable them to critically engage the powers that be, with a sense of the history and contingency of this work in language. Students who would be trained in the use of language's powerful and critical tools, also deserve an education in how literacy has assumed its hold on our language and lives. The critical issues in language and literacy are all about the power to delimit people's worlds. These literate abuses of power are the result of long-standing historical projects, like European imperialism, that often draw on the institutional support of the schools. The critical literacy to which this work of mine aspires asks that we become better students of our very ideas about language and literacy. This critical literacy is concerned with identifying the bad habits and profound prejudices in the language that are clearly in need of redressing by teachers and students alike. In this way, my arguments here would augment the critically literate tool-kit, proposed by Luke and Fairclough, which is aimed at helping students analyze how certain institutional uses of language in the media and elsewhere fails them, as it excludes and diminishes the lives of some, and aimed at enabling students to use this critical awareness of how language works to seek redress and remedy.

My contribution is concerned with how such powerful concepts as race and culture have taken shape in the language. Teachers and students need, I am arguing, to understand the history of struggle and promise that has above all marked literacy's critical democratic project. The project is then to identify what can be done within their own sphere of influence to rewrite and reread language's seeming determinations of the world. It can be a matter of small works for a larger cause.

For example, I recently found myself helping a class of high school students in an English literature class transform the school's official sources of knowledge, at least when it came to poetry anthologies, from a decidedly monolingual and monocultural state into a multilingual literary exchange. That is, we ended up creating a hand-made alternative literature anthology for classes to use in the school which featured student and parent translations and analyses of poems from a wide range of languages and nonstandard dialects. Even as the project challenged the school's literary canon, it resonated with literary history, as Chaucer, among others, had found poetic translation greatly enriching of his own work, just as it has always been the broad boast of English that it is a magpie language.[8]

Perhaps the real moment of critical literacy came at the end of this translation project with the high school students, when they took it on themselves to present to the other English teachers in the school why and how they had developed this alternative poetry anthology as a class set for these teachers to use. These students button-holing teachers outside their classes to pitch what these new anthologies offered may have fallen short of what Luke describes as the "Freirian agenda [that] places great stock in the capacity of critical literacy . . . to mobilize larger social movements toward progressive, if not revolutionary, social transformation."[9] Yet it seemed a positive and constructive way of mounting a critique of what the teachers in that school had long been teaching from. Here was a literate act that both challenged (in its non-canonical selection of poetry in other languages) and accommodated (following the textbook-anthology genre) the order of the school. The students became students of the schools' primary literate form, the textbook, in order to mount their critique of this form of knowledge, as it then stood so out of touch, as a Canadian anthology, with the culturally diverse student population. The students turned their critique into an effort to make the school a more inclusive public space, as it would teach students to appreciate how well literature can represent a larger world.

The translation project also did its share, then, to make good on public education's promise to advance democracy.[10] This is an important point, as little enough thought is given to what literacy means for democracy, beyond a basic ability to mark a ballot in an age of sound-bite politics, is rarely considered (with even the ability to properly mark a ballot coming into serious dispute with the United States presidential election in 2000). Luke rightly worries that literacy programs without a critical edge will "make one just literate enough to get in real trouble," referring not to an ability to write one's way into infamy but to a vulnerability that leaves the student susceptible to being "ripped off, ideologically deceived."[11]

Yet I am uneasy with this assumption that this society's dominant voices and texts are written in bad faith and designed to take advantage of people's uncritical literacy. It may just be age, with its onset of creeping liberalism, but I now think that harboring such suspicions as the critical point to literacy is not the best tactic in the struggle for social justice within a democracy. We need a literacy, rather, that encourages students to read the values and interests by which people live. This does mean thinking about what writers are attempting to accomplish with their texts, which may indeed lead one to suspect that ideological deception is at the heart of a text. But harbouring a basic respect for what others are about is a strong starting point, whether for a critical reading of a literary work or a process of democratic deliberation.

This is only to say that we need forms of literacy that work well with the opposition of ideas and the struggle over values in ways that can make greater sense of these differences for more people.[12] More attention could be paid to the special responsibilities of a literacy dedicated, in part, to the expression and extension of democratic justice, responsibilities that we need to explore and develop in our research, scholarship, and pedagogy. Historically, we can trace with students this literate engagement with democracy through the development of the press, popular and public education, paperbacks, and public libraries. We can see the responsibilities owed to one another revered and resisted, embraced and refused, through literature's power to write out our lives. And we can begin to inquire how this literate approach to democracy is going to work in the brave new world of information technologies as well as advocacy politics and global capitalism. The essays in this book provide their own background to this literate formation of our world, as they demonstrate, for example, how such basic concepts as identity are matters of reading and writing each other, and as such are subject to revision.

Extending this idea of literacy as inviting deliberation among people—while dwelling on just how it can work in political and expressive (and in expressively political and politically expressive) contexts—seems to me a suitable end for a literacy that comes after literacy. It leaves us facing a number of challenges in crediting the power of literacy to shape this world.

As teachers, we have tended to focus on improving students' literacy skills (or on stocking their literate tool-kits) largely through lessons and exercises that work best in preparing them for, well, the next year of schooling, if not, perhaps, for a lifetime of school teaching. In the first dozen years of a child's education there is time, I suspect, to do more with these skills and tools than exercise them in anticipation of what is to come. We need to find ways of beginning with the young the very rereading and rewriting of the world that falls to each generation. This is our privilege and responsibility as teachers who are, after all, working directly on the future.

I have also come to realize in recent years that, as scholars and researchers, we may be contributing too little, ourselves, to what follows from this overcoming of illiteracy, too little to foster and enrich the public's education that follows their schooling. In our research on the schools, we have produced a considerable body of research and writing about an institution that the public cares greatly about, yet this writing amounts to a literacy that over the last century has added woefully little to what people know. If the fault is largely ours, so then is the opportunity. As scholars and researchers, we do indeed work hard at rewriting the schools for the better, offering a wide range of ideas about advancing this critical social institution, with much of the work publicly sponsored. Now we need to ensure far more open and intelligible access to the resulting work, as a way of informing public and professional deliberations over education. We need to use our understanding of literacy and learning to organize and support this knowledge, with the help of new information technologies, so that the public and scholarly value of this work will be increased. This is only to say that my next project, as a student of literacy, is concerned with how the research that we do at the university can contribute to a larger sense of public education and public literacy. Whereas the present book is taken up with how literacy works on the world, what follows for me is finding new ways of increasing the chances that the larger body of research and scholarship can make a far more vital and critical contribution to the future of democratic literacy, deliberation, and action.[13]

Notes

1. Given that this testing and standards approach to literacy tends to favor palliative, remedial approaches, the research supporting the phonics-first approach is still not as strong as is suggested by, for example, the flawed but highly influential survey of Bonita Grossen's white paper "Thirty Years of Research: What We Know about How Children Learn to Read," Center for the Future of Teaching and Learning, Santa Cruz, Calif., 1997. For a critique of this work as well as a review of its legislative influence, see Richard Allington and Haley Woodside-Jiron, "The Politics of Literacy Teaching: How 'Research' Shaped Educational Policy," *Educational Researcher* 28, 8 (1999): 4–13, with a countering response in Patricia Mathes and Joseph K. Torgensen, "A Call for Equity in Reading Instruction for All Students: A Response to Allington and Woodside-Jiron," *Educational Researcher* 29, 6 (2000): 4–15.

2. See my *The New Literacy: Redefining Reading and Writing in the Schools* (New York: Routledge, 1990).

3. See the following articles, all in the *New York Times*: Kate Zernike, "Gap Widens Again on Tests Given to Blacks and Whites" (August 25, 2000), A14; Jodi Wilgoren, "With Ideas and Hope, a School Goes to Work" (August 23, 2000), A1; Jacques Steinberg, "Test Scores Rise, Surprising Critics of Bilingual Ban" (August 20, 2000), A1; and Jodi Wilgoren, "National Study Examines Reasons Why Pupils Excel" (July 26, 2000), A14.

4. Barbara M. Taylor, Richard C. Anderson, Kathryn H. Au & Taffy E. Raphael, "Discretion in the Translation of Research to Policy: A Case From Beginning Reading," *Educational Researcher*, 29, 6(2000), pp. 16–26, available at http://www.aera.net/pubs/er/arts/29-06/forman01.htm *versus* Barbara R. Foorman, Jack M. Fletcher, David J. Francis & Chris Schatschneider, "Misrepresentation of Research by Other Researchers" *Educational Researcher*, 29, 6(2000), pp. 27–37, available at http://www.aera.net/pubs/er/arts/29-06/forman01.htm

5. See Norman Fairclough, "Global Capitalism and Critical Awareness of Language," *Language Awareness* 8, 2 (1999), draft available at http://www.schools.ash.org.au/litweb/norman1.html; Allan Luke, "Critical Literacy in Australia," *Journal of Adolescent and Adult Literacy* 43 (2000), available at http://www.btr.qld.edu.au/papers/critlit.htm; and New London Group, "A Pedagogy of Multiliteracies: Designing Social Futures," *Harvard Educational Review* 66, 1 (1996): 60–92.

6. Diane Ravitch, *Left Behind: A Century of Failed School Reform* (New York: Simon & Schuster, 2000).

7. Luke, "Critical Literacy in Australia."

8   See my *Empire of Words: The Reign of the OED* (Princeton, N.J.: Princeton University Press, 1994), 104–10.

9   Luke, "Critical Literacy in Australia."

10 Fairclough puts considerable weight on how critical language awareness is necessary for "effective democratic citizenship" in "Global Capitalism."

11 Luke, "Critical Literacy in Australia."

12 See Ian Shapiro, *Democratic Justice* (New Haven, Conn.: Yale University Press, 2000): "A democratic conception . . . aims at enabling people to live by their values, but always in ways that permit opposition and take due account of the affected interests of others" (p. 232).

13 As every introduction is an act of self-promotion, this work on research's contribution to public literacy is found in my *Technologies of Knowing: A Proposal for the Human Sciences* (Boston: Beacon, 1999) and *If Only We Knew: Increasing the Public Value of Social Science Research* (New York: Routledge, 2000).

Chapter 2

Postmodern Literacy: A Primer

It may seem that for the sake of literacy, postmodernism is too much fashion and too little education. Postmodernism is about the new, artful, clever. It wants for serious didactic purpose; it plays too far from the school grounds. It is more cluttered than modern, and not so much cool (that was modernism) as ironically engaged. What could such fashion offer classrooms—a theory of conspicuous consumption or a consumption of conspicuous theory?

I can appreciate the suspicion, the due sense of caution. Fashion in school has always meant trouble. Yet fashion is hardly absent from the way we do schooling. Fashion has come and not yet gone in education. School stockrooms are stacked with once fashionable instructional packages and textbooks that no one now seems to know what to do with. And not all of those dated ideas are in storage. Walk the terrazzo corridors of any school and overhear, classroom by classroom, a short history of modern teaching techniques presented in random order.

Perhaps fashion is not the problem. Consider the other side of its reversible jacket. Fashion is renewal. It is a self-conscious effort at redefinition. It recycles whole periods in what must strike us today as an ecologically sound idea. It restores the disregarded and enriches the taken-for-granted environment. Fashion is a form of cultural labor, and postmodernism is currently a working fashion, working hard. But at what precisely?

The postmodern deals in styles, trades in theories, and plays with language parenthetically. It is a cultural development and an environmental issue. The mixed-period skyscraper, with stone and brass, skylight and gargoyle, is postmodernism's building block. The neoclassical shopping mall, a simulacrum of the village marketplace, is its consumptive playground. The rock video, with *American Bandstand*–style lip-synching and computer-cut graphics, is its musical wallpaper. The shelves of the chain bookstore carry a small section of self-de(con)structing literature, each book speaking to itself about the futility of its own theory of fiction, with Kathy Acker's *Empire of the Senseless* shelved next to Julian Barnes's *A History of the World in 10 1/2 Chapters*. These are snapshots from the popular culture of the postmodern. Even a substantial footnote could only begin to define it, but then this entire paper is a working definition of postmodernism's potential contribution to the literate culture of a classroom.[1]

Given the mark made by postmodernism on the skyline, airwaves, and bookshelves, I think it is time to consider what classrooms can gain by this current wave of cultural expression. This is to ask what sorts of lessons for education lie in current cultural events; it is to ask what literacy can learn from the sister arts. On these grounds, I want to experiment with postmodernism's offerings, especially as they might further the pleasures of the text for the young.

Clearly, postmodernism is not without its dangers. One has to be selective, strategic, political, committed. I would follow E. Ann Kaplan (1988), for example, in favoring postmodernism's utopian instincts over its grossly commercial inclinations. Henry Giroux (1991) seems on the right educational track in promoting the critical virtues of postmodernism that arise from freeing ourselves from the determinations of self and essence, seeking out the potential for this way of thinking to extend the democratic sphere. But within this political agenda, I also favor postmodernism's literary project, with its self-consciously playful regard for the workings of the word. Think of Milan Kundera opening his novel *Immortality* by describing how he came to invent the book's hero, Agnes, from the gesture of a woman he happened to see at a swimming pool: "Just as Eve came from Adam's rib, just as Venus was born of the waves, Agnes sprang from the gesture of that sixty-year-old woman at the pool who waved at the lifeguard and whose features are already fading from my memory" (1991, p. 35).

Postmodernism's critical, democratic, pedagogic, and playful utopianism would seem to warrant a hearing when it comes to discussing the future of literacy, and this seems the right time to consider what it has to offer. A decade ago, art critic Clement Greenberg could refer to postmodernism as "a rather new term" (1991, p. 43); now, after infusing the entire cultural scene, the first exaggerated rumors of its demise can be found among the headlines of the *New York Times:* "As It Must to All, Death Comes to Post-Modernism" (Grundberg, 1990). Linda Hutcheon, who championed it in *A Poetics of Postmodernism* (1988) and *The Politics of*

Postmodernism (1989), has now coauthored a seemingly nostalgic *Remembering Postmodernism* (Cheetham & Hutcheon, 1991). Before we forget postmodernism, I want to argue that there is something of educational value to this cultural movement.

We might begin by booting up postmodernism's program and working with its menu of *appropriation, history, irony, ornament, pastiche,* and *production values.* The principle of appropriating style and history to create new forms of education seems amenable to easing stressed school budgets as well as to furthering a sense of democratic, imaginative, critical, artful, and restorative participation. It is a familiar story of curriculum profiting from outside cultural influences. What is perhaps most radical about the self-conscious, if irreverent, postmodern approach is its potential to foster not only more literate students but, in what has become a key phrase for me, *students of literacy,* who are interested in how various forms of the written word dominate a culture.

Let me show you how this might work by demonstrating throughout this chapter a little of postmodernism's eclectic style. To create this primer on postmodern literacy, I've decided to appropriate two rhetorical devices: the principle and the story. Both principles and stories are handy mnemonic devices, the one offering an aphoristic tidiness and the other a seductive grip. Certainly with principles, no less than with commandments, there should be 10.

The First Principle of Postmodern Literacy

Approach cultural movements with an eye to the opportunity and advantage inherent in their forms.

It may still seem that postmodernism is one cultural fashion that does not bode well for literacy. "Postmodern literacy" sounds oxymoronic amid sound bites, rock videos, promos, miniseries, and zapper games. The prevailing ethos seems to be aliteracy bordering on literaphobia. "Today we can speak of an Image World," art critic Lisa Phillips observes, "a specific media of culture of teletransmissions, channels, feedback, playback, and interface that has produced a televisual environment" (1989, p. 57). Not only do we continue to read the Image World to find our way, but we do so only by virtue of inference, deduction, and hypothesis testing, not to mention irony and skepticism.

This ineffable visuality has been exceedingly scripted. Do not forget that it is written out first, not only metaphorically but literally too. As it now stands, we are read to constantly by the media, like patient children of attentive parents. Bedtime stories—can we go to sleep without them? The word moves through a dozen hands, from script to teleprompter to our ear as we sit propped up on our pillows. At the heart of it remains writing, draft by draft, composed, rehearsed, and revised to maximize its effect. Postmodernism is postliterate *only* in this sense of the word writ large, beyond the page. I take from Andrew Ross's clever quip that postmodernism is "the continuation of modernism by other means" (1988, p. ix) that it is also the continuation of literacy by other means. Teletransmission has given the written word that much greater a power to proliferate. Gutenberg invented only one in a series of public broadcasting systems.

If postmodern culture extends the reach of the word in fact, it does no less in theory. Those who work in postmodern theory could not make more of the text. To understand the extent of this textuality, a distinction needs to be introduced between the modern and the postmodern. Modernity, at its theoretical best, offered us structuralism. Structuralism read the world as if it were a text. Think of the French anthropologist Claude Lévi-Strauss's close reading of the raw and the cooked, stories told round the campfire, and the incest taboo in *Tristes tropiques* (1961). He practiced a form of literary criticism on the cultures visited by Western intellectual tourism.

Postmodern theorists go an extra step, beyond reading the world *as if it were a book*. In the continuation to which Ross refers, they have it that our knowing is best understood as itself a text, composed, written, fabricated out of what is always already there, awash in history and culture. We live within the text(ure) of the world; it is what makes the world sensible. The ways in which we come to the world, as we wake up in it each sleepy morning, are responses to the daily script(ure) of our lives. Can we really stand face-to-face with an immediate, untexted reality without turning it into one of our stories?

The notorious French philosopher Jacques Derrida is the exemplary postmodern.[2] Derrida both revels in this textualization of our understanding and dares to undo the certainty to which texts aspire. Texts come undone in Derrida's hands, and he rebinds them, inserting his own pages. For Derrida, the search for the truth about our lives—seemingly the heart of the writing project—can be grounded neither in some nontextual, extrahuman sphere nor in some secure inner soul of human certainty. But do not lose hope. Deconstruction's bark is worse than its nip. It is about the play of texts, after all, and language is child's play for Derrida.

He puns his way deeply into the language, troping in many tongues. At the extreme, in *Glas* (1986), for example, he breaks up the page to sustain multiple analysis, each set in its own typeface, each offering its own mode of inquiry on a common theme as if there was always more than one story to tell about any given story.

Yet what can deconstruction mean for the classroom? a number of critics have asked Derrida. Although Derrida has been involved with a group dedicated to the teaching of philosophy in the schools, he identifies his abiding interest in language as the very thing the schools may not be able to tolerate: "What this institution cannot bear is for anyone to tamper with language. . . . It can bear more readily the most apparently revolutionary ideological sorts of 'content,' if only that content does not touch the borders of language and all of the juridico-political contracts that it guarantees" (1974, pp. 124–125). I am arguing against these Derridean doubts, in the hope that a postmodern interest in the border country can find a place in more than a few classrooms. An education in the language is at issue and, contractually, we can and must hold the schools to their promise of an education.[3]

(Think of a student beginning to write a report for school about the coyote, the prairie wolf, Canis latrans, in the measured prose of her reference books. There are facts, maps, and photographs. She starts making notes and tracing maps as she has done many times before. In reading the entry in the *Canadian Encyclopedia* on coyotes by a professor of zoology, she is given pause by his concluding sentence: "They are considered, mistakenly, a threat to livestock" [Churcher, 1985]. This stops her cold. Something has gone wrong. Her father has lost more than 120 sheep on their Cape Breton farm to coyotes over the last two years. She has seen the slaughtered sheep lying in the field, spotted with blood, as she rides the morning bus to school, and she has seen the coyotes at dusk running free over the ridges of the hills on her way home. The killings have been written up in the newspaper [Bruce, 1991], and her father clipped the article out and stuck it on the fridge. Feeling a break between these different versions of the coyote in both the facts and in her own feelings, she decides to divide the pages of her project in half. She reserves the top for the encyclopedic "facts" describing these proud creatures of nature but sets aside the bottom of each page for a story of a Cape Breton sheep farmer whose life and livelihood have become a battle with a coyote pack. When her father notices one of the charts she has prepared, which situates the coyote's indisputable role in nature's web, he begins to wonder if the prairie creatures that have invaded the island are coming between his daughter and him. But for her, the whole project still carries an air of uncertainty.)

The postmodern inquiry into literacy reveals the ways in which writing does not so much mirror or reflect a given reality but begins to *constitute* reality and the realms of possibility. We live by texts. We are written by them, and some we write. This calls for close readers and careful writers. It asks the world of them. The seriousness of writing's constitutional work is made sharply apparent by sociologist Dorothy Smith (1990). She speaks of the "documentary realities" established by social agencies, bureaucratic as well as educational. These agencies are adept at constructing a "textual surface of objectified knowledge" that tends to govern their clients' lives (p. 101). Smith examines instances in which women in professional positions are discounted as informed speakers while other women turning to the health professions for help are made to feel their dependence and subordination in the home. These, too, are reading and writing lessons. "Objectified knowledge," Smith goes on to say, "as we engage with it, subdues, discounts, and disqualifies our various interests, perspectives, angles, and experiences, and what we might have to say speaking from them" (p. 80). The challenge is to sort through the texts, to choose among them, and to find a place for one's own story as well as a form to make it stick—all in the face of those who have the power to write that story otherwise.

The Second Principle of Postmodern Literacy

The diffuse and unsteady realm of text constantly works through forms of authority to define the world within us and without us.

Although one might expect it to be otherwise, this postmodern absorption in textuality turns out rather badly for the author. If the world is so much text, it proves to be so little author. Thus, French critic Roland Barthes is only too happy to celebrate the "death of the author" (1986). Again, this may not seem to bode well for literacy. However, it turns out to be a staged death, a timely, melodramatic end for romantic conceptions of the grand author, banishing the vision of text as a solitary expression of creative genius born ex nihilo and whole out of the furrowed brow of the troubled writer. In *S/Z* (1974) for example, Barthes deflates the author image of Honoré de Balzac by asking of his novella *Sarrasine*, "Who is speaking here?" The question is posed to reveal the degree to which Balzac's novella is spoken, in fact, by the various cultural codes that constituted the realm of meaning for the author and his readers: "Each code is one of the forces that can take over the text (of which the text is the network), one of the voices out of which the text is woven" (Barthes, 1974, p. 21). How strange this is. The world is made text by postmodern text(ile) workers; writing is reduced to a labor of scissors and paste in a Borgean library of endless texts. Balzac's towering genius is virtually buried, as if folded within his great housecoat, as in Rodin's sculpture of the man. He is treated at best as an amanuensis, a transcriber of the already written. Yet Barthes's motives are highly literate. He would keep the book from being contained by the writer's own intentions, meanings, experiences, and language as the origin and thus final arbiter of its meaning. Barthes spills the book over the page, revealing the social, literary, and sexual codes that have written the writer as much as vice versa.[4]

I want Barthes in my postmodern classroom to bring the craft of writing back to earth, from its scared realms of Romantic genius. Barthes appreciates Balzac's skillful rendering of the codes, and his deft weaving of those codes makes its own contribution to the already written, a weaving which other writers will take from in turn: "The artist is infallible not by the sureness of his performance (he is not merely a good copyist of 'reality') but by the authority of his competence; it is he who knows the code, the origin, the basis, and he becomes the guarantor, the witness, the author *(auctor)* of reality" (1974, p. 167). Barthes offers a new job description for the writer—"*pasticheur,*" "a public scribe." But then we, all of us, are workers in codes. To write, as to speak, is to feel the limits of a certain set of codes; it is also to push against their form (as I push here).

But, Balzac aside, what of the young *pasticheur?* Think of the curricular implications for a composition class. Students are invited to work with the codes that we live within, to pick up the pieces of what is already written and begin arranging them on the page afresh, drifting away from the models as far as they dare. This, surely, is a lot less intimidating than asking the young to call on the font of genius from deep within. Yet it is no less than what Chaucer and Shakespeare did to set English literature in motion. The terror of the blank white page, that great floundering Moby-Dick, is exchanged for a Barthean "copying a (depicted) copy of the real" (1974, p. 55). *Copying*—the very code word of less-than-dedicated students. This form of re-creation is still work—copying requires craft—but the metaphysical burden of originality is sent safely heavenward. It is not that we live within a fixed universe of meaning and energy, but that for too long we have not given credit to how incremental the gains are and how they are based on an infrastructure of the already written.[5]

(The Cape Breton student working on her coyote project leafs through a stack of materials on the coyote, some dating back to the 1940s, which she obtained by writing to a number of provincial ministries of wildlife and game. There are bounty and warning notices, pamphlets on rabies and protective fencing, bumper stickers, copies of eradication and protection motions brought before the provincial legislatures. With each decade, the state seems to have taken a different bearing on the creature, as friend or foe. As she sorts through these documents, she catches the mournful baying of the coyotes moving about the foothills at the edge of the farm. She begins to imagine the coyotes' mottled coats as pages of print in motion. How is she to read them, as they circle round the sheep that form part of her life on that Cape Breton farm, as they slip through the trees, as they run free by the sea? She hears her father going for his hunting rifle in the back porch, hears the chains of the leghold traps rattle as he gathers them up, and it is clear to her that she doesn't know what to think of "the wily coyote." But she is beginning to see how the animal has been put together in many versions, some she can abide by and others she has begun to abhor. She re-sorts her papers and documents in different orders, watching how the meaning of them seems to change, as she hears the back door quietly close.)

In the word was the beginning. The postmodern temperament, in theory and practice, still possesses a passion for producing text. Postmodernism makes a hypertext of what is painted, designed, composed, played, acted, and filmed. This interest in textual production accords well with progressive literacy developments already afoot in the schools. With the rise of the writing-process and reader-response movements, students are producing considerably more writing, a writing in which they have a far greater stake than in traditional composition exercises (Willinsky, 1990b). The postmodern classroom that I envision only adds to this trend, extending the students' literate reach electronically as well as historically. The postmodern interest in production values, its playful and crafty attention to details and design, serves as an incentive for exploring new vehicles of expression.[6] This approach takes advantage of the fact that most schools are gradually acquiring the technical resources of a small publishing house and the electronic ability to network with the world. It should be enough to send students scurrying to the prop room of history to dress their work in aspects of Aesop's fables, Shakespeare's sonnets, or the chapbooks, manifestos, and graphics of the eighteenth, twentieth, and twenty-first centuries respectively. The right to cite—in fact its very necessity and artfulness—is understood as literacy's way, as if to recover afresh words and codes of other times.

Such a playful literacy cannot please everyone. Fredric Jameson, for one, bemoans the loss of the "monumental" work at the hands of the scatterbrained postmodernist who, in Jameson's colorful language, "ceaselessly reshuffles the fragments of preexistent texts, the building blocks of older cultural and social production, in some new and heightened bricolage: metabooks which cannibalize other books, metatexts which collate bits of other texts" (1987, p. 223). Yet is this not also the literacy of the Romantics in their feeling for the ruins, fragments, and traces of the idyllic past? Gregory Ulmer rebuts these concerns of Jameson's by pointing to the cannibalism by which scholarship cites and thrives (1989, p. 13). This is reading and writing drawn from the resources of the already written and made new. Acts of representation and events of signification, metatexts and hungry writers ready to consume their own kind are the constant topic of study and purpose of activity–the power and the pleasure. Writing and reading. It is as E. M. Forster, albeit a mere modernist among novelists, had it—*only connect*.

The Third Principle of Postmodern Literacy

We participate in the circulation of meanings as readers, first of all, and then as writers and critics.

No one drops out of circulation. Certainly, the young are already plugged into this "textual circuitry." Hip-hop and rap music are citation-prone and allusion-proud. It is only for us to join them in understanding how far the linking of cultural efforts on different fronts can go. The postmodern is a mixed economy of art and commerce, of what were once discretely elite and popular cultural forms.[7] As clip art abounds in the postmodern, the value of the creative act becomes an intellectual, legal, and economic battlefield. Yet this exchange is not a matter of free trade in ideas. It runs on an intricate credit system that students also need to learn. This is an age of intellectual properties, the real estate of the mind. Intellectual property has become the best investment in town, and disputes over it are a regular stay of the courts. However regrettable this may seem to anyone who has lived on the open road, the economy of the imagination speaks to the worldly powers of the word.

Raymond Williams offers an illuminating metaphor for bringing our visions of art down to street level in a postmodern fashion. As a literary critic interested in the relationship between literature and society, he found it best to treat writing as, in effect, a "means of production" (1980). If this cultural materialism seems to diminish the likes of Balzac, it elevates what students do when they write; they are producing texts, texts that should, on occasion, enter into the circulation of meanings in their community and beyond. For Williams, the question was always simple enough, and really a variation on Barthes's: Who is given the opportunity to communicate to whom about what? The question carried Williams through the complex fabric of England's social history, in which the disenfranchised, through the press and education, gradually obtained a measure of public voice as a result of a "long revolution" (1961). This question is part of the social history of literacy and it seems yet another lesson worth teaching to those finding their own, often difficult way into the language.

My brief with intellectual property rights is to teach the young in a frank manner how the word works in an economic as well as a political and moral fashion.[8] They can explore how cultural production invokes legal rights/rites and gives rise to certain responsibilities for what is represented. Postmodernism speaks as well to the writer's renewed liability for acts of representation, for the use of codes and texts, history and artifact. This postmodern textualization adds to the importance of representation as a defining or constituting process. Salman Rushdie's literary postmodernism is, of course, the most provocative point for considering how literature continues to participate in the documentary reality of the world and on a global scale. Our shock at Ayatollah Khomeini's deadly review of Rushdie's postmodern efforts to rewrite the texts of Islam is due in some part to the West's current regard for the word. It is, no less than other goods, a commodity to be attractively packaged and promoted for quick sale. What is the fuss? nonbelievers insensitively seem to ask their Moslem friends who were not prepared to buy Rushdie's words as art. The West's dominant economy of signs and goods calls for careful reading lessons of the means of literate production.

The Fourth Principle of Postmodern Literacy

Appreciate that pop songs, literary works, billboards, TV news, and the law are means of cultural production situated, more than ever, at the busy intersection of commerce and state.

There remains another postmodern tenet that can be drawn from Williams's treatment of communication as a means of production. Having questioned the writer as the pure originator of texts, the postmodern is willing to allow that readers and writers are produced by writing. What can be made of this rewritten self, especially among those who aren't given to writing in classrooms, is, in effect, a question Shannon Bradley Green and I asked of junior high school students when we recruited a number of them into a magazine-publishing project (Willinsky & Green, 1991). One student offered us his answer by writing about his brush with the law. Sam's editorial about police disregard for teenagers illustrated the point by telling of his arrest for being in a car with a boy who shot someone with a BB gun. Appropriating both legal and editorial language, Sam constructed the certainty of his innocence and the miscarriage of justice that the incident represented. As we encouraged him to write his piece—and he was indeed a "reluctant writer"—we could see him build a case out of the language of others, the language of power: "We both didn't own the gun, neither of us fired the gun and we didn't aid them [the shooters] in any way." Utilizing the aid-and-abet language of the legal system allowed him to construct himself as innocent, that is, within the system's categories and yet on his terms.

A young woman in the study accomplished as much through her editorial on the issues separating teachers and students in her school. Linda positioned herself at the center, resolving differences through a policy of mutual respect between the two parties:

> Perhaps if we could just take into consideration that the teachers have a job to do educating us and that we make it difficult by being hard to get along with, then maybe we wouldn't get hassled so much. As well, if teachers wouldn't assume that we are guilty until proven innocent and realize that treating us with respect will get them a lot further than bullying us, then perhaps some peace could come to the education system, and both parties could enjoy school a lot more than they do now.

Her subtle, repeated "perhaps" holds out the possibility of reconciliation to both parties. As a handicapped student recently "mainstreamed" into the school, Linda presumably had not had the chance previously to take up such a form of discourse. She turned her status as an outsider to her advantage, adding a leaf to her own book and to the circulation of meanings in the school.

This is not a whole-language discovery of students' own story; it is the making of a new one, a public one, out of the available language of others. The magazine articles written by Sam and Linda became, if only for a moment, part of who these young writers were—the part of them they had made against many of the expectations others had for them.

The Fifth Principle of Postmodern Literacy

You are made, and made over, by acts of expression and assertion.

Writers have always known and done this. To focus on this aspect of cultural production, in postmodernism's self-conscious manner, is to add to the teacher's responsibility for encouraging students to get their words out where they can see them moving others. The hope of the postmodern for education, and the state at large, is its extension of participation in culture and the resulting proliferation of expression. To let students in on the contest of meanings, to see how the forms that dominate the realm of public discourse can be appropriated, challenged, and rewritten in other people's images, would seem to hold a promise of a certain good beyond the classroom. Postmodern literacy, when kept to this sense, examines how power is written and circulated. It is committed not just to forms of pluralism but also to understanding how the differences are encoded forms of power and that the high and the low, the center and the margin, the dominant and the silent need cutting and repasting.[9]

A student of literacy should be more than a little interested, for example, in the wave of democratic revolution that has swept Eastern Europe. The changes have been underwritten, truly, by *samizdat*, the constant struggle of an underground-press movement and a community of writers in exile that continued to smuggle the word back and forth through the Iron Curtain until it was so perforated that it collapsed from its own weight. Closer to home, there have been the "counterpropaganda" efforts of ACT UP, the AIDS Coalition to Unleash Power, founded in 1987 (Crimp & Rolston, 1990). Beginning with the chilling equation "Silence = Death," this group has mounted a massive graphics campaign to end significant mistreatment amid the AIDS crisis. The power of word and image in the group's work has turned more than a few heads. The disease is no longer met with silence. It is finding tragic expression in journalism, theater, music, and many forms of creative writing. The representation of AIDS and those who suffer with it becomes part of what the disease means and part of how it will be treated.

The key to tying together Eastern Europe's and the gay community's disparate literacies is, perhaps, Jean-François Lyotard's analysis of the postmodern condition (1984). He finds in our time a certain unraveling of the "grand narratives" of legitimation, of which he identifies principally two: the narratives of scientific progress that underwrite accounts of knowledge, and narratives of emancipation that legitimate state actions. The grand plots of history, whether written by Christian, Enlightenment, imperialist, or Marxist interests, are giving way to local assertions of autonomy that explore new forms of expression and confront the old stories with new ones. Communities have always had their many texts, but not all of them have been openly spoken. Clearly, the emerging sense of polyphony to which Lyotard draws our attention amounts to a utopian vision of postmodern literacy. There remain economic and religious signs that Lyotard's obituary for the reign of the master narratives may be a little premature.[10]

One challenge this literacy faces is finding another language that extends beyond the dominant stories, and many teachers know that this is not always easy in the local setting of the classroom: "Talking with students, with people who come to lectures," bell hooks observes, "I have had the pain of fragmentation deeply impressed upon my consciousness. The alienation felt by many people who are concerned about domination—the struggle we have even to make of our words a language that can be shared" (1988, p. 3). The postmodern interest in language and literacy, as I am casting it, is to understand how some texts more than others constitute reality. But it is also to find ways of "talking back," to take up hooks's theme. As a youngster, she learned that "to make my voice, I had to speak, to hear myself talk—and talk I did—darting in and out of grown folks' conversations and dialogues, answering questions that were not directed to me, endlessly asking questions, making speeches" (pp. 5–6). Hooks may have been duly punished, but she was on her way to a more promising form of literacy.

The centers of a former certainty cannot hold. The postmodern academy is gutting and remodeling the dilapidated mansions of critical theory and literary canon. Boundaries are blurred between the literary and the critical. Criticism has taken on a new life, and literature resounds with fresh voices issuing from new categories of hyphenated expression—native, postcolonial, immigrant. Defenders of the old order, perhaps shaken by the loss of the once tidy "five-foot shelf" of classics, maintain the investment value of their own cultural literacy. Yet many educators welcome the proliferation of expression for the doors it opens to new works and to the constant reworking of the world by the silent and dispossessed, with many students surely among them.

The Sixth Principle of Postmodern Literacy

You no longer need to take your story from that narrow shelf of master narratives.

Not all is deconstruction and demise in the postmodern. Down fall canon and author; up go broader principles of the text amid a new wave of architectural splendor across city centers. (Arche)texture has been the most prominent breeding ground of postmodern élan. Stylized inscriptions borrowed from other periods dominate the cityscape in a return to arches, cornices, porticoes, gargoyles. The blank page is no longer an architectural motif. Buildings have become texts, line by line, detail by detail. They begin to tell stories again in their play with tradition. False walls speak volumes. Fictional rather than functional representation prevails. At first glance, it may well seem the perfect match for the schoolroom. The young take easily to the decorative, finding delight in show and tell, elaboration and intricacy. Yet, of course, there is something more at stake with postmodern architecture than this seemingly innocent pleasure.

While embellished skyscrapers and renovated houses add visual interest to the city, postmodern architecture often houses the wealthy at work and home. In this way, the stylish use of classical order, built beyond the reach of the homeless, still harks back to the original, if now lost, meaning of *sacrifice* (Hersey, 1988). These structures delineate and contain those who would remove themselves to their own self-celebratory world financed by an increasing disparity between the rich and the poor that has been the pathetic but persistent economic theme of the last two decades (Phillips, 1990). Or as Heinrich Klotz notes in properly architectural terms, "the monumentalization of portico" becomes symptomatic of an "orchestration of decorative embellishments for the surface of containers—in short as a packaging aesthetic" (1988, p. 425).

But what and whom are architects and their clients packaging? Here again arises the particular politics of pleasure (Jameson, 1988). Knowingly, cautiously, take beauty and the return of human shapes to architecture. Read them as a writing out of interests. Watch for the counterreadings, the rewritings. Martha Rosler, for example, has organized a critique of the postmodern city that amounts to a cultural assault on an economy that favors the building of high-rise "fortresses" as "enclaves of wealth on the terrain of the poor" (1991, p. 17). Rosler brought together a number of artists and community activists in a project entitled "If You Lived Here," which was made up of public forums, exhibitions, and alternative-housing plans, all in search of ways of returning the city to its constituents. Her project amounts to keeping alternative texts and reversed perspectives in circulation.

The Seventh Principle of Postmodern Literacy

What is at stake in the poetics of cultural forms is the packaging of power in a regime of truth that can, on occasion, be told otherwise.

Just as buildings under the postmodern spell take on new textures that speak to the classroom project, so visual artists turn their canvases to the word. Their artful use of words, consistent with the postmodern theory I have discussed, is a rejection of art's claims to direct representation.[11] The painting is framed, the postmodern artist reminds us, to set it off from the world. It exists in its own order of signs. It, too, signifies the text(ure) or codes we search for in living. John Constable's romantic landscapes signify a lost English Eden, Jackson Pollock's a confronted angst. The picture re-presents a theory, a text, that would count as the world; it is no window on the countryside (itself a common and telling romantic theme from the art of the 19th century). Recognizing that the well-painted tree is no more real than the word *tree,* many artists are finding the power of the word, the slogan, and the telling phrase as a way of extending their palette.

Jenny Holzer is a particularly dedicated instance of a postmodern literacy at work. She shows remarkable courage in situating her art in new arenas of the public sphere, as if her art mattered enough to get it out of the gallery. Imagine sitting in the stands at a ball game or pulling into the Caesar's Palace parking lot in Las Vegas as the electronic display begins to flash a series of her "truisms": "MONEY CREATES TASTE," "ABUSE OF POWER SHOULD COME AS NO SURPRISE," "TURN SOFT AND LOVELY ANY TIME YOU HAVE THE CHANCE." In *The Survival Series,* the aphorisms not only appear on electronic signs but also are printed on stickers for easy distribution across the urban landscape. When placed on parking meters and garbage cans, they become part of the environmental press, participating in that cityscape even as they represent and appropriate it: "Go where people sleep and see if they are safe"; "It is in your self interest to find a way to be very tender"; "When there is no place to sleep you're tired from walking all day and exhausted from the night because it's twice as dangerous then." Art seems to be doing and renewing the work of thoughtful language—caring, pointed, and somewhat ironic, if not bemused.

What is Holzer trying to sell? Her texts may seem, at first, to be fish out of water. But we soon realize that they cause us to take stock of the language environment that we have been swimming in. Her insinuating messages of social commentary ("PROTECT ME FROM WHAT I WANT") turn up in contexts that we have learned to read as if they couldn't mean anything, really, but that now clearly do at a number of new levels. Her work constitutes a postmodern decoding lesson of the first order. This appropriation of literacy is in the name of art's engagement with meaning and representation. It occurs at the very point where language is losing any hope of the free and dangerous play of meaning in its public display. "In a dream you saw a way to survive and you were full of joy" (cited in Waldman, 1989, pp. 68–81).

The Eighth Principle of Postmodern Literacy

Ask after language in public forums: What is it up to? What does it make of us? Then try turning it to different purposes.

How is it, you might ask, that public discourse is reduced to the one-liner posted in rented space? The marginalization of art in the public landscape is troubling, but that should not prevent educators from seriously considering where the public life of language is headed and how this development can be challenged and played against itself, as Holzer is doing.

(The deadline is approaching for the coyote project, even as our student of the creature is increasingly unsure of what the project should be about. She keeps getting drawn away from the given categories of the report—description, habitat, range, food, reproductive cycle, and related species. First there were the troubling facts in the encyclopedia, and now she has been thinking about the fading bounty notices for coyotes that remain stapled to fence posts along the road. She did not pay any attention to the notices before, but now when she comes across them, they rile her as rifle shots did when she was walking over to one of the neighboring farms. She wonders what else an official notice could say about the coyote as the government rules on life beyond the fenced perimeter. She considers creating a new set of notices with the computer at school, not to hand in with her project but to tack to fence posts and to post at the store. What would they say? She considers excerpts from her favorite book, Jack London's *Call of the Wild*, bits from her story about her father's plight, notices from animal activists on leghold traps. Suppose, she imagines, I could then video what happens when people see these new notices, their rethinking of coyotes. Could she hand in a report on her contribution to what people in the community were thinking about coyotes?)

As postmodern students of literacy read and write the larger text of a this-space-for-rent culture, they have waded into what is known as media studies.[12] Yet again postmodernism offers an engaging approach, one summed up by cultural critic John Hanhardt when he points to a move "from the oppositional stance toward mass entertainment taken by modernism to a postmodernist appropriation of those media" (1989, p. 95). What can come of such appropriations? Richard Serra, in his 1973 videotape *Television Delivers People,* uses the screen to rethink the medium. At one point in the tape, there appears the televised text "You are the product of t.v." with an accompanying explanation: "You are delivered to the advertiser who is the customer." Serra is turning on its head both medium—placing text where images should be (recall postmodernism's textual bias)—and message—TV is not so much for us to watch as to deliver us to others.[13] He is using the medium to expose the inner workings of this economy of images. If his artful immersion in the televisual is still on the margins of cultural expression, margins remain the place where critical commentaries are penciled in as the reader writes back to the text.

Serra and Holzer are engaged in forms of "conceptual" art. This is not all that postmodern artists are doing ("representational" painting has made its own ironic return, for example, in the work of Eric Fischl and David Salle). But conceptual art seems the very thing called for in our schools. As we might say, teach the young the concepts, and the facts will teach themselves. But if that is the case:

Select the statement that best constitutes the postmodern lesson–
a) facts represent certain *concepts of activity*
b) conceptual art is the *art of conceptualizing*
c) teaching is the business of melting concepts *subject to expression*
d) there is time in a dozen years of schooling for many lessons
e) all of the above

Let students become conceptual artists. Let them immerse themselves in a medium—video, broadsides, self-help books, lyrics, short stories— with the purpose of making a statement about how that medium has traditionally operated, turning it on itself. Recall our postmodern design formula: *appropriation, history, irony, ornament, pastiche,* and *production values.* To work within the medium affords appreciation with critique, in a mix of creative and intellectual pleasures. One who has risen to the challenge of bringing this sensibility to the classroom is Gregory Ulmer (1989). The result is that Derrida's "grammatology" meets the age of video in what Ulmer terms "teletheory." He goes so far as to offer a ready-to-use assignment for students based on the production of a "mystory," which is Ulmer's special deconstructive mix of history, mystery, herstory, and my-story:

> Write a mystory bringing into relation your experience with three levels of discourse—personal (autobiography), popular (community stories, oral history or popular culture), expert (disciplines of knowledge). In each case use the *puncture* or sting of memory to locate items significant to you; once located, research the representations of the popular and expert items in the collective archive or encyclopaedia (thus mixing living and artificial memories). (p. 209)

Following the assignment, Ulmer offers his own engaging instance in the form of a script and a few of the visuals for a film compilation, *Derrida at the Little Bighorn*. It warrants full marks for working with the three prescribed discourse levels. But more to the point, Ulmer speaks of himself as the "first reader": "The desired effect is surprise . . . at the associations produced by the juxtapositions" (p. 211). This therapeutic pleasure aside, the postmodern aim for literacy, as I have been describing it here, goes beyond filling in the categories of discourse, the already prescribed, in search of self-fulfillment.

The Ninth Principle of Postmodern Literacy

Reach into the screen and appropriate the mechanisms that govern discourse, creator, and consumer.

It is not hard to see that the advertising industry is both source of and subject for conceptual art and postmodern style. Art and advertising take from each other. But the two forms are also competing for the spaces of meaning. Of course, advertising holds most of the leases; it has spent a century purchasing formal control of public spaces. But advertising also comes close to art on rare occasions. In magazines of not too long ago, the Gap clothing company offered stunning sepia-toned photographs exuding an artfulness that played off celebrity endorsement and artistic expression: "GAP pocket-t $10.50, as worn by SHEILA METZNER, photographer. Photographed by Herb Ritts." This selling of T-shirts as a *way of being* collapses commerce and art in a way that is not out of line with the larger World of Art: "Passion. It's how you craft a flawless definition of yourself from everything you touch. Classic Gap for individuals of style." This striking mix of romantic individualism and postmodern design values represents Madison Avenue's considerable absorption of talent and craft. We may decry the purchasing power of the corporation or perhaps applaud the beautification of bus-stop shelters and magazines, sponsored by Gap pocket-tee wearers. But such is the social text, the common cultural legacy, the marriage of art and commerce. If the world is a text, then a good deal of it is the work of copywriters. Things come to mean for us, after all, as we consume them.[14]

"If we consume the product as product," writes French political economist of the sign Jean Baudrillard, "we consume its meaning through advertising. . . . Through advertising mass society and consumer society continuously ratify themselves" (1988, p. 10). We are in the business of consuming signs that others have created out of objects. According to Baudrillard's algebra, "in order to become object of consumption, the object must become sign" (p. 22). We consume text, never quite satiated by signs. Our relationships are embodied by consumption, or as Baudrillard unsentimentally asserts: "A couple's ultimate objective becomes the consumption of objects that previously symbolized the relation" (p. 23). Students of this culture must attend to the organization of its sign systems. The advertising industry is postmodernism's political economy of signs, and the state is one of the consciousness industry's biggest clients. Postmodernism is dangerously consumptive—it is the proliferation of goods and signs. Treat it as an invitation, an invasion; treat it warily, with curiosity and jest. We are not without our principles.

The Tenth Principle of Postmodern Literacy

The contest of sign and significance is the subject of a literacy that will be written in the future tense.

These postmodern lessons, in principle and story, are drawn from the passing moment. They are ambivalent at times, idealistic and cynical by turn. Of itself, postmodernism is no educational elixir. It contains no set program for attacking problems of sexism, racism, and economic disparity within which the schools remain trapped; it fails to offer specific help to those who suffer their schooling badly. But aspects of postmodernism can be drawn on to address these problems: its critical reading of culture and economy, its undoing of the master narratives, its invitation to history. Postmodernism is about the critical and artful enterprise of literacy. Out of such lessons arise rewriting projects. In yet other ways, postmodernism is a source of educational opportunity. Think of the walkway it forms from school to uptown, from student to writer; its style is open to student appropriation in ways that might extend the intellectual and public reach of the student's work.

(She has been sitting with a group of her friends in the library watching a National Geographic special on wolves. Her friends are very taken by the wolf cubs tumbling about their earthen den, but they drift into chatter during an interview with a farmer and his wife whose livestock have been hard hit by wolves. She has been taking notes about the television program as it carefully balances "the issues." But she gradually realizes that the way her friends are paying selective attention to the program again tells her what is being made of the animals. She watches her friends' eyes, and notes their comments in her book. She realizes that this scene could be added to the video that she is thinking of making, or at least the script for it. It is going to take something like that video to weave together what she has learned about coyotes, encyclopedias, the province, her father, and school projects into a kind of knowledge ecology that works on tensions and contradictions to sustain its shifting web of meaning. She wonders for a moment whether it shouldn't open with a clip from the cartoon series *The Road Runner*.)

There is no great educational secret here, no postmodern promised land. But there is a premise. Schools do well to look to the world, not for what is fashionable so much as for what is vital and set within larger cultural enterprises. If postmodernism is not itself multicultural or transhistorical, it is deeply interested in what is made of culture and history. If it often wears corporate colors, it still has an eye for graffiti. The postmodern literacy of greatest interest shows a critical regard for mapping the cultural processes by which some gain and others lose. The contest of meanings in postmodernism, as in a culture generally, is about the forms of language that will prevail, that will be heard, and that amount to the array of stories from which we have to choose. Education is part of that contest of meanings, insofar as it teaches the young to read and write more than one version of their lives. Postmodernism's connections, both fashionable and critical, require a good deal of imaginative and literate work to get them right so that they do some good. But they offer to teach us, in turn, new, expanded lessons about literacy that seem entirely worth our consideration.

Notes

1. Of definitions of *postmodernism*, there are terse academic ones requiring their own glossary, such as Linda Hutcheon's, "where documentary historical actuality meets formalist self-reflexivity and parody" (1989, p. 7), and book-length efforts, such as Charles Jencks's *What Is Post-modernism?*(1986). All told, I find Umberto Eco's analogy most helpful: "I think of the postmodern attitude as that of a man who loves a very cultivated woman and knows that he cannot say to her, 'I love you madly,' because he knows that she knows (and that she knows that he knows) that these words have already been written by Barbara Cartland. Still, there is a solution. He can say, 'As Barbara Cartland would put it, "I love you madly."' At this point, having avoided false innocence, having said clearly that it is no longer possible to speak innocently, he will nevertheless have said what he wanted to say to the woman: that he loves her, but he loves her in an age of lost innocence. . . . Both will consciously and with pleasure play the game of irony. . . . But both will have succeeded, once again, in speaking of love" (cited by Jencks, 1986, p. 18).

2. I cannot begin to provide an adequate citation for deconstruction, but I would offer one exemplary text by Derrida, *Limited Inc* (1988b), as among the cleverest instances of a textualization of the world (and a needlessly bitter attack on fellow philosopher John Searle). However, I would balance it with a lesser known but carefully argued book of criticism on the seemingly infallible movement, *Against Deconstruction,* by John Ellis (1989). For a brief "teacher's introduction to deconstruction," see Crowley (1989).

3. Problems still remain. If texts rather than truths prevail, we seem poised on the brink of relativism. Here, American pragmatist Richard Rorty (1988) is most helpful in pointing out how readers may embrace one text (truth) over another, for its artfulness or sense of justice, while remaining open, in good pragmatist fashion, to the arguments posed by contrary texts. A second concern is the association of two of deconstruction's prominent figures, Martin Heidegger and Paul de Man, with National Socialism in Nazi Germany, a problem of intellectual responsibility which has only begun to be worked out (Derrida, 1988a, 1990; Lacoue-Labarthe, 1990).

4. Cheryl Walker identifies critical dangers to this demise of the author and offers an alternative reading that does not return to older romantic notions: "My own brand of *persona criticism* assumes that to erase a woman poet as the author of her poems in favor of an abstract indeterminacy is an act of oppression. However, every version of the persona will be a mask of the author we cannot lightly remove. . . . How representative is this mask and what contradicts it?" (1990, p. 571).

5. In making sense of Barthes's and Derrida's dethroning of literature and philosophy, Rosalind Krauss has characterized their work as "paraliterary" (1986). This, too, might be seen as adding to the possibilities of a postmodern literacy, as it

creates an imaginative continuum between the literary and the critical: "The paraliterary space is the space of debate, quotation, partisanship, betrayal, reconciliation; but it is not the space of unity, coherence or resolution that we think of as constituting the work of literature. For both Barthes and Derrida have a deep enmity towards that notion of the literary work. What is left is drama without the Play, voices without the Author, criticism without Argument" (p. 293).

6   Although I am not arguing at this level of specifics in this chapter, recent research comparing whole-language to basal-reading programs does suggest that a greater attention to the form of written language in the first grade, for example, would be a helpful addition to whole-language programs (Stahl and Miller, 1989).

7   Examples are legion. William Burroughs, for instance, was a Beat author and dedicated word forger who worked around the boundaries of induced perception, perhaps, but he was a denizen of that dedicated effort to find the words and to fashion the books that tell it like it has been for the writer. Burroughs is also, it turns out, the inspiration for a half dozen rock-and-roll bands, most notably the Soft Machine, which takes its name from his novel. The bands have created albums for his novels and have read his novels into their albums. Words and music—cultural studies.

8   I have discussed in some detail the educational relevance of intellectual rights and properties (1990a). In terms of a scholarly interest in the material relations of power and economy that constitute a culture, the "new historicism" has taken the lead. It seeks, in Stephen Greenblatt's terms, a "poetics of culture" in the form of "an interpretive model that will more adequately account for the unsettling circulation of materials and discourses that is, I have argued, the heart of modern aesthetic practice" (1990, p. 13).

9   The argument for a "radical democracy" along these lines has been made in some detail by Ernesto Laclau and Chantal Mouffe (1985), socialist students of the times.

10 The postmodern economic system has been variously styled as "late capitalism" marked by an expansion of the culture industry by, in Fredric Jameson's terms, "the multinational apparatus, the great suprapersonal system of late capitalist technology" (1988, p. 73), and as "fast capitalism," which Ben Agger feels so commodifies the realm of meaning that it deactivates such serious forms of thought as the book, in favor of "money, science, edifice, and figure which increasingly encode significance" (1989, p. 6). 1 would also add that Lyotard's master theorizing seems to demonstrate the concentration on theoretical as opposed to social struggles that Nancy Fraser and Linda Nicholson (1988) point to as the feminist contribution to postmodernist work.

11 Art's use of print has its origins in dadaism. In rebellion against the archseriousness of art early in the 20th century, dada embraced the typography of popular culture, rendering absurd the conventions of representation and culture by adding a mock philosophical labeling. Francis Picabia's *Paroles,* to take one instance from 1919, contained the assertion "La verité ressemble à la mort," written into a diagram of some obscure mechanism (cited in Freeman, 1989, p. 118). Perhaps the most paradoxical confrontation of this representation is René Magritte's 1926 painting *Céci n'est pas une pipe,* in which the assertion "This is not a pipe" is

carefully written out beneath what to all appearances, we might say, looks like a pipe; it presents a theme on the nature of representation that Michel Foucault (1982) has considerable fun exploring.

12   Media studies was the invention, one could argue, of literary critic F. R. Leavis, arch defender of the "great tradition." In 1938, he penned an assuming textbook with Denys Thompson, *Culture and Environment,* which tore into "the media," making no bones about the need to protect the best of the young against the barbarian hordes lined up at the cinema, glued to their radios, and, in effect, storming the gates of culture. Media studies has for the most part remained a negative and highly competitive assault on the seductive elements of popular culture.

13   As it is, advertisers are gaining greater control of television programming; they have recently begun purchasing entire programs rather than time slots, recalling the "golden age" of television when the networks could be mistaken for an extension of the advertising industry (Kleinfield, 1990, p. F1).

14   There is always the countertext: Performance artist Karen Finley, looking at another side of the Gap, will have none of it: "Well, I'm here to tell you The Gap is the devil. Having everyone look as inoffensive as possible, having everyone be as together as possible though the wearer is as offensive as possible on the inside. You want everyone to look the same, so maybe they'll feel the same and they'll be easier to control, to take over" (1990, p. 6).

References

Agger, B. (1989). *Fast capitalism: A critical theory of significance.* Urbana: University of Illinois Press.

Barthes, R. (1974). *S/Z: An essay* (R. Miller, Trans.). New York: Hill & Wang.

Barthes, R. (1986). The death of the author. In R. Howard (Trans.), *The rustle of language* (pp. 49–55). Berkeley: University of California Press.

Baudrillard, J. (1988). The system of objects. In M. Poster (Ed.), *Jean Baudrillard: Selected writings* (pp. 10–28). Stanford: Stanford University Press.

Bruce, A. (1991, January 12). Wily coyote thrives in East. *Toronto Globe and Mail,* D2.

Cheetham, M. A., & Hutcheon, L. (1991). *Remembering postmodernism: Trends in recent Canadian art.* Toronto: Oxford University Press.

Churcher, C. S. (1985). Coyote. *The Canadian Encyclopedia* (Vol. 1, p. 235). Edmonton, AB: Hurtig.

Crimp, D., & Rolston, A. (1990). *AIDS demo graphics.* Seattle: Bay Press.

Crowley, S. (1989). *A teacher's introduction to deconstruction.* Urbana, IL: National Council of Teachers of English.

Derrida, J. (1974). Living on: Border lines. In H. Bloom, P. de Man, J. Derrida, G. Hartman, & J. H. Miller (Eds.), *Deconstruction and criticism* (pp. 75–176). New York: Continuum.

Derrida, J. (1986). *Glas* (J. P. Rand & R. Rand, Trans.). Lincoln: University of Nebraska Press.

Derrida, J. (1988a). Like the sound of the sea deep within a shell: Paul de Man's war (P. Kamuf, Trans.). *Critical Inquiry, 14,* 590–652.

Derrida, J. (1988b). *Limited Inc* (S. Weber, Trans.). Evanston, IL: Northwestern University Press.

Derrida, J. (1990). *Of spirit: Heidegger and the question* (G. Bennington & R. Bowlby, Trans.). Chicago: University of Chicago Press.

Ellis, J. M. (1989). *Against deconstruction*. Princeton: Princeton University Press.

Finley, K. (1990). *Shock treatment*. San Francisco: City Lights.

Foucault, M. (1982). *This is not a pipe* (J. Harkness, Trans.). Berkeley: University of California Press.

Fraser, N., & Nicholson, L. (1988). Social criticism without philosophy: An encounter between feminism and postmodernism. In A. Ross (Ed.), *Universal abandon: The politics of postmodernism* (pp. 83–104). Minneapolis: University of Minnesota Press.

Freeman, J. (1989). *The dada and surrealist word-image*. Cambridge, MA: Massachusetts Institute of Technology Press.

Giroux, H. (1991). Modernism, postmodernism, and feminism: Rethinking the boundaries of educational discourse. In H. Giroux (Ed.), *Postmodernism, feminism, and cultural politics: Redrawing educational boundaries* (pp. 1–59). Albany: State University of New York Press.

Greenberg, C. (1991). The notion of postmodern. In I. Hoesterey (Ed.), *Zeitgeist in Babel: The postmodernist controversy*. Bloomington: Indiana University Press.

Greenblatt, S. (1990). *Learning to curse: Essays in early modern culture*. New York: Routledge.

Greenblatt, S. (1989). Towards a poetics of culture. In H. A. Veeser (Ed.), *The new historicism* (pp. 1–14). New York: Routledge.

Grundberg, A. (1990, September 16). As it must to all, death comes to post-modernism. *New York Times*, H47.

Hanhardt, J. G. (1989). Film and video in the age of television. In M. Heiferman, L. Phillips, & J. G. Hanhardt, *Image world: Art and media culture* (pp. 95–111). New York: Whitney Museum of Art.

Hersey, G. (1988). *The lost meaning of classical architecture: Speculations on ornament from Vitruvius to Venturi*. Cambridge: Massachusetts Institute of Technology Press.

hooks, b. (1988). *Talking back: Thinking feminist, thinking black*. Toronto: Between the Lines.

Hutcheon, L. (1988). *A poetics of postmodernism: History, theory, fiction*. New York: Routledge.

Hutcheon, L. (1989). *The politics of postmodernism.* New York: Routledge.

Jameson, F. (1987). Reading without interpretation: Postmodernism and the video-text. In N. Fabb, et al. (Eds.), *The linguistics of writing: Arguments between language and literature.* New York: Methuen.

Jameson, F. (1988). Pleasure: A political issue. In *The ideologies of theory: Essays, 1971–1986: Vol. 2. Syntax of History* (pp. 61–74). Minneapolis: University of Minnesota Press.

Jencks, C. (1986). *What is post-modernism?* London: Academy.

Kaplan, E. A. (Ed.). (1988). *Postmodernism and its discontents: Theories, practices.* London: Verso.

Kleinfield, N. R. (1990, July 29). The networks' new advertising dance. *New York Times,* F1, 6.

Klotz, H. (1988). *The history of postmodern architecture* (R. Donnell, Trans.). Cambridge: Massachusetts Institute of Technology Press.

Krauss, R. E. (1986). Poststructuralism and the paraliterary. In *The originality of the avant-garde and other modernist myths* (pp. 291–296). Cambridge: Massachusetts Institute of Technology Press.

Kundera, M. (1991). *Immortality* (P. Kussi, Trans). New York : Grove Weidenfeld.

Laclau, E., & Mouffe, C. (1985). *Hegemony and socialist strategy: Towards a radical democratic politics.* London: Verso.

Lacoue-Labarthe, P. (1990). *Heidegger, art, and politics* (C. Turner, Trans.). Oxford: Blackwell.

Leavis, F. R., & Thompson, D. (1938). *Culture and environment.* London: Chatto & Windus.

Lévi-Strauss, C. (1961). *Tristes tropiques: An anthropological study of primitive societies in Brazil* (J. Russell, Trans.). New York: Atheneum.

Lyotard, J.-F. (1984). *The postmodern condition: A report on knowledge.* Minneapolis: University of Minnesota Press.

Phillips, K. (1990). *The politics of rich and poor.* New York: Random House.

Phillips, L. (1989). Art and media culture. In M. Heiferman, L. Phillips, & J. G. Hanhardt, *Image world. Art and media culture* (pp. 57–95). New York: Whitney Museum of Art.

Rorty, R. (1988). *Contingency, irony, and solidarity.* Cambridge: Cambridge University Press.

Rosler, M. (1991). *If you lived here: The city in art, theory, and social activism: A project by Martha Rosler* (B. Wallis, Ed.). Seattle: Bay Press.

Ross, A. (1988). Introduction. *Universal abandon: The politics of postmodernism.* Minneapolis: University of Minnesota Press.

Smith, D. (1990). *The conceptual practises of power: A feminist sociology of knowledge.* Toronto: University of Toronto Press.

Stahl, S. A., & Miller, P. D. (1989). Whole language and language experience approaches for beginning reading: A quantitative synthesis. *Review of Educational Research, 59,* 87–116.

Ulmer, G. (1989). *Teletheory: Grammatology in the age of video.* New York: Routledge.

Waldman, D. (1989). *Jenny Holzer.* New York: Harry Abrams.

Walker, C. (1990). Feminist literary criticism and the author. *Critical Inquiry, 16*(3), 551–572.

Williams, R. (1961). *The long revolution.* Harmondsworth, UK: Penguin.

Williams, R. (1980). Means of communication as means of production. In *Problems in materialism and culture* (pp. 50–63). London: Verso.

Willinsky, J. (1990a). Intellectual property rights and responsibilities: The state and the text. *Journal of Educational Thought, 24*(3A), 68–82.

Willinsky, J. (1990b). *The new literacy: Redefining reading and writing in the schools.* New York: Routledge.

Willinsky, J., & Green, S. B. (1991). Desktop publishing in remedial language arts settings: Letting them eat cake. *Journal of Teaching Writing, 9*(2), 223–238.

Chapter 3

Qualities of Student-Adult Electronic Communication: Immediate, Pedagogical, Aberrant

The Internet offers students not only a wide range of educational resources but also a whole new level of engagement with peers, professionals, and other sorts of experts. This opportunity to engage students in new communities of practice and to have them work with mentors in forms of authentic and integrated learning seems an encouraging extension of the school's regular program. As students increasingly use the Internet to open a new world of educational resources, educators need to consider what these resources add to their experience and learning. As part of that effort, this chapter identifies the qualities that distinguished a two-year computer-mediated communication (CMC) project between a class of high school students and a group of technology professionals on the West Coast of Canada during 1991–92. Their correspondence was intended to help the students learn more about the writing tasks professionals face and was focused on the students' gathering sufficient information about the professionals to compose personal profiles of them for their corporate newsletter.

In analyzing the correspondence, three themes emerged—immediacy, pedagogy, and aberration—that may help educators to focus on what is gained and risked by having students use the Internet to correspond with the larger world. Each of these themes raises questions about how literacy entails forms of responsibility for the way one engages with and comes to represent those with whom one is corresponding. The responsibility that comes of making connections has to do with the power of the word at such close range. The lessons for students in CMC were about literacy as a form of social involvement, as Deborah Brandt (1990) has characterized it, and the responsibility that follows from that involvement.

Previous research on CMC has pointed to its notable impact on interpersonal relations. In one of the new electronic journals, *Interpersonal Computing and Technology*, for example, Swanson (1993) reports how CMC tends to alter the organizational hierarchy in ways that frustrate managers and please subordinates as it opens far more direct channels of communication. Laboratory studies have established that electronic communication, when compared to face-to-face meetings, takes more time but offers a greater sense of equality and encourages the sharing of more ideas, albeit sometimes in the form of "flaming" (Sproull & Kiesler, 1991, p. 119). At the postsecondary levels Beadle (1996) and Anderson (1995) have both used CMC to create structures that enhance student communication and participation.

Canada's Writers in Electronic Residence program has allowed students from across the country to have their writing critiqued by a pool of established authors in an interaction that the students find inspires their writing (Owen, 1990). The Bread Loaf School of English in Vermont has long used CMC; William Wright (1992) describes a series of its projects, including international reading groups, that bring together teachers and students on a national scale. Without offering a detailed analysis of the interactions, Wright argues for the sense of a real audience that the network provides and the sense of real purpose that comes of connecting to others beyond the classroom. The point is also made by Barbara Sanchez and Judi Harris (1996), who stress the importance of basing the communication between student and adult on a clear purpose and topic while also allowing for the role of developing friendships in the communication.

The Project

The study reported here was situated in a West Coast high school located in a middle-class urban neighborhood in Canada. One of the school's six Grade 10 English classes was volunteered by its teacher to correspond with employees at a corporation who had agreed to participate in the project. The class was made up of 13 boys and 15 girls, of which total 24 had computers at home. For 9 of the students in the class, English was a second language. Createch, Inc., the corporation involved, is a Canadian corporation that integrates technology systems for such clients as airlines and the post office. The 28 employees who volunteered to participate in the project ranged from secretarial staff to the senior executive level, and in age from their early 20s to mid-40s.

In the first year of the study, we set up informal links among employees and students to begin conversations about the nature of work in the corporate world. However, although the students formed a few links toward the end of the school year, it became apparent that both teacher and employees felt a need for more structure to the connection. For the next round of exchange, the students were asked to compose a profile of an employee through email interviews and consultations, to be published in the branch newsletter, *Createch Pacific News*. Students examined a series of personality profiles drawn from the *New York Times*, *Forbes*, *Rolling Stone*, and *Thrasher* (a skateboarding magazine) as models for creating their sketches of life in the corporate fast lane. The educational goals for this unit included demonstrating the potential of CMC for developing communication and literacy skills, as well as increasing career awareness. Students were encouraged to consider a blend of imaginative and expository writing styles that would take them into the realm of literary nonfiction and the New Journalism (Wolfe, 1982). Once they were connected, the distinguishing aspects of this collaboration between students and adults demonstrated (a) *immediacy,* in quickly achieving a remarkable degree of engagement; (b) *pedagogy*, in implicitly and explicitly teaching each other through their exchanges; and (c) *aberration*, in one case that of a student running unquestionably askew in the communication, suggesting, in its own way, the extent of the responsibility entailed in operating this powerful medium.

Immediacy

The initial inquiry that the students sent out to the employees at Createch was marked by the degree of assumed connection, of immediate and direct communication, that can be struck up between virtual strangers with only a linked computer between them. The students recognized that this act of connecting was the first challenge in working on the project, and they came at it from a number of different angles, including a takeoff on the New Age restaurant waiter who is open about the need to break the ice: "Hello, my name is Anne and I will be your interviewer. Let me start by introducing myself to you so as to make this a little less awkward!" (A. Barlow, 9 Nov.). Others found their point of connection in objecting to the assignment, as a way of sharing their burden of connection while at the same time finding, by this sleight of hand, the means of overcoming it, as student and employee could be said to share responsibility for working on the assignment:

> I've never really done anything like this, so it feels a bit strange. I guess I'm just not used to communicating with someone that I've never met or even seen before. . . . Are you married? Do you have a family? (I feel really nosey asking all of these questions, but it's what I'm supposed to be doing!) (T. Sears, 9 Nov.)

> I mean how do I communicate with somebody without the slightest idea what they are. This is ridiculous, I've never had such a ridiculous assignment and they call it technology? I'm so glad that I wasn't born any later than 1976. (P. Chin, 9 Nov.)

The tone of equality and immediacy that infuses the students' communications with the employees of Createch was afforded by both the medium, which equalized their physical presence screen-to-screen, and the assignment, which acted as a bond between them, creating, at least initially, what we might term "screen equals." The students had rarely worked with an assignment for an English class that had drawn them into this sort of contact with a "subject."

Another form this directness took was the focused request, from student to employee, for assistance with the assignment. Here too there appeared to be an absence of more formal protocol, as if to say, "Here's what I need to get this task done and I know that you can help me." In sending an early draft copy of her profile to Jason at Createch, Susan included parenthetical questions that struck me as taking a refreshingly direct and at times imperative tone, as one might expect from a collaborator on a corporate proposal:

> As Jason Davis, dressed in his trendy suit and tie, gets off the elevator on the 27th floor, he enters the familiar environment of his workplace. . . . Createch. (*what does the office look like when you get in every morning, is it really busy or slow*) Jason who was born twenty-four years ago in far away Winnipeg would not be getting off that elevator almost every morning each week if his family hadn't decided to move to Vancouver when Jason was eight years old.
>
> (*Right here I need some thing to say about the dreams you had in your childhood!*) As his high school years finally came to an end, Jason decided to enroll in a computer systems program at Douglas College. . . . (S. Taylor, 25 Nov.; emphasis added)

There is something of both the collegial and collaborative spirit in these inquiries, along with the doggedness of a determined reporter after a story. Taking his cue from Susan, Jason responded to a later draft with his own inserts, pointing out what he felt were "factual errors" in Susan's story that he would like to see corrected ("I wasn't really 'an aspiring basketball player,' I just played it and other sports sometimes" [J. Davis, 27 Nov).

This quickly achieved immediacy also took place, not surprisingly, outside of the task at hand, as the conversations between students and employees explored aspects of each other's interests and lives. As one employee commented to her student, "For some reason, it seems easier to talk about myself through email. Interesting. . . ." (N. Fleck, 13 Nov.). Here I want to point out that what at first seemed to be digressions were, to a degree, contributions to the project. Before tracing one exchange in more detail, I offer the following excerpt from one of the students in the first two weeks of correspondence. It points to how literacy in this situation meant not only articulating one's own position but also learning more about the thinking of the person one was addressing:

> You hurt me. I think Madonna is rad. I agree that maybe she is lonely but as a christian you shouldn't be putting anyone down whether or not you agree with their values. I don't really think that the way she portrays herself is really what she is like. I think it is a front cause in hollywood it's not smart to let anyone know who you really are.
> So how did the big date go. I am sorta seeing this guy who is to me wonderful although he is often a jerk!! His name is Julian. (A. Barlow, 23 Nov.)

The camaraderie and directness in this student's response to the employee indicates she has stumbled onto an important aspect of the workplace, as this sort of connection can make for successful collaboration on the job.

In communicating across school and corporate worlds, the power of connection seemed capable of overcoming barriers that keep a distance between people, which added to the responsibility for the relationships that were acted out on the screen. The exchange between student Lynn and employee Steve began shakily enough, with Steve failing to respond ("I am way behind because I missed a class before and would really, really appreciate it if you replied" [L. Wong, 26 Nov) but grew in a few weeks to a mutual exchange of biographical information:

> As to my appearance I'm chinese and very short 5'2, or 5'3 actually. Obviously I have long black hair parted down the middle and brown eyes. I have chapped lips and a lot of tiny moles on one side of my face. Hardly noticeable, though. Um . . . I weigh 109lb to be exact and love vintage clothing and cool shirts. I don't have any dimples but I have three holes in my left ear (for earings). (L. Wong, 24 Nov.)

As part of the remarkable sensitivity she brought to this correspondence, Lynn spoke of her reluctance to actually meet Steve on the class's planned field trip to Createch: "They say we might meet you people at Createch one day and I don't know if I want to do that. I don't know why" (L. Wong, 30 Nov). Literacy, within this medium, is about exercising a power over how you are perceived, how you present yourself as you would have others see you —not necessarily dishonestly, but on your own terms, where blemishes are "hardly noticeable, though." Here, Lynn was in control and connected in a way that she could not imagine happening between an adult and herself in person. Here the machinery appears to isolate the other variables that speak to impossible differences. The electronic medium allows for a degree of control and connection that would otherwise be broken or disturbed by who the participants are in the actual rather than the virtual world.

Lynn's finished profile includes a biographical introduction to Steve and a concluding interview that deals far more with the humanity of the high-tech corporate employee than the nature of his work at Createch. But what is most striking about the profile is how it dramatically captures the spirit of their correspondence, as the reporter is made fully present in the reporting. In the process of creating the piece, Lynn transposed and projected their electronic meeting into a real, adult-world setting:

> Around 6 pm I was sitting casually in the dark atmosphere of Naam, a vegetarian establishment, at a candlelit table. Steve had mentioned that he was a junk food person and after chatting on the phone a while I thought he would appreciate healthy food if he tried it so I suggested this place. The door opened letting in a cool breeze and an extremely tall man entered and looked quizzically around, probably searching for a particularly small, oriental girl.
>
> I stuck my hand up hesitantly and relaxed when I noticed he was wearing faded blue jeans and a rugby shirt, what he said he would be wearing. He walked tentatively between the small spaces of the tables and reached my table safely.
>
> "Lynn?"
>
> "Yep, and you must be Steve."
>
> He smiled and sat down opposite me, peeling off his jacket in the same motion. Silence followed as we peered at each other through the flickering light. Steve was obviously tall, about 6', and had brown hair which was speckled modestly with grey on the front and sides. He had clear brown eyes and sported a sweet dimple in his chin. We laughed as we realized that we both knew what the other was doing.
>
> He asked what was good to eat and I recommended the french fries with miso gravy and the salads. We ordered our food, him, the french fries and Thai noodles, and me, the Caesar salad and soup of the day.
>
> I nestled myself into the chair and brought out my notepad and a pencil which I stuck behind my ear for the interviewer effect. I took a sip of my juice.

Qualities of Student-Adult Electronic Communication

> "Now let's get down to business shall we?" I started off. I had already asked him the serious things so it was easy writing from there.
> "Sure but I want to ask you some stuff later, okay?" (L. Wong, 30 Nov.)

The article then slips into an interview format, breaking back into narrative as the food comes to the table, only to have the conversation interrupted by the inevitable beep of Steve's pager:

> "Hey, I have to go and dial in on the ol' laptop to fix a problem. This can be a real drag sometimes. It's been great meeting you though and I hope I helped with your project. Toodles!" We shook hands and with that he swept out the door and disappeared. I sat at my table and sipped the last drops of my juice and then left homebound to finish my article. (L. Wong, 30 Nov.)

The whole piece reflects Lynn's control over the writing process, taking advantage of the connections she made to create a better, more engaging story for the newsletter, as part of the journalist's primary responsibility. This was an exploration in literacy, a correspondence that allowed her to explore far more of the reporter's life in an adult work world than she might otherwise have achieved in visiting offices or meeting in restaurants. The lesson here is also about how much the assignment, the external impetus to connect, sustained a relationship that the electronic medium had sped up in the first instance. The correspondence between Lynn and Steve, as well as between the others in the project, produced some exceptional journalism helped by the immediacy of the connections achieved through CMC.

Pedagogy

The connections achieved in this project also proved rich in pedagogical opportunities for both students and adults. That is, aside from what the students needed to learn about Createch, both sides used CMC as an instructional medium, garnering some excellent lessons on how to ensure effective and well-received communication.

We had built into the project a time for the students to submit a draft of their work to the employees for fact checking and other editorial assistance. In this first instance, the employee Jennifer, who was responsible at Createch for "typing huge and small documents" as well as "editing" them, brought a series of nuanced suggestions to the student's profile of her, reflecting a level of sensitivity to the demands of literate language:

- "soon to be born" could be "soon-to-be-born"
- "her co-worker Christine discuss" could be "her co-worker, Christine, discuss"
- after the "T.V. that flickers" you could put in a comma
- "parents which live a few blocks away" should be "parents who live a few blocks away"
- "hope to one day get married" should be "hopes one day to get married" (J. Hawson, 9 Dec.)

It became apparent to the student that not only English teachers fuss about hyphenation and split infinitives, as the student's collaborating editor moves from "could be" to an imperative "should be" in her suggestions. The learning process proved to be a two-way street, however, as the people at Createch discovered just how teaching is, as someone once said, learning twice. In reflecting on the process after the project, Jennifer commented that she "learned about other people here and how to communicate better—instead of correcting and returning, I was explaining to her *why* to change" (J. Hawson, 11 Jan.).

A number of the employees, when they were asked afterward to reflect on the profile-writing process, concurred with this sense that in communicating with the young, for whom very little technical knowledge can be presumed, one has to assume responsibility for assisting one's audience. Our initial promotion of the project to Createch had been on the grounds that this self-consciousness over clarity of expression formed its own learning connection, which would cause the employees to experiment more with means of explanation, from metaphor to analogy. Here are a series of the responses, in the truncated phrasing of experienced emailers, to our question about the challenges that the employees felt they faced in explaining their job to a student:

> Terms were hard to explain—maybe because there is no good explanation—only when you talk to an outsider do you realize how many there are. (K. Huang, 27 Nov)

> A challenge communicating in layman's terms—easy to slip into technical jargon—big step backwards to explain my job to a 16 year old and to try to keep notes humourous / entertaining / not boring poor girl. (L. Andre, 28 Nov)

> Challenge explaining to those I work with!—he didn't understand what I did. This is a general challenge in our job—no different in this case. (M. Shields, 28 Nov)

> It's all very abstract, I find. It's hard to explain to anyone what we do here, if they are not in the business (does that mean I'm a poor communicator?). (T. Kennedy, 30 Nov)

> Challenging to express on paper, in writing, what you do—watching how you word something—pay careful attention to your message—easily misquoted—but it got better—"handy skill." (R. Wilson, , 29 Nov)

In the last instance, Robert Wilson's sense of needing to "pay careful attention to your message" and of being "easily misquoted" also came up more than once in my discussions with the employees. They were surprised not only by the students' taking imaginative liberties with their materials, as we saw earlier when Jason corrected his student about being "an aspiring basketball player," but also by how easily they had been misunderstood and misread. This called for a much greater effort at making explicit what was intended and in checking that this intention had been communicated, all of which added to the theme of responsibility that emerged from the lessons on writing fostered by the project. The distance that sometimes has to be bridged in communicating is something that corresponding with these students brought vividly to all of the employees' minds. As Dave put it, describing his interactions with his student:

> I felt like I was from another planet —he'd say "You do what?" or I'd say "Do you understand?", he'd say "No, not really". But he did say at the end: Boy it's tough out here, I'm going to have to work. (D. Smith, 12 Dec)

It appeared that both employees and students were learning to think about audience in a new way. For the employees, it was by taking full responsibility for explaining in the simplest language possible the nature of their work, while collaborating with the students to ensure they were fairly and clearly represented in their work and lives. The students learned about being responsible to the subject of their writing, which in turn was linked to their subject's sense of responsibility to the wider audience of the newsletter, their coworkers and superiors. When Craig, for example, wrote in his profile that Amy "started out at Createch as a developer and has worked her way up to managing," Amy was quick to respond to him that "this sounds as if I have managed a large project on my own. I have been part of the management team on a large project, not the project manager. Please fix this" (3 Dec). Similarly, when Craig went on to say about her job that, "although she enjoys it she would really like to go to Australia and Europe before she starts a family," Amy corrected, "You don't need to say 'Although she enjoys it' as this sounds as if I would prefer to travel over my career, this is not true." The sense she insisted on, of both teamwork and commitment to the job, is part of a sensitivity to the form of expression, to the subtle use of a word such as *managing* and the placement of an *although*. These are fine-grained lessons in representation and responsibility that arose not so much from the medium per se but from the connections that it afforded between writer and subject in ways that might not otherwise have arisen in these students' educational experience.

What proved an added bonus among the lessons learned in this project, within the context of the students' English class, were the exchanges over literature, prompted typically by questions about favorite books. The most extended instance of this literary interest arose over *The Rubáiyát of Omar Khayyám,* which the employee Tracy explained to her student, Steph, that she "went home last night and dug out" in order to inform her discussion of her favorite book. Tracy explained, "Omar Khayyam is 'The Astronomer-Poet of Persia,'" going on to quote that "he was born in 'the latter half of our Eleventh, and died within the First Quarter of our Twelfth Century'" (T. Dish, 30 Nov.). Then, rather remarkably, Tracy transcribed three different translations of the famous "A Jug of Wine, a Loaf of Bread —and Thou" verse from Edward FitzGerald's 1859, 1868, and 1872 editions of the poem, adding at the end:

> Like I said, looks like Fitzgerald was obsessive compulsive. Can you imagine re-translating the same works 5 times? Didn't he have anything better to do? But I do appreciate Omar Khayyam's works, whichever translation you read. (T. Dish, 30 Nov.)

Tracy went on to cite a few more verses. Steph responded by commenting favorably on the line "The Moving Finger writes; and, having writ, / Moves on," and by reporting on her search for the book:

> I can't find the Rubaiyat in our school library. I think I looked for it and the original copyright was date in the 1800's (I think). That's pretty old! I guess too old for our library. But I'd really like to read some of it, so I will look for it in the public libraries. (S. Nelson, 3 Dec.)

In Steph's profile of Tracy for the newsletter, Tracy's poetic interests do not appear, although her interests in learning and teaching do come through:

> Starting off as a lowly key-punch operator, Tracy "Jay" Kennedy quickly became interested in computers. . . . Known under intimidating titles such as Senior System Analyst and CEM (Career and Education Management program) Coordinator, Tracy is actually "a jack of many trades," teacher, facilitator, organizer, and motivator. . . . She is part of helping clients learn how to manoeuvre through the twists and turns of today's technology. . . . Only knowing Tracy through the email system, she shines through as an outgoing and lively personality—a person of many interests. (S. Nelson, , 3 Dec)

As Tracy worked with Steph's draft, she corrected Steph's simplification of the job that Tracy was doing, while encouraging her experiments in literary style, in another show of her interests in the poetic touch: "I really like your alliterations (all the "t"s at the beginning of those words, it's great imagery to me—twists and turns and tongue twisters!!)" (T. Dish, , 3 Dec).

One student and one professional also came to collaborate on turning the assignment into a pedagogical project, resulting in the article "The Du & Steven's Method to Success in the Corporate World" for the newsletter. The article included a guide to "the definitions of words that are a must for success" in order "to dazzle your co-workers with your impressive knowledge of corporate speech," complete with a self-scoring quiz. Here is a sample question:

6. The Channel is (a) Y[outh]TV
                   (b) the marketing process from supplier to customer
                   (c) the cologne

This glossary-and-quiz pedagogy represented a different sort of profile of the professionals at Createch, suggesting, perhaps, that one is only as good as one's language skills and know-how. The lessons that took place around language and communication were varied, if rarely so explicitly handled as in this final case. The medium was seen to be part of a learning environment, and in a short period the professionals assumed responsibility not only for teaching but also for learning from this interaction. One advantage to bringing adult mentors in connection with students is opening this two-way street of teaching and learning, which can occur in the course of simply working together on a writing project. That these lessons occurred speaks to the quality of educational experience engendered from the connections struck during the short period of this phase of the project.

Aberration

For all of the immediacy and pedagogy achieved, there were also bound to be less favorable results, at times, from a class of 28 lively students. Some of the misuses of the email system amounted to little more than the passing of electronic notes in class among the students in the project. A few, inadvertently sent to the research file, covered the events leading up to, and the consequences of, a teacher's apprehending two students smoking marijuana. Another illicit message consisted of a love poem that suggested how new mediums end up carrying forward traditional forms.

Of a far more serious nature was the behavior of what I took to be a troubled student, Chris, who managed to put the employee with whom he was corresponding, Pam, into an awkward and uncomfortable position. Chris began his correspondence with the immediacy that I was quick enough to praise earlier but that, in his hands, revealed a certain twist: "My name is chris kende, I'm about sixteen years old and my neighbor next to me loves life. I however do not. I don't understand life, so there" (C. Kende, 9 Nov.).

Although Pam was a little taken aback by this introduction to her student, she took his initial message in the spirit of what we both originally thought might be a slightly odd sense of humor. She replied thus:

> Well, given the options of Life or Death, I'd have to choose Life. I don't understand it either, but then again neither do I understand Death. But if I were dead, I don't think I'd be capable of understanding anything. So there! What don't you understand about it? I am told that some of my co-workers offer after-hours psychiatric evaluations for a small fee. Interested? (P. Veitch, 12 Nov.)

Chris continued in his original vein, also making inquiries about where Pam lived. At this point Pam contacted us. His teacher spoke to him about sticking to his responsibilities in completing the profile, while at the same time Pam handled it from her end with a message to Chris about another sort of lesson on life in the business realm:

> Chris, I can appreciate the fact that you have a wild imagination, but the purpose of the Learning Connections Project is to communicate with someone in the corporate world. Well, in the corporate world, we don't appreciate time-wasters, and that is what the substance of your emails have become. I am a very busy person right now, and I don't have time to answer emails about dead cats and chopping trees. Can we communicate on topics that deal with your assignment and the corporate world?
> I do enjoy communicating with you, but I don't like where it is going. Let's get back on track. (P. Veitch, 4 Dec.)

This worked to a degree. Yet Chris went on to produce a profile that set Pam's life within a fictionalized episode of industrial espionage, secret-selling, and murder that went beyond what Pam could live with in a newsletter distributed to offices throughout this international company. The profile was not published, and the reasons were explained to Chris. He still reported finding the project interesting but took it as "kind of offensive" that his piece was not published, suggesting that our explanations of its rejection were only partially accepted.

This was another lesson in responsibility and writing that arose directly out of the student's work with his subject, although not without some direct intervention on both the teacher's and the subject's part. In the first year of the project, we had discussed with the students how participation in this network community depended upon a form of responsible citizenship, given the power and autonomy that their computer accounts afforded the students. Although we had seen little abuse, Chris's case of dead cats and trees served as a reminder that it still falls upon those in charge of such programs to be vigilant in what amounts to an extended field trip in time and space.

Conclusions

When students were asked to reflect on their impressions of the *Createch Pacific News* project in relation to typical English lessons, the responses were uniformly positive. Qualifications were added by a few students about the technical problems they experienced, and, as one student politely put it, the "experiment was a little rough around the edges." The 26 employees at Createch who completed the project (2 had transferred to other locations) also expressed support for the project, accompanied by a few reservations, mainly about the difficulty the students had in grasping what the nature of this work was, with only one expressing some concern over a student's abilities in English as her second language. The employees' sense was that the learning connection proved more helpful from a vocational point of view, as it helped "students to learn about workforce and corporate life," as one employee put it. Another said, "Wish I could have done it in Grade 11—maybe I wouldn't be in computers." They also judged that the project was more beneficial for the students than for themselves, although they seemed to appreciate the chance, as one put it, "to feel like a peer and help someone out."

The quality of learning and connection arising from the project remains, however, in the profiles that the students produced for the newsletter. In addition to Lynn's fictionalized interview and Du and Steven's quiz, there were a number of experiments in literary nonfiction, as well as more traditional encapsulated biographies. In the two years of the project, amid a number of focused exercises that included interest groups, response to literature exercises, and poetry-writing sessions, the newsletter profiles proved to be among the most productive activities undertaken.

We do not want to minimize the amount of effort it currently takes to connect to the world in this fashion. Yet just as the technology continues to develop, so too have the partnerships between business and school, as an expression of corporate responsibility to the community. We need to track the educational qualities of this extended communication system so that we might keep to the forefront why it is that we seek to deploy these new systems, what it is that they add to the students' powers to connect, and what they can teach both us and them about this larger process of communication.

This project extended students' reach and learning connections, even if frustrations and aberrations were bound to occur. A school's participation in the Internet not only can create a bridge between school and workplace, as well to other cultures and countries, but also can contribute to a greater sense of responsibility in the writing process —a responsibility to the subject one is writing about, to those to whom one is writing for, and to those whom one is trying to help and learn from. The benefits of such responsible writing, which became apparent in this CMC project, can extend to other forms of writing and communication, as well as to other sorts of projects involving communication technology. Although the Internet is just another technological device with educational potential, and not the next great revolution in learning, it appears to have value, judging by this instance, in how it can lead us to think again about important qualities of learning and connection that have always been at the heart of the educational enterprise.

References

Anderson, M. (1995). Using computer conferences and electronic mail to facilitate group projects. *Journal of Educational Technology Systems, 24*(2), 113–118.

Beadle, M. E. (1996, March). Strategies for a communication course using the Internet. *Tectrends*, 17–20.

Brandt, D. (1990). *Literacy as involvement: The acts of writers, readers, and texts.* Carbondale: Southern Illinois University Press.

Hull, G. (1993). Hearing other voices: A critical assessment of popular views on literacy and work. *Harvard Educational Review, 63*(1), 20–49.

Owen, T. (1990). Waiting to connect: The writer in electronic residence. *The Computing Teacher, 17*(5), 46–49.

Sanchez. B., & Harris, J. (1996, May). Online mentoring: A success story. *Learning and Leading with Technology*, 57–60.

Schwartz, J. (1990). Using an electronic network to play the scales of discourse. *English Journal, 79*(3), 16–24.

Sproull, L., & Kiesler, S. (1991, September). Computers, networks, and work. *Scientific American, 265*(3), 116–123.

Swanson, D. J. (1993). Toward a policy for managing the use of Computer Mediated Communication in the workplace. *Interpersonal Computing and Technology: An Electronic Journal for the 21st Century, 1*(1), unpaged.

Wolfe, T. (1982). *The purple decades: A reader.* New York: Farrar, Straus, Giroux.

Wright, W. W., Jr. (1992). Breaking down barriers: High schools and computer conferencing. In G. Hawisher & P. LeBlanc (Eds.), *Reimagining computers and composition.* Portsmouth, NH: Heinemann.

PART TWO

CULTURAL

Chapter 4

The Paradox of Text in the Culture of Literacy

It is now generally recognized, at least among those who study education, that Shirley Brice Heath has opened a whole new uncharted nation of literate practice. In *Ways with Words* (1983), she breaks through the divide normally struck between states of literacy and orality. She does not describe what may be wistfully lost and intellectually gained by crossing the borderline to literacy, she demonstrates that the divide disappears if one actually visits the countryside where people carry on with books and talk. Her work suggests that the importance placed on literate/oral cultural divisions may well be at the political convenience of educational and research interests.

For the last two decades, this great divide between literate and oral states of mind has been worked through a number of projects in history, anthropology, and linguistics, from the glory that was alphabetic Greece to contemporary preliterates in the days before they enter school. Yet recently the "great-divide theory" between oral and literate states has suffered a certain erosion: first, there was Ruth Finnegan's head-on attack (1973); then, some years later, Sylvia Scribner and Michael Cole's cautionary tales about the restricted intellectual impact of literacy on the Vai of Liberia (1981); and next, Shirley Brice Heath's portrait of the oral/literate blend in Trackton and Roadville. We have begun to distinguish different sorts of cultural features besides divides.

However, as Harold Rosen (1985) points out in reviewing Heath's book, she has left relatively untouched what she refers to as mainstream culture–presumably the home of what we commonly mean by terms like *literacy*. What Heath has taught us about the complex place of oral and literate language within working-class communities, and what Scribner and Cole have taught us about the Vai, has only begun to be realized in the context of understanding literacy among the mainstream.[1] Caught somewhere between a psychological process and an intellectual capacity, the social nature of literacy that pervades middle-class culture remains elusive. Because the concept of literacy is one that often guides our search for the ideal educational experience both here and abroad, it seems worth examining how the idea has been worked up against what it is not—the preliterate society, the oral culture, the child's utterance.

Resettling the Relationship between the Oral and the Literate

One of the notable contributions to a description of literacy in the mainstream classroom is found in the work of David R. Olson. His investigations into children's acquisition of literacy and into the nature of textbooks have led him to certain conclusions about the relation between oral and literate forms of expression and culture. His conceptualization of literacy and the divide between these two cultures holds a special importance for educators. He stands to touch the classroom in a way that others working this divide—anthropologists, historians, and classicists—are unlikely to do. As Olson talks about the nature of literacy, educators come to study and understand what it means for children to learn to read and write.

As a way of exploring the underlying roots of Olson's conception of literacy, I wish to take up his seminal piece "From Utterance to Text: The Bias of Language in Speech and Writing" (1977a). In the tradition of Jack Goody and Ian Watt (1962–1963), Olson provides a sweeping survey of the literacy events that account for the remarkable achievements of our civilization. His historical vision of literacy is one of intellectual advancement: "My central claim is that the evolution both culturally and developmentally is from utterance to text" (1977a, p, 89). As a result of his research, Olson has decided that the distinguishing features of text, when compared to utterance, are the high degree of autonomy and explicitness it is able to achieve. These two strengths of the text, he maintains, facilitate the considerable progress that has been achieved in the modes and range of our thinking in the West. Taken together, autonomy and explicitness extend the possibilities of textual coherence and abstraction, which in Olson's cosmos are the necessary elements of our intellectual accomplishment thus far.

In the first part of this chapter, I wish to challenge the nature of the textual distinction put forth by Olson. In the second part, I will propose what I hold to be a legitimate and necessary supplement to his view by introducing a text in Judaism known as the Haggadah, which has guided the Passover service for nearly two thousand years. My queries begin with Olson's essay because it is an instance of the strong case still being made by those who work the divide between the oral and the literate, though, to be fair, Olson has since declared that the split he originally described "is somewhat exaggerated" (1980, p. 187). The overlooked lessons about the culture of literacy that I will introduce stem from my experience of growing up with the Haggadah. What transpires during Passover services, I have come to realize, introduces a challenge to our perception of the intellectual tradition in literate culture. This tradition, I believe, is far more rooted in the oral—and is, in fact, what I wish to construe as an oral ideal of interpretive concern—than is currently acknowledged in the work on literacy. The oral basis of the texts I describe comprises interruption and interpretation, challenge and commentary. This underplayed nature of the text could have a profound bearing on our approach to literacy in educational settings, a point I will consider briefly toward the end of this essay. The textual paradox I wish to expose lies in the fact that the level of sophistication of the highly literate text is dependent on sustaining an oral sensibility.[2] To reset the relationship between the oral and the literate, I have decided to get both textual and personal in this essay, bringing together the blend of cultures in my own life.

I must acknowledge the considerable intellectual risk I undertake in bringing lessons learned at home to the academic front. Olson has pointed out, as part of his argument, that the essayist has increasingly set aside the personal perspective that Montaigne, who is credited with inventing the genre, first introduced: "I speake unto Paper as to the first man I meete" (Montaigne, 1909, p. 1). The marginalizing of personal reference has afforded us, in Olson's terms, the full play of abstract ideas in all their logical intricacies and connections, free from the constraints of "intuition, common sense, or authority" (1977a, p. 105), which are for Olson the bane of utterances. To make a contribution to our knowledge and theoretical understanding, we must grow impersonal, which, in Olson's terms, means to become explicit and to set the text in an autonomous (anonymous?) state. The goal is a text that can travel without the crutch of context, a sentence that can become a thing explicitly in itself. This impersonal autonomy creates the text's own source of authority, particularly as it is brought to bear in the textbook found in the school setting (Olson, 1980).

A Strong Case for the Divide

Olson draws on three historical moments that he deems crucial to literacy's contribution to our intellectual advancement. The first among these was the Greek perfection of the phonetic alphabet, somewhere around 700 B.C.E., which then permitted the transcription of speech into print. The second leap occurred some time later, with the Reformation in Europe. In this instance, Martin Luther fixed his place in the divide between text and utterance with his principle *sui ipsius interpres*—scripture is its own interpreter (Olson, 1977a, pp. 85–86). The third historical achievement was the British essayist tradition that emerged in the 17th century, especially as it was developed in the philosophical writings of John Locke. Olson gives credit for this final breakthrough in literacy to what is sometimes termed the plain style in writing, a style that eschews rhetorical flourish. The result, in Olson's terms, is that "this use of language made writing a powerful intellectual tool by rendering the logical implication of statements more detectable and by altering the statements themselves to make the implications both clear and true" (1977a, p. 96).

Olson's stance toward what he has observed in the evolution of Western literacy tends to waver. At times in his work, he seems intent on simply carefully recording the historical development of the common attitude toward literacy: "Knowledge was taken to be the product of an extended essay" (1977a, p. 96); or "An understanding of Western scientific and literate thought would be a description of 'schooled' forms of competence" (1977b, p. 70). At other times, he seems quite happy to partake of this attitude and to accept the development of the essay form as the natural evolution of the human mind to a more advanced state: "The Greeks perfected the alphabetic system and began developing the writing style that, encouraged by the invention of printing and the form of extended texts it permitted, culminated in the essayist technique" (1977a, p. 97). It is this aspect of his work which suggests a certain element of ethnocentrism, a charge that Brian Street, in his recent review of literacy theories, levels directly at Olson: "The ideological purpose of such work is to justify and defend Western educational practice" (1984, p. 35). The claims for literacy made by Olson and others working in this fashion, Street suggests, "derive from the writers' own work practice and belief system and serve to reinforce it in relation to other groups and cultures" (p. 39). As part of his analysis, Street has postulated an alternative great-divide theory, this time between literacy researchers. Street sets apart those such as Olson who hold to an autonomous model in which literacy of itself is seen as bringing change, whether cognitive or economic, from those such as Harvey Graff (1979) who sense the ideological context and hold to a model in which literacy is shaped and bound within the limits of the culture.

Olson is both a recorder of the natural history of writing and an advocate of his own favored form of expression, especially as it has blossomed among the community of scholars. In his view, text "culminates in the essayist technique," whereas aspects of oral culture and all other forms of literate expression appear to be relegated to the intellectual infidelities of "utterance." Although he has been critical of the textual bias in the schools' approach to literacy, boldly declaring the epistemological and pedagogical unsoundness of this tendency, his very call for a renewed balance sustains the sense of fixed boundaries between the oral and the literate (1977b, p. 86). In an introduction to a set of essays on literacy, he has more recently stated his continuing commitment to this autonomous model of literacy, to "the conviction that oral language was different in important respects from written language and that those differences would help account for the difficulties some children have in becoming fully literate" (1985, p. 13). Yet, later in the same piece, he declares as part of a revised vision that "what matters is what people do with literacy, not what literacy does with people" (1985, p. 13)— though the book's subtitle, *The Nature and Consequences of Reading and Writing,* suggests otherwise. In a different sense, I am taking up here what people do with "literacy."

I do not doubt that Olson has accurately described some of the distinctive features of text, when compared to utterance, yet I feel he has overlooked the continuing cooperation between them. To point to Yugoslavian oral poets and to Bob Dylan as remnants of peaceful coexistence between the two cultural states (Olson, 1977a, p. 91) is to slight the sustaining part that oral practices play in the "dominant literate traditions." To begin to recover the ongoing rather than remote oral sources of textual forms, my approach is to begin with my own reading of Olson's text.

Oral Practices in Literate Culture

My commentary arises out of the marginalia I wrote while reading Olson's article; these interjections first occurred as scribbled remarks bound to his text, sentential perhaps but not yet autonomous sentences. By that process I began reading and interpreting his work, denying rather than affirming his conception of the autonomous text by setting his comments in the context of other readings, such as Street's work. The practice of marginal interjection goes back to the manuscript culture of the Middle Ages in which glosses and commentaries, as well as illuminations, filled the borders of manuscripts and quietly challenged the text. Interrupting the text in this manner might be taken as a reflection of the Renaissance dispersal of argument and the silencing of discourse, something Elizabeth Eisenstein has described as a product of a new print culture (1979, p. 129 *passim*). But though the technologies of communication change the tone of discourse, the ideals of challenge and exchange remain.

I would contend that Olson has violated the autonomy of his own text through the use of the citation, in which a bibliographic reference serves to substantiate the argument. He brings in other voices to support his case while at the same time setting his work in the larger context of a particular academic community. The citations resemble an utterance, an interjection, far more than a text. This reminds us that the meaning of one text is sustained by a community of texts, and not by any given sentence, as Olson suggests. The logical deliberations that the essay form makes detectable are in some ways obscured by this shorthand extraction from others' arguments; the citation serves a number of purposes, one of which is to name an authority that lies outside the autonomy and logical argument of the text. This scholarly apparatus, as it is sometimes termed, is reminiscent of the requirement in medieval England that twelve good men were needed to testify to land ownership at a time when written documents were not yet trusted (Clanchy, 1979). The judgment of these twelve was later sustained in the jury system; their presence became a trusted, authoritative source of interpretation in the ways of language and justice.

Law as a whole provides an interesting example of the continuing importance of oral practices in a literate culture. The law continues to cling openly to a blend of oral and written traditions, a practice that holds generally in literate culture but is often obscured in other forums. Certainly, texts are as central to the culture of the law as they are to scholarship. Yet the law is based on an acknowledgment that the meaning of a text—whether constitutional or legislative—is found in the *interpretation* to which various parties are allowed to speak. The internal logic and coherence of the law are attended to, but its interpretation is still wrapped in a reading of human intention that may be modified by context, as often happens, for example, in American constitutional cases. Meaning in these texts is achieved through a consideration of the culture of the law and the interpretation of human intention, which are brought to bear in the oral forum of the courtroom. This mix, I am suggesting, weighs heavily against granting any single sentence the sort of autonomy Olson ascribes to the state of advanced texts and literacy.

The same is true with the scholarly essayist tradition. With the academic essay, the hearing given to the interpretation of uncertainties and possible ambiguities unfolds in a series of steps proceeding from collegial lunches, through conference presentations, and on to the refereed journal forum until, perhaps, the work is finally settled between hard covers. Along this path, Olson's regard for the autonomy that those texts have achieved is rarely respected, and we are the richer for it. Although Olson's claim that "statements can become relatively free from judgement or interpretation only with a highly explicit writing system such as the alphabet" (1977a, p. 93) cannot be disputed, this potential autonomy must be qualified by the actual culture of literacy. The situation is much the same with older, well-established texts. Commentaries and countercommentaries bind us in the very way that Olson has claimed the Greek alphabet should have freed us; the commentaries are reminders of what we have gleaned or should have gleaned in our reading, to "aid [us] in getting the right interpretation" (1977a, p. 93). This is the function that Olson, citing Eric Havelock, ascribes to texts made from prephonetic alphabets. In the socialization of children and students into the culture of literacy, these elements of extratextual authority and meaning are a part of what has to be mastered and learned by those who would do well, a point that has been brought to Olson's attention by Luke, de Castell, and Luke (1983).

In establishing the linguistic features of the written text that have promoted intellectual development, Olson singles out the alphabet and the sentence. The important feature of the Greek alphabet is its ability to transcribe speech with case and exactitude, though within greater limits than is suggested by Eric Havelock's reference (1976) to the alphabet's capabilities for perfection and accuracy (cited by Olson, 1977a, p. 92).[3] The contention is that out of this technology of the phonetic alphabet, anchored in the sound of speech, there was launched a new level of autonomy and an internal, self-sufficient logic. Yet this very fidelity to the spoken word as the basis of intellectual progress must surely reinforce the oral roots of language and argument rather than undermine the role of utterance. As a measure of the alphabet's ability to resolve the ambiguity present in utterance, Olson cites the French homonyms *cette* and *sept* in otherwise identical sentences (1977a, p. 92). But, in fact, this question of ambiguity works both ways. As Olson acknowledges, homographs, such as *lead* and *lead,* have a similar built-in ambiguity, though these are perhaps no less a trivial case than homonyms. On the side of increased explicitness, speech has the ability to be interrupted and interrogated for an ongoing resolution of doubts and the achievement of a certain clarity, as Socrates is made to point out in Plato's *Phaedrus*. With respect to written words, Socrates states, "If you ask them anything about what they say, they go on telling you just the same thing forever" (Plato, 1952, p. 158). On another front, French philosopher Jacques Derrida has taken up both a style—"If we are to approach a text, it must have an edge" (1979, p. 83)—and a project of philosophical subversion that would undo Olson's claim that advanced texts minimize "the possible interpretations of statements" (1977a, p. 95). Perhaps this simply points to how strongly Olson is holding to the British intellectual tradition of the essay, which seeks the definitive statement and the rhetoric of philosophical closure.

Strong indications of the limits on the autonomy and the resolution of ambiguity achieved by written language are to be found in the extralinguistic practices of philosophy and science. The symbol systems employed for logical relations and truth tables in philosophy, as well as for relationships in science and mathematics, are more than a shorthand for language; they are symbolic representations of the concepts at hand, representations which are intended to escape what I call the sociable ambiguities of language. Olson recognizes this representation as yet another step to cover "the remaining lack of explicitness" (1977a, p. 92) in written language, but he is inclined to see the difference as one of degree. Unmasking the rhetoric of the text's comprehensiveness, Derrida has taken issue with this view. He sees comparisons of written language with the language of mathematics as an expression of an uncritical metaphysical claim: "The practice of scientific languages challenges intrinsically and with increasing profundity the ideal of phonetic writing and all its implicit metaphysics" (1974, p. 10). Wittgenstein (1958) realized a similar distinction after recognizing his mistaken attempt in the *Tractatus* (1961) to establish the limits of language by regarding it as a logical representation of the world. The inadequacy of language (spilling over into literacy) amounts to a continuing failure to sustain its own logic, both in grammar and in argument. Stripping language of this veneer was a central theme of Continental philosophy during the 20th century. But the apparent ill determinacy of language is no less present in the primary historical events that Olson records—in the break with orality encouraged by the Greek phonetic alphabet; and in Luther's biblical injunction, which as soon leads to religious fundamentalism as to textual modernity.[4]

I am not denying that elaborate texts can construct systems of thought that, both in audience and in explicitness of detail, go beyond anything uttered. Yet I am not so certain about the essay's exclusive claim to this achievement. The British essay, of the analytic sort practiced so well by John Locke and R. S. Peters, does achieve an admirable degree of directness and coherence that, admittedly, is uncommon in other texts and utterances. But it is guided by conventions of expression and form that act as a rhetorical force, a means of conviction, quite apart from its logical integrity. Part of the essayist's skillfulness is foreseeing the probable points at which a reader will pose counterarguments or ask for clarification. In this fashion, as the essayist foresees, so he quiets the reader's urge to interrupt. Locke was an early master of this rhetorical device: "I must therefore beg a little truce with prejudice, and the forbearance of censure, till I have been heard out in the sequel of this Discourse, being very willing to submit to better judgments" (1972, p. 40). In a number of ways, the analytic texts of this tradition transcend neither the language nor the social practices of the utterance. Their intellectual strength is to be found not in the distance they have traveled from utterance but in the systematic accomplishments of a critical and interpretive culture that embraces the social practices of both utterance and text.

Challenging the Conventional View of Literacy

With these initial disruptions of the intellectual line drawn between utterance and text in place, I would like to continue the commentary in another vein. The question is still the one Luther addressed with his *sui ipsius interpres;* but in this instance neither the text, the Passover Haggadah, nor the commentator, Rabbi Elazer, is well known. This rich and peculiar text openly challenges, to my mind, the conventional view of our literate culture, including its tendency toward ethnocentrism. At the least, it reminds us of the actual variety of roles that texts still play in our proudly post-oral (and soon to be postliterate?) culture. My argument may seem tenuous at this point, and not just because it grows more personal. The influence of Judaism on the intellectual development of the West, as Leon Roth (1954) has gone to some trouble to point out, is as undeniable as it is difficult to specify.[5] Though the Haggadah is a living trace of this past, I am not in a position to claim that it has directly influenced the development of our literate culture, after the fashion of Luther or Locke. Rather, this text has struck me as unique in its *representation* of the oral root and the oral essence of the intellectual enterprise.

To provide a little background: The Hebrew word *Haggadah* is the nominalization of *le-haggid* which means "to say" or "to tell."⁶ The Passover service is based on this stricture found in the Torah: "And thou shalt tell thy son in that day, saying, It is because of that which the Lord did for me when I came forth out of Egypt" (Exod. 13:8), referring to the escape led by Moses from the state of bondage in Egypt. The Passover Haggadah, as the source of that telling, is used in a service conducted in the home with the family seated around the dining-room table before the evening meal on the eve of the Passover holiday. The tribute to God is an act of questioning and telling, traditionally in a dialogue between fathers and sons set in a domestic scene fashioned by mothers and daughters. (That tradition, too, is currently the subject of questioning and telling in many families.) In Joshua and Second Kings, there are references to the telling of the Passover story—the first of a series of self-referential aspects of this service. Yet the Passover Haggadah is said to have served as a written guide only with the beginning of the common era.

The Haggadah is a book I grew up with. I heard it read in the same version, the same edition, year after year while I looked at the same pictures, first at my grandparents' table and then at my parents' (*Form of Service*, 1859). The books were handed down, not as a legacy but simply because they were the books we used. Gathered between marbled-paper covers and cloth spine, each page was split between the thick gothic Hebrew and the thinner English typefaces, representing an accommodation of the split in our cultural allegiances. The fine-lined engravings accompanying the text struck me as medieval in temperament, the biblical characters seemingly pasted onto European land- and cityscapes. The engravings were often dramatic: helpless babies and hapless Egyptians struggling and drowning, though on different pages and in different waters; plagues grouped in a neat but chilling set of 10 . . . but, as I shall explain, not only 10.

For a child, the moment of attention and anxiety in the Passover seder comes with what is known as "the four questions." These questions, the Haggadah instructs, are to be asked by "the youngest in the company," which meant in my household the youngest who could read them, preferably in Hebrew. The seder is opened by and shaped around the query "Wherefore is this night distinguished from all other nights?" elaborated by four questions on the reason for unleavened bread, bitter herbs, dipping in salt water, and relaxed postures. Though I can no longer read the questions in Hebrew, I can still recite the first one from memory, and I recall, too, that it was also one of the few sentences in Hebrew that my father could recite, intoning the question of why this night differed from all others whenever my mother served an unusual dish for dinner. I have never heard my mother use the lines. My father and I each in our time played that leading role in the service, memorizing the questions and feeling the importance of our place in raising them at the table. That the service should open, after a number of initial blessings, with such a demand from the youngest is at the root of the telling, a telling prompted by questions rather than simply told. The "whole company" is asked to respond in this 19th-century edition of the Haggadah: "Because we were slaves unto Pharaoh in Egypt, and the Eternal, our God, brought us forth from thence with a mighty hand and an outstretched arm."

This response to the questions is immediately followed in the Haggadah by a short section that has always struck me as perversely out of place. Sitting at the dining-room table with aromas escaping from the oven, and already waiting for the service to end and the supper to begin, I was vastly impatient with this particular passage, which struck me, even as a child, as a disruption, a digression. As I got older, I began to find its apparent incongruity in the service something of a joke, a bit of sloppy bookmaking, a blooper. Finally and only very recently, I have come to realize that this short section is a vastly important part of the text:

> And thus is related of Rabbi Eleazar, Rabbi Joshua, Rabbi Elazer, the son of Azariah, Rabbi Akiba and Rabbi Tarpon, that they once met (on the night of Passover) and continued discoursing of the departure from Egypt, all that night, till their disciples came and said: "instructors it is time to read the morning Shema [prayer]."
>
> *Rabbi Elazer, the son of Azariah, said, "verily, I am a man of seventy years of age, and have hitherto not been able to proof [sic], that the narration of the departure from Egypt, ought to be related at night, till expounded by the son of Zoma; after this manner is it said, that thou mayest remember the day of thy going forth from the land of Egypt ALL the days of thy life." From whence he observed, that the expression of, the days of thy life, signifies the days only; but ALL the days of thy life, denotes the nights also. But the sages say, the days of thy life, denotes this life only; but ALL the days of thy life denotes even at the time of the Messiah.*

That an aside about these five rabbis should interrupt the service (to discuss a point of the conduct in the very service they were interrupting) initially seemed absurd.[7] Each year, I listened to Rabbi Elazer's argument about what "ALL the days of thy life" actually denoted, but never heard the point resolved. It was left hanging there between all the days and, possibly, all the nights. Each year, I listened to how these rabbis absentmindedly spent the entire night "discoursing of the departure from Egypt," with Rabbi Elazer particularly perplexed over this seemingly moot point—how attentive can one actually be, day and night?

The Broken Reading of the Passover Haggadah

More recently I have recognized that in this interruption there is embodied an unusual critical regard toward sacred texts. This regard becomes a part of the telling which the service constitutes. In addressing the spiritual focus of the Passover service, Philip Goodman has summed it up as "one of longing for redemption and freedom, a belief in the survival of the Jewish people and an unyielding confidence in divine salvation" (1973, p. 70). But here I am focusing on what might be termed the textual spirit that pervades the service. That is, what is significant in the two paragraphs about the rabbis is that rather than granting self-sufficient, canonical authority, the interruption disrupts the text such that we are compelled to consider its interpretation. What is significant is the interruption's final, frustrating state of irresolution; it suggests that neither from the wisdom of rabbis nor from that of sages will definitive interpretation of "all the days of thy life" be "proofed." And finally, what is significant is its reflexivity as it comments on the endless but desirable struggle to interpret the text in which we, as well as the rabbis, are a part of the questioning process. The Haggadah is amazingly frank—or explicit, in Olson's terms—about how the canonical text, of which it is a part, is to be regarded and read.

I should add another textual note on how this section of the Haggadah text is handled. Typographically, its centrality to the service is reinforced. My Haggadah is printed in three sizes of typeface for both the Hebrew and the English. The smallest type serves as a guide for procedures ("Then fill the cup with wine"), the middle for the special parts of the service required if the seder falls on the Sabbath, and the largest for the main body of the service. The story about the five rabbis is set in the largest typeface and fits without break between the collective response to the four questions and the blessing for the bequeathal of the law. It serves neither as a supplement nor as a footnote to the service; it is part of the substance of the text—part, in fact, of the questioning that begins with the young and then moves to the old as the service progresses.

Baruch Bosker (1984) has recently discussed the rabbinic standardization of the Passover service, which gradually took place after the destruction of the Temple in 70 C.E. He notes that the wording of the opening questions became fixed along with other parts of the service. This is not a surprising path for a ritual to take over the centuries, but what is paradoxical is that preserved in this fixing is the spirit of an approach in which "intellectual discussion [is] a central activity incumbent upon everyone" (Bosker, 1984, p. 67). It might be argued that this approach addresses what Socrates so feared of the written text: that it cannot be interrupted and questioned. As Frank Kermode (1986) has pointed out, the encouragement of interpretation rooted in text, which Olson grants to the historical period of Martin Luther, had been vigorously sustained by Jewish readers and scholars for well more than a millennium before the Reformation. With deliberate intent, the Jewish text does not flow seamlessly as does, say, the British essay tradition. It does not hide its collective making and its construction through interpretation. It insists upon digression, a broken reading.

Philip Goodman has suggested that rabbinic discussion was added to the Haggadah, along with other matters of interpretation, somewhere between the 6th and the 11th centuries (1973, p. 75). 1 certainly found it included in a number of modern editions I consulted. Yet I did find one edition, *An Israel Haggadah for Passover,* which had omitted it because, I suppose, it did not fall within the edition's purpose: "to restore to our Passover observance something of its earlier tradition of spontaneity of connection to current life and hence to universal freedom efforts" (Levin, n.d.). In the search for a connection with current life, this section might seem expendable (it certainly struck me so as a youngster), yet in the fight for freedom it might still represent an uncowed spirit of critical inquiry.

Though the lucubrations of the five rabbis seem strikingly incongruous, they actually comprise the first instance of many such moments, as the service maintains a central concern with questioning and interpretation. After the discussion of the five rabbis, the text turns to the inquiries of the four sons: "the wise, the wicked, the simple, and he who hath not capacity to inquire." Clearly, the service suggests that we are to explain ourselves just as we are, as we question each other. We are to participate in the text, helping those who do not have what it takes to inquire (as if this questioning were the test of mental capacity). At another point, the service boldly advocates to "search and inquire." Yet along with the questioning, there are sections given to straightforward exegesis, which continue to explain the story we are compelled to tell.

The five rabbis emerge again, this time with the counting of the plagues visited upon the recalcitrant Egyptians. Rabbi Akiba puts forward his case, concluding that "it is deducible, that in Egypt they were smitten with fifty plagues, and at sea they were smitten with *two hundred and fifty* plagues." He is preceded in this discussion by Rabbi Jose, who establishes the figure at sea as 50 plagues, and Rabbi Eliezer (not to be confused with Rabbi Eleazar) whose reading has led him to estimate 200 plagues. The intrusion of this debate did not impress me in the same way that the opening discussion of the rabbis did. I had been prepared by the previous instance, and, furthermore, the point of this dispute is somewhat more clear, as the section concludes, "What abundant favors hath the Omnipresent conferred on us!" Yet here, too, in another unresolved intrusion in interpretation, the nature of the *sacred text* retains its spiritual importance while defining our relationship to it—it is inviolable but not untouchable, perhaps reminding us that the term *Israel* means "to wrestle with God."

As a concluding instance, I cite this powerful supplement, or rereading, from a final Passover seder conducted in the Warsaw ghetto on the eve of its destruction in 1943:

> Passover has come to the ghetto again
> As always—the German snarls his commands.
> As always—the words sharpened and precise.
> As always—the fate of more Jews in his hand:
> Who shall survive, who shall die the Passover night.
> But no more will Jews to the slaughter be led.
> The truculent jibes of the Nazis are past.
> And the lintels and the doorposts tonight will be red
> With the blood of free Jews who will fight to the last.
> (Fredman, 1981, p. 153)

Interpretive Compulsion and the Literate Enterprise

The textual spirit of the Haggadah, which is common enough to Judaism, also has a parallel (steering clear of the concept of source) that continues to exist within the culture of literacy in general and, more specifically, with regard to the important texts in our civilization. To explain why I find this spirit exemplified in Judaism, it is not enough to say that the Jews are a people of the book; rather, it is that a people who have been singularly dependent on what might be termed a textual cohesion, rather than a geographical one, have necessarily found a way to live within and through their books as a means of attending to their cultural identity. Thorlief Boman (1970) has described how the ancient Hebrews regarded understanding as a form of hearing, an approach which differed from that of the Greeks, who relied on what could be seen.[8] In Judaism, the urge to give a hearing to different interpretations goes back to the "oral Torah," which developed around the sacred texts and which only during the third and fourth centuries of the common era evolved into the extensive written commentaries of the Talmud. Gersholm Scholem, in summing up this cultural practice, has pointed out that "commentary thus became the characteristic expression of Jewish thinking about truth" (1971, p. 290). With the Passover Haggadah, the tendency to intrude on the already interrupted text is found in one marvelous edition in which the service is augmented by no less than 238 commentaries (suggesting a seder I would be reluctant to attend).

Harold Bloom's work provides one modern instance of how this Judaic influence has directly shaped a critical theory of the text. Drawing heavily from the Jewish mystical tradition of the cabala, Bloom has created a body of literary criticism that is blended with elements of Freudian psychology. He has applied this critical reading to the English literary canon, though not without some controversy and conversion, both of which are interestingly exemplified by feminist critics Susan Gilbert and Sandra Gubar (1979). In a statement that summarizes the nature of text that I have found in the Haggadah, Bloom cites Scholem at one point in his argument: "Everything that we perceive in the fixed form of the Torah, written in ink on parchment, consists in the last analysis of interpretation or definitions of what is hidden. . . . . There is no written Torah, free from the oral element" (Bloom, 1979, pp, 7–8). Bloom has taken this spirit and used it to create what he terms an aggressive reading of the literary text: "There is no reading worthy of being communicated to another unless it deviates to break form, twists lines to form a shelter, and so makes a meaning through that shattering of belated vessels" (1979, p. 22).[9] Bloom would interrupt and shatter the given forms of autonomy as the most effective means of engaging the sense of the text. His contribution to the community of texts is a commentary that opens up the form and provides continuity with older voices heard alongside his own.

Today, it might be said that interpretive commentary and community are sustained principally through our educational systems and, most ideally, in our universities. This extended educational and intellectual community is the source for those texts which Olson admires for their evolutionary distance from utterance. Yet, as I have already pointed out, within this community we have retained many vestiges of an oral ideal—of the sort brought to my attention by the Haggadah—that are intended to ensure intellectual rigor. The paradox of the text lies in the fact that the interplay with oral traditions is essential to the vitality of what is termed academic discourse. Interpretive intrusion moves the reader past the autonomy and authority of the text; it amounts to a thoughtful outspokenness within a community of discourse.

In the classroom—itself another blend of oral and literate cultures—it would seem incumbent on us to examine the regard for texts and for literacy that we encourage among our students. My examination of Olson's history of the text in light of my own personal history suggests a missing lesson in literacy, a lesson on the interpretive compulsion that is at the heart of the literate enterprise. As Olson has noted in his investigation of the text in the school setting, "Textbooks, like religious ritual . . . are both devices for putting ideas and beliefs above criticism" (1980, p. 194). In the Passover service, we have a ritual that suggests that even the sacred text demands both telling and questioning, both inquiry and critical argument. The authority and ritual of the textbook can be met through an introduction to the cultural tradition of commentary. Students can be encouraged in their urge to interrupt if teachers make it clear that this is a common and healthy practice in taking hold of texts, rather than being thoroughly taken as a reader. This encouragement should begin at the age when students feel comfortable with the seamless flow and authority of the text. By this point, many will already have taken their first critical steps, if only by recommending one book to a friend and throwing down another. Yet will they come to realize that the object is not so much to pull "the" meaning from the text as it is to endlessly challenge that meaning?

As I stated at the beginning of this chapter, my reading of the Haggadah is intended to provide a cultural supplement to Olson's analysis of textual qualities. My desire has been to bring to the fore at least one aspect of how we conduct ourselves with texts. In the face of the text's authority in the schools, I certainly agree with Olson's primary recommendation that students become strong writers as well as strong readers: "The development of competence as a writer may again win for [the student] the social role of equal participant and critic, but this time in the community of writers" (1980, p. 195). Yet I feel that this writerly approach should be informed by a renewed regard for the text, that writing should move from interruption to inquiry. This regard can become the basis of competence within the community to which Olson refers. But in aspiring to join this group, students need to appreciate its power; an "interpretive community," to use Stanley Fish's term (1980), acts to constitute the processes of interruption and interpretation. In the field of literary studies, Fish and

Frank Kermode have worked in quite different styles to establish that with a text in hand, "interpretation is the only game in town" (Fish, 1980, p. 355), and that "it is by recognizing the tacit authority of the institution that we achieve the measure of liberty we have in interpreting" (Kermode, 1983, p. 184).

The teacher's responsibility in light of this urge toward interpretation and community would seem to extend beyond instruction in the skills of literacy; otherwise, we bring students to the door only to leave them outside of the community, disenfranchised. There is a need to introduce students to the textual attitudes, practices, and communities that have guided the advancement of knowledge over the centuries. If we need a model for textual discourse in the classroom, we might well turn to J. F. Molitar's assessment of the sustaining role of the oral element in a literate culture: "The spoken word, as well as life and practice, must therefore be the constant companions and interpreters of the written word, which otherwise remains a dead abstract concept in the mind, lacking all vitality and tangible content" (cited by Scholem, 1971, p. 290).

If we are to keep these two companions of the tangible—the spoken and written word—present in our classroom work with texts, we should also push them to the fore in our research into literacy. Certainly the interplay of the two lies at the heart of Shirley Brice Heath's sensitive ethnography of the Trackton and Roadville communities. In less obvious ways, these oral and literate companions remain part and parcel of literacy in other communities as well. To go after the distinguishing marks of literacy in language and culture, we need to balance the tireless search for a cognitive model of linguistic processes with an attentiveness to how these processes work in our literate culture. The literacy lessons that should inform our educational concerns can be found both in sitting down with the family around the dining-room table or with a child in the corner of the classroom, and in reading the graffiti at the bus stop on the way home or bedtime stories after the sun goes down.

Although autonomous and explicit qualities of language may be part of a literate bias in text, the bias in literacy is more surely in us and in what we make of it. We can take these linguistic qualities as the basis of an educational ideal for reading and writing, or, as I have attempted, we can challenge them for their certain narrowness, their partial deafness. The act of recovering this sub-rosa chapter in the development of a literate tradition is meant to remind us of the range of possibilities literacy contains. The paradox of the utterance underlying the text is that it opens, rather than confounds, the scope of our textual experiences and the direction of our investigations. Since all of this has been said as an interruption of David Olson's essay on utterance and text, I offer him the courtesy of the final word by resuming his sound advice: "What matters is what people do with literacy."

Notes

1. Deborah Tannen's research within the mainstream on differences between oral and literate language (1982) has broached the divide by striking a continuum; Suzanne Romaine (1984) has applied this concept in her studies of adolescent communicative competencies, though she still holds to a literacy that "centres on decontextualized non-participation," which divides from the oral mode in a fashion that this chapter is intended to challenge.

2. In exploring the continuing traces of oral culture, Walter Ong has found a certain persistence to "orality," as he terms it (1980). Yet he describes a definite drop in the oral approach to literacy-reading as an oral activity-in the 19th century. He identifies in current culture a "secondary orality," which thrives through the media; but what I am focusing on is the survival of an oral spirit that remains at the source of the intellectual strength in our approach to texts. Although Ong (1982) advises against treating the oral as an ideal, I am not so much harking back to a golden age of vocalism as emphasizing the value that has been sustained.

3. For what seems a more rigorous assessment of the Greeks' accomplishment with the phonetic alphabet, particularly in relation to the earlier achievements of the Semitic consonantal alphabets, see Geoffrey Sampson (1985). It almost goes without saying that the oral intellectual ideal embodied by Socrates in the dialogues of Plato represents another sort of textual paradox.

4. Elizabeth Eisenstein (1979, p. 130) points to this Lutheran instance of distortion by way of reminding us that few simple propositions hold on the impact of print and the spread of literacy.

5. Roth (1954) points out that this inheritance includes the notion of study as a form of worship, which is central to the tradition of the Haggadah. Noting "how familiar Jewish thinkers seem to have been to the educated public of Europe from the thirteenth century to the seventeenth century," he mentions the project of Maimonides as exemplary for the European intelligentsia: "It is an attempt by a Jew, steeped in the literature and the traditions of his people, to solve an intellectual problem, of urgent importance for the thought of the day, in the spirit of that tradition and with its help" (p. 57). More recently, Hartman and Budick (1986) have accused both church and university of "misconceiving or misappropriating the Hebraic elements in our culture" (p. x), although they also point out that since the 19th century, these elements have been recognized, albeit in some confusion, by the likes of Matthew Arnold as "one of the countercritiques [along with Hellenism] by which western civilization has been kept vigorous and creative" (p. ix).

6. Though the term *Haggadah* is also used to refer to an entire genre in the Judaic tradition, covering a range of commentary that does not relate specifically to Jewish law (Heinemann, 1986), in this instance *Haggadah* is used to refer to a specific text in this tradition, the Passover Haggadah, which incorporates biblical story, liturgy, and postbiblical commentary.

7   These five disruptive rabbis receive no introduction in the service; they are simply a part of its telling. As it turns out, they were from the second century C.E., and Rabbi Akiba is certainly the most notable. It is told that he remained a shepherd until the age of 40, when his wife inspired him to study. Out of his oral roots he became a great Talmudic scholar; his courage eventually led him to martyrdom, after leading the Bar Kokhba rebellion against the Romans under the emperor Hadrian (Ben-Asher & Leaf, 1957, pp. 16-17).

8   In bringing to the modern conception of literacy the Judaic reminder of an oral core, I have inadvertently stumbled into an ancient debate about the intellectual roots of the West. Apparently, Josephus, a Jewish historian at the time of Christ, declared that Homer could not write. Walter Ong points out that "he did so in order to argue that Hebrew culture was superior to the very ancient Greek culture" (1982, p. 18). The fact that Josephus was right came to be accepted only in the 20th century; Eric Havelock (1982) has described how important the literacy of Homer was to the European conceptions of ancient Greece during his own early education. Although Havelock has made much of the Greek perfection of the "true alphabet" as the instrument of a new state of mind, he cautions against a treatment of Hellenism that is "by definition assumed to be an ideal one expressive of the intellectual values of modern Europe as these have been nurtured by philosophic idealism and literary romanticism" (pp. 29-30).

9   A related theory on the question of engagement is the reader-response school of reading, which postulates a transactional or creative experience between reader and text (Tomkins, 1980). Absent from its account is the matter of aggression or interruption raised here; the reader is said by some to experience the text and by others to write the text. Something more is implied by Bloom and by the Haggadah: an endless wrestling with the interpretation that is reading. For a recent interruption of the complacency in reader response, see Patracinio P. Schweickart (1986).

References

Ben-Asher, N., & Leaf, H. (Eds.). (1957). *The junior Jewish encyclopedia.* New York: Shengold.

Bloom, H. (1979). The breaking of form. In H. Bloom, P. de Man, J. Derrida, G. Hartman, & J. H. Miller (Eds.), *Deconstruction and criticism* (pp. 1–38). New York: Continuum.

Boman, T. (1970). *Hebrew thought compared with Greek* (J. L. Moreau, Trans.). New York: Norton.

Bosker, B. (1984). *The origins of the seder: The Passover rite of early rabbinic Judaism.* Berkeley: University of California Press.

Clanchy, M. T. (1979). *From memory to written record: England, 1066–1307.* London: Edward Arnold.

Derrida, J. (1974). *Of grammatology* (G. C. Spivak, Trans.). Baltimore: Johns Hopkins University Press.

Derrida, J. (1979). Living on. In H. Bloom, P. de Man, J. Derrida, G. Hartman, & J. H. Miller (Eds.), *Deconstruction and criticism* (pp. 75–176). New York: Continuum.

Eisenstein, E. (1979). *The printing press as an agent of change: Communications and cultural transformations in early-modern Europe.* Cambridge, UK: Cambridge University Press.

Finnegan, R. (1973). Literacy versus non-literacy: The great divide. In R. Finnegan & R. Horton (Eds.), *Modes of thought.* London: Faber.

Fish, S. (1980). What makes an interpretation acceptable? In *Is there a text in this class? The authority of interpretive communities* (pp. 338–355). Cambridge, MA: Harvard University Press.

Form of service for the two first nights of the feast of Passover (new illustrated ed., with English translation). (1859). New York: J. Rosenbaum, successor to H. Sakolski.

Fredman, R. G. (1981). *The Passover service.* Philadelphia: University of Pennsylvania Press.

Gilbert, S. M., & Gubar, S. (1979). *The madwoman in the attic: The woman writer and the 19th-century literary imagination.* New Haven: Yale University Press.

Goodman, P. (1973). *The Passover anthology.* Philadelphia: Jewish Publication Society.

Goody J., & Watt, I. (1962–1963). The consequences of literacy. *Comparative Studies in Society and History, 5,* 304–345.

Graff, H. (1979). *The literacy myth: Literacy and social structure in the 19th-century city.* New York: Academic Press.

Hartman, G. H., & Budick, S. (Eds.). (1986). *Midrash and literature.* New Haven: Yale University Press.

Havelock, E. (1976). *Origins of Western literacy.* Toronto: Ontario Institute for Studies in Education.

Havelock, E. (1982). *The literate revolution in Greece and its cultural consequences.* Princeton: Princeton University Press.

Heath, S. B. (1983). *Ways with words: Language, life, and work in communities and classrooms.* Cambridge, UK: Cambridge University Press.

Heinemann, J. (1986). The nature of Aggadah. In G. H. Hartmann & S. Budick (Eds.), *Midrash and literature* (pp. 41–56). New Haven: Yale University Press.

Kermode, F. (1983). Institutional control of interpretation. In *The art of telling: Essays on fiction* (pp. 168–184). Cambridge, MA: Harvard University Press.

Kermode, F. (1986). The plain sense of things. In G. H. Hartman & S. Budick (Eds.), *Midrash and literature* (pp. 179–194). New Haven: Yale University Press.

Levin, M. (n.d.). *An Israel Haggadah for Passover.* New York: Abrams.

Locke, J. (1972). *An essay concerning human understanding* (M. Cranston, Ed.). New York: Collier.

Luke, C., de Castell, S., & Luke, A. (1983). Beyond criticism: The authority of the school text. *Curriculum Inquiry, 13,* 111–127.

Montaigne, M. (1909). *The essays of Michael, Lord of Montaigne* (J. Florio, Ed. & Trans.). London: Oxford University Press.

Olson, D. R. (1977a). From utterance to text: The bias of language in speech and writing. *Harvard Educational Review, 47,* 84–109.

Olson, D. R. (1977b). The language of instruction: The literate bias of schooling. In R. C. Anderson, R. J. Spiro, & W. Montague (Eds.), *Schooling and the acquisition of knowledge* (pp. 65–89). Hillsdale, NJ: Erlbaum.

Olson, D. R. (1980). On the language and authority of textbooks. *Journal of Communication, 30,* 186–196.

Olson, D. R. (1985). Introduction. In D. R. Olson, N. Torrance, & A. Hildyard (Eds.), *Literacy, language, and learning: The nature and consequences of reading and writing* (pp. 1–15). Cambridge, UK: Cambridge University Press.

Ong, W. (1980). Orality and literacy in our time. *Journal of Communication, 30,* 197–204.

Ong, W. (1982). *Orality and literacy: The technologizing of the word.* London: Methuen.

Plato. (1952). *Plato's Phaedrus* (R. Hackforth, Trans.). Cambridge, UK: Cambridge University Press.

Romaine, S. (1984). *The language of children and adolescents: The acquisition of communicative competence.* Oxford: Blackwell.

Rosen, H. (1985). The voice of communities and the language of classrooms. *Harvard Educational Review, 55,* 448–456.

Roth, L. (1954). *Jewish thought as a factor in civilization.* Paris: UNESCO.

Sampson, G. (1985). *Writing systems: A linguistic introduction.* Stanford: Stanford University Press.

Scholem, G. (1971). Revelation and tradition as religious categories in Judaism. In G. Scholem (Ed.), *The messianic idea in Judaism* (pp. 282–303). New York: Schocken.

Scribner, S., & Cole, M. (1981). *The psychology of literacy.* Cambridge, MA: Harvard University Press.

Schweickart, P. P. (1986). Reading ourselves: Toward a feminist theory of reading. In E. A. Flyn & P. P. Schweickart (Eds.), *Gender and reading: Essays on readers, texts, and contexts* (pp. 31–62). Baltimore: Johns Hopkins University Press.

Street, B. (1984). *Literacy in theory and practice.* Cambridge, UK: Cambridge University Press.

Tannen, D. (1982). The oral/literate continuum in discourse. In D. Tannen (Ed.), *Spoken and written discourse* (pp. 1–16). Norwood, NJ: Ablex.

Tomkins, J. (Ed.). (1980). *Reader response criticism: From formalism to post-structuralism.* Baltimore: Johns Hopkins University Press.

Wittgenstein, L. (1958). *Philosophical investigations* (G. E. M. Anscombe, Trans.). New York: Macmillan.

Wittgenstein, L. (1961). *Tractatus logico-philosophicus* (D. F. Pears & B. F. McGuinness, Trans.). London: Routledge & Kegan Paul.

Chapter 5

Curriculum after Culture, Race, Nation

"Culture" has long been taught, mapped, displayed, and tested in schools. We all know the routine. Culture is what students study when they learn how people in other lands live, work, worship, and play. Culture is not what students learn when they do long division, mastered "Ode to Joy" on the recorder, or whack a ball with a stick. Which is only to say that the schools worked with traditional anthropological conceptions of a world divided into different cultures.[1] Many schools now take a multicultural approach that extends the study of culture by, in effect, bringing it on back home. The study of culture now includes not only those living in far-off lands, but also those living within the school neighborhood.[2] This is certainly not all that multiculturalism is about. But this expanded appreciation of culture does represent a more democratic and inclusive approach to the cultural diversity of both schools and the nation. Culture, then, has become a way of thinking about identity and difference in schools and in scholarship.[3]

To better understand the progress that has been made in the name of culture, I wish to draw a few lessons for educators and students about how this concept has come to organize pervasively the way we see the world. Although much fascinating work is being done on culture's hybrid, hyphenated, and migratory relation to identity, I think there is also value in stepping away from these psychological interests and asking how culture, as a concept, an idea with its own history of use, stands as a force for good and evil. I am interested here in the strategic use of this concept, especially in relation to its powerful complementary terms of race and nation. Although it may seem that for as long as there have been humans there has been culture, we need to think about how the word has come to be used in the way we now use it. The idea of studying human differences as an expression of different cultures was originally posed a century ago by the anthropologist Franz Boas in what can be identified as an antiracist strategy. Although the concept of culture has provided a powerful testimony to the power of words and ideas in its reduction of racism in his field and in education more generally, it has continued to carry forward residual ideas of race and nation that need to figure in the thinking of educators who bear the torch of culture as a liberating force that readily overlaps with ideas of race and nationality.[4]

My modest hope is that the stories I have to tell here about the conceptual work that culture does will help the schools expand what they teach about human differences by including lessons on how ideas such as culture are used to divide people and how they might overcome those divisions. The schools could surely do more to help students understand how education has contributed to the weight of culture, race, and nation, no less than gender, on the shape of their lives.[5] As they learn to detect and resist popular forms of racism, the work presented here may help them to also appreciate how the study of culture continues to work within and against the racial and national divisions that were among the most studied objects of European imperialism.[6] Students can see that what otherwise seems past can be carried forward in the language by which we come to know ourselves and others. They may also see that changing the future may entail just that pragmatic project of working with more imagination on our vocabulary (Rorty, 1989). This is an invitation to join in an archaeology of knowledge of the sort described by Michel Foucault, which, if it could possibly be captured in a single phrase, consists of treating all that has been said about culture, for example, "as practices that systematically form the object of which they speak" (1972, p. 49). If the study of culture systematically forms the object of which it speaks, it also has the effect of objectifying the differences that divide people. What follows, in other words, concerns what we teach about when we teach about culture.

Before going any further, I should make it plain that I am not somehow against studying differences among nations, spiritual beliefs, or genetic structures. It is only that the ways we divide the world should not be exempt from historical and critical inquiry. That we are endlessly fascinated by variations and deeply attached to the familiar seems no more than a characteristic of how we live. My interest here is in how we learn to read these perceptions and practices, variations and familiarities, in ways that do not serve everyone equally well, and how these differences are made to produce an otherness in a confluence of culture, race, and nation. Still, you may wonder whether questioning culture in this way doesn't undermine the spirit of multiculturalism in the schools. Now that the prize of cultural recognition is more widely shared, am I doing to culture what feminists have charged postmodernists with doing to subjectivity, that is, "decentering" it only after women made a claim to it? I think it a fair caution, yet victories are good times to ask about the terms under which the race has been run, about what comes after culture, if it has not already come, in this ongoing struggle against discrimination. After all, Boas did not hit upon the true nature of humanity with his idea of people possessing their own cultures; he only found a way of characterizing differences that diminished the place of race in the social sciences at the turn of the 20th century.

In trying to understand this need to question the way culture is used as a concept, the study of gender offers interesting parallels. In the recent past, social scientists were as keen to determine the *nature* of gender differences as they were with culture. Treating the male as the norm, they generated a body of research that furthered, in effect, the disadvantage and containment of women.[7] It took the dedicated efforts of feminist scholarship, some of which I draw on later in this chapter, to rethink what had become a scientifically enhanced form of common prejudice. The world according to gender has since been shaken, if not shattered, and biology is no longer destiny. What then of the divisions inspired by the study of culture, which has formed such an explicit part of the school curriculum in a way that gender has not (however much it continues to dominate the hidden curriculum)?[8]

The schools have already proved to be a critical forum in the ongoing fight against racism. They are currently caught up in debates that pose a national culture against multiculturalism, but they have yet to deal with what nationalism means for students whose world of identification is inevitably larger than the nation and who are about to step into a Microsoft-Disney era of transnational economies and global cultures. Educators need to take stock of what culture once was, and they need to ask how this fin de siècle idea is equipping those about to step into a new century. There seems no better time to invoke—let us say in memory of Franz Boas's progressive accomplishments with culture—a centennial retrospective on the state of the concept.

Culture against Race

It could readily be said that European imperialism combined a strange dedication to exploitation and education. Although I have developed this theme elsewhere (1998), let me just say briefly here that imperialism's most daring adventurers, no less than its most ruthless administrators, proved keen observers of what we now think of as cultural differences, and their ethnographic records and collections initiated an ordering of humanity on the basis of race and culture. What began with Columbus's landing in San Salvador as a captain's logbook of fascination and desire—"They all go naked as their mothers bore them, including the women, although I saw only one very young girl" (1969, p. 55)—was gradually transformed into the disciplined gaze of an edifying science of human difference. By the 19th century, these itinerant students of human nature had created a man-headed science that was devoted to positioning the races of humankind within an evolutionary narrative (Baker, 1974; Banton, 1987; Hannaford, 1996).

During the Victorian era, as Christopher Herbert has described it, this idea of culture, which suggested that all people lived by a set of rules and practices that possessed their own logic and order, was posed as "a scientific rebuttal" of the "myth of a state of ungoverned human desire" among savage and primitive peoples (1991, p. 29). Culture, Herbert goes on to say, was "one of the most lethal instruments of dissidence from Victorian thinking," dispelling the idea of primitive life as representing a state of moral anarchy and debacle in favor of evolutionary development (p. 44). Yet this scholarly interest in the study of culture and cultural differences was still about subjecting colonial peoples to the knowing gaze of the West; as Herbert asks at the outset of his book, "Does 'culture' embody purely and simply the imperious will to interpretation?" (p. 6). The answer may well be "not necessarily," yet imperialism's intrepid adventurers-cum-anthropologists were very much a part of the empire's governing apparatus well into the 20th century. And when anthropologists began to prove less than loyal to the imperial cause in their fieldwork and began siding with the interests of native populations, they faced their own regulation and governance by colonial regimes (Burton, 1992).

This idea of culture began to disrupt the rule of race, diminishing the scope of human difference from an evolutionary force to a history of social practices, while still providing the European educated classes with a basis for paternalism and acquisition. That is to say, cultures were to be studied and collected, and in that way, it was imagined, they were being revered and protected. Yet this also meant that cultures were yet another source of Western wealth within imperialism's scheme of things.[9] Imperialism's shiploads of cultural artifacts fed a will-to-know that had its heart set on the whole of the world, much like the bibliophile mad to own great and small books in order to pursue the whole of humankind's artful mind. But this wasn't simply about collecting culture for its own sake. James Clifford notes how the value of the resulting collections, museums, and exhibitions was focused on "accumulation [that] unfolds in a pedagogical, edifying manner" (1990, p. 144). This educational function formed an important part of the rationale for the acquiring, ordering, and preserving of cultures. It attested to the West's ability to instruct the world about its own true nature and gave a fine polish to what might otherwise seem to be the obsessive and greedy work of sail and cannon.

Yet consider how imperialism's global economy had already undone the imagined integrity of the cultures that made up the empire. This possessive study of culture was already an act of nostalgia, a longing for a world of isolated communities that imperialism had destroyed. The exhibition of these cultures obscured the damage done to them by imperialism, while reinforcing the boundaries of the primitive and the civilized, which were essential to the moral economy of imperialism. What appears to lie behind this tireless drive to delineate the precise nature of difference—first as race and then as culture—is not a history of scientific development but a shift in political economy, especially in its relation to knowledge and education. The use of culture as a concept for organizing difference emerged within a specific struggle for global domination that had reached its peak with the turn of the 19th century and was about to enter a period of reconfiguration and transformation, as the imperial states recognized that they could not remain in power on the same moral basis as they had for the previous four centuries.

The decisive moment in the contest between race and culture as the best interpretive framework for making sense of human differences within the imperial mind-set that held the world in thrall came in the final years of the 19th century. It was then that Boas decided to stop using race, as his colleagues did, to analyze the way the peoples he studied lived. He chose instead to speak of culture; more specifically, he began by the simplest of grammatical acts to speak of cultures, distinct and integral cultures, in a way that other anthropologists had not. People responded to the world through the form of their own culture. They were not simply acting out a reflection of their race or their evolutionary development in their progress toward culture, both of which were held to be the great determiners of destiny and character. Boas freed people from the continual reference to the accomplishment of Western civilization (Degler,

1991). His "anti-evolutionist, anti-racialist empirical study of cultures," as George Stocking has characterized Boas's work (1982, p. 287), offered a new direction for the social sciences that eventually became the basis for what we take for granted as culture.

However, Boas knew that it was not enough simply to offer this idea of integral cultures as an alternative to the racial study of humankind and wait for his colleagues to change their ways. He also set out to design research studies that would undermine the principal and prized concepts of his race-focused colleagues. Boas undertook studies of immigration in America that demonstrated how the body responded to cultural changes rather than being racially fixed. He also challenged the field to produce any real proof that race figured in the "mental characteristics" of a people, spawning a contest that goes on to this day (1940, p. 10). The third step to what I am identifying as Boas's approach—after proposing culture as an alternative conception of difference and refuting and exposing the claims made on behalf of race—was to inspire a generation of scholars to explore the implications of this new tack. Still, it would take Boas and those who studied with him, including Margaret Mead, Alfred Kroeber, and Ashley Montagu, decades to overcome resistance in the social sciences to the idea that culture rather than race should be the principal object of study.

In his 1931 presidential address to the American Association for the Advancement of Science, Boas reminded his audience that "racial traits are unimportant compared to cultural conditions" (1940, p. 13). But by then, the science of race was approaching its most terrible moment, and this scientist-as-social-activist felt compelled to attack what he described as "the strong emotional reactions and varied types of legislation" then being mounted against "the intermingling of racial types" in the United States (p. 3).[10]

When it comes to helping students understand that this now prevalent idea of culture was the work of anthropologists, who did not so much uncover the culture of a people as fashion it out of the raw materials of their lives, the best lesson aid or instrument of epiphany that I have found is a field note by Margaret Mead. She is remarkably perceptive and candid about the process in a way that can help us get a distance from a concept that now seems a fact of nature. First published in the *American Anthropologist* in 1932, Mead's field note has since been reprinted by James Clifford more than once; still, I think it worth doing yet again to appreciate what went into establishing the bounds of a "culture" by a profession intent on bringing an unruly world to order:

Note from New Guinea
Aliatoa, Wiwiak District, New Guinea
April 21, 1932

We are just completing a culture of a mountain group here in the lower Torres Chelles. They have no name and we haven't decided what to call them yet. They are a very revealing people in spots, providing a final basic concept from which all the mother's brothers' curses and father's sisters' curses, etc. derive, and having articulated the attitude toward incest which Reo [Fortune] outlined as fundamental in his Encyclopedia article. They have taken the therapeutic measures which we recommended for Dobu and Manus—having a devil in addition to a neighbor sorcerer, and having got their dead out of the village and localized. But in other ways they are annoying: they have bits and snatches of all the rag and tag and bob tail of magical and ghostly belief from the Pacific, and they are somewhat like the Plains in their receptivity to strange ideas. A picture of a local native reading the index to *The Golden Bough* just to see if they had missed anything, would be appropriate. They are very difficult to work, living all over the place with half a dozen garden houses, and never staying put for over a week at a time. Of course this offered a new challenge in method which was interesting. The difficulties incident upon being two days over impossible mountains has been consuming and we are going to do a coastal people next.

> Sincerely yours,
> Margaret Mead (cited by Clifford,
> 1990, pp. 151–152)

In a series of inside jokes, Mead reflects both the well-intentioned desire to learn about others and the world-weary professional work of "doing" another culture. The anthropologist completes and names the culture that the natives unknowingly reveal. The professional apparatus of anthropology—gathering, naming, ordering, and classifying—was devoted to taking possession of the natives' lives in a way that the natives could never hope to acquire.[11] The natives' lives ranked among gold, tomatoes, and tobacco as the fruits of conquest. Their lives contributed to what I have characterized, in my study of imperialism (1998), as a form of "intellectual mercantilism," in which the raw materials for grand theories were imported from the colonies for refinement and redistribution.

Not long after Mead wrote her note, culture may have reached a culminating moment in its climb to being the central focus in the study of humankind, when Bronislaw Malinowski proposed a "scientific theory of culture" (1944). Although Franz Boas had made culture into a system of meaning, he was not given to theory building. This fell to Malinowski, who is best known for his fieldwork in the South Pacific, which set new scientific standards for "authenticity" in the efforts of ethnographic fieldwork to capture the culture of the native. His intent was to distance the profession from the gentleman curio hunters, who were drawn to the exotic and the sensational, as well as the anthropologists for hire, who conducted surveys of native life at the behest of colonial administrators.

After years "in the field" observing the readily apparent wholeness of other people's lives, Malinowski was able to see in culture "a vast apparatus, partly material, partly human and partly spiritual" (1944, p. 36). Culture was "obviously . . . the integral whole" of a society, and this sense of obviousness spoke to culture's ability to establish new boundaries after this turning away from a reliance on racial distinctions. "Each culture owes its completeness and self-sufficiency," Malinowski wrote, "to the fact that it satisfies the whole range of basic, instrumental and integrative needs" (p. 40). Culture's integral vitality could be found in any given artifact, behavior, or belief, which could always be shown to reflect the completeness of the whole. It meant that culture could account for the whole of the "difference" that set one people off from another. Culture was a way of naming and naturalizing the boundary that set people apart. The study of a culture was about realizing how the way that a people lived constituted a distinct and self-sufficient organism. This differed from the traditional study of race, which was focused on determining the near-species distinctions between the races, yet it still treated the differences as integral to people's lives. This continuing relationship between race and culture will be treated in the next section of this chapter.

Malinowski's contribution also makes clear how this anthropological interest in culture tended to create a body of knowledge out of a body of desire. His posthumously published field diary makes it painfully clear that an intimate study of another culture could as soon give rise to hostility and loathing as to the sort of longing he records after following a native woman through the forest.[12] Fieldwork could mean translating bodies of desire into bodies of knowledge; it could mean identifying the cultural integrity of the body as a way of bringing both the body and the one naming the body within the order of knowledge.[13] While Malinowski explored the personal struggle that came of this fascination with difference, the public line on regulating the sexual divide was focused on policing "miscegenation," which proved a constant theme for the science of race. It was a fear, recall, that Boas had had to address in the 1930s when the eugenics movement was afoot in America. In studying imperial themes of desire, purification, and repression, Ann Laura Stoler (1995) points to an array of educational programs, colonial regulations, and scientific studies that were clearly intended to feed the fascination and desire while educating people in the risks that befell those who did not adhere to the "natural" distinctions among peoples.[14]

Finally, there is the therapeutic value of cultural study, which, Marianna Torgovnick argues (1990), drove both Mead and Malinowski to use their anthropological studies to work through their own alienation and sense of homelessness. Malinowski found, as Torgovnick explains, "the means of objectifying his feelings, of converting his feelings into the magisterial observations guided by pure, untainted theory," even as his alienation provoked, in her words, a "furious desire for the primitive" (p. 231). In Mead's study of Samoans, Torgovnick finds "a model of alternative social organization in which psychological integration is a birthright" (p. 240).[15] As I have suggested, native lives were treated as a natural resource to be used, in this case, to improve the mental health of American society. As Mead wrote in *Sex and Temperament*, "If we are to achieve a richer culture, rich in contrasting values, we must recognize the whole gamut of human potentialities" (1963, p. 322).

By this point, what had begun as a way of talking about how people lived within different cultures had grown into the central scientific concept of anthropology and sociology. By the end of the Second World War, Stuart Chase could hold up culture as "the foundation stone of the social sciences" in his book *The Proper Study of Mankind* (1948, p. 59), although I hardly need to add that there were social scientists who kept alive the focus on race and racial differences.[16] Culture, for Boas, Mead, and Malinowski, was about giving meaning, order, and structure to the way people lived, and thus to who they were. It was about searching for the laws and nature of human development. What had been cast as a matter of race during the 19th century became for them, as it is in large measure for us today, a matter of culture. This renaming of difference was aimed at clearing the slate of racial prejudices in the study of humankind without giving up on the study of difference and division. In expanding what we teach under the name of culture, we need to compare it to the barrier that race constructed around people's lives.

The schools, in turn, did their part during the 20th century to spread this idea of integral cultures. Social-studies textbooks eventually dropped illustrated tables that compared the different qualities of each race, in favor of guides to the strange and fascinating cultures that made up what was often entitled "our world." Although the 1960s saw racial notions of "cultural deprivation" used to explain inequalities in educational attainment, American schools by and large endorsed the stance of the Supreme Court, which, following the civil rights movement, held the law to be color-blind. The specter of racism continued to haunt the daily lives of people of color, but when it came to the rule of knowledge in the schools (no less than with the rule of law), race was said to have no place.[17]

Now, it's true that anthropology began decades ago to do penance for these earlier sins by critiquing its own part in the imperial enterprise (Asad, 1973; Hymes, 1974). The museums have not been long in following suit, asking about their own acts of appropriation and display in the name of culture (Karp & Lavine, 1991).[18] As a result, many museums are now rethinking how they display artifacts (as well as about their ownership of those artifacts), no longer treating them as a window into the lives of those at a distance in time and space from us. We are now invited to think about how the objects we are looking at are also very much about those who assembled and arranged them. I think it is fair to ask whether the questioning of culture that is going on among anthropologists and museum curators has found its way into the schools, which have long proven enthusiastic markets for ethnographic exhibits in many different forms, from *National Geographic* and its spin-offs to Web-based simulated travel adventures.[19] A century after Boas turned culture into such an effective alternative to the racist construction of difference, we have to ask ourselves whether it has taken us as far as it possibly can down the road of human equality. We ought to pause and consider what it continues to bring forward from that earlier time.

Culture after Race

It can seem that when people refuse to have their rights denied any longer, as happened with the civil rights and national independence movements in the 1950s and 1960s, the educated classes take it as their duty to rustle through the scattered concepts of identity for the least volatile of containers, brush it off, and see if it will hold people together in less damaging ways. This is a matter not of selecting what is finally the right name for who we are but of reworking the language (or inventing new vocabulary, as philosopher Richard Rorty would have it [1989]), that it might advance the long-haul political project of achieving ever greater degrees of human equality. In this way, Boas turned culture into a way to discuss differences that was removed from the abuses of denigration perpetuated in the name of race. But there is no walking away from this idea of race. However discredited by the human and biological sciences that once paid it such attention, race is still something more than an itch in a vestigial limb of the body politic. It is not about to be reasoned or written away, not about to be finally displaced by culture. For culture and race bleed into each other, as the divisions of culture are made to resemble those of race.[20]

Walter Benn Michaels offers a convincing instance of how race still lies with culture when he examines the common concern that *one can lose one's culture* (1993; 1994). If culture describes a way of life, a set of behaviors and beliefs that give life meaning, then how could one lose it, except by death or dementia? This sense of potential loss suggests that culture, rather than "describing beliefs people hold and the things they actually do," forms an original essence within each of us, leading Michaels to conclude that "cultural identity is actually a form of racial identity" (1994, p. 758). Does culture really detach difference from biology? If it does, how can one think of culture as operating as a specific set of differences that are inborn and integral to a life? When culture is thought of as the soul of a people, how far removed is it from the idea of race as a quality of character that cannot be escaped? Given this tendency in the use of culture, Michaels tries to do Boas one better by calling for an end to the use of the categories of both race and culture. It is not going to work, but then maybe such a desire is wrongheaded.[21]

This liberal interest in transcending forms of race consciousness has come under serious critique, first by black power advocates in the 1960s and, more recently, by critical race theorists in legal studies, who take exception to the civil rights movement's focus on integration (Crenshaw, Gotanda, Peller & Thomas, 1995). Liberalism's successes with integration were taken to signal that the courts and schools were color-blind and, as such, that they should form a refuge from racial struggle and the prejudices of ignorance. This located the problem of racism elsewhere, in redneck and other localized prejudices, while obscuring the cultural (and racial) character of the courts and the schools that claimed to be rational and professional in their judgment of a case or a student. Race consciousness itself was transformed into the problem by this liberal stance, undermining affirmative action and placing those who had no choice about their race identity in an untenable situation. It pushed the underground, unspoken routines of racism, no less than the daily struggle against them, outside the scope of the law and the curriculum.

For well more than a century, dating back to Martin Delany's antebellum call for black separatism, the vital alternative to this integrationist stance has been black nationalism based on the distinct cultural identity of the black people. With the resurgence of black nationalism in the 1960s, Stokely Carmichael's call for freedom was about, in his words, "preserving the cultural integrity of the black community," and Malcolm X defended the idea of all-black schools equipped with books that carried many of the otherwise "missing ingredients" of African American culture (cited by Peller, 1995, pp. 139, 128). Culture was again being used as a point of refuge against the demeaning spirit of racism, yet black nationalism was never simply about cultural preservation. The assertion of nationhood was about African Americans achieving a greater degree of political sovereignty over their own lives. It was about recognizing a "nation within the nation" directed at liberating "forcibly transplanted colonial subjects," as C. Munford put it a 1970 address, "who have acquired cohesive identity in the course of centuries of struggle against enslavement, cultural alienation, and the spiritual cannibalism of white racism" (cited by Peller, 1995, p. 137). Even though such was the rhetoric of an earlier age, it effectively dramatizes how identities are forged in a struggle for place, rather than being simply an expression of the neighborhood in which one grew up. Black nationalism brought race, culture, and nation into close association in the fight for fundamental political power. The master's tools *can* be used to take down the master's house. And although I do not want to gloss over the Nation of Islam's disquieting bouts of anti-Semitism, I do think the critical-race-theory movement and other expressions of black nationalism are effective responses to the continuing force of a racism that uses this category of race to name what is outside the norm.[22]

The educational challenge, as I see it, is to help students to see how what is often portrayed as a struggle between the races is as much a contest over how the categories are defined and controlled, a contest in which the schools, among other institutions, have long participated and have long needed to reexamine their role. The lesson here, for me at least, is to imagine a time *after* culture, race, and nation, a time when these categories no longer stand as the necessary and natural divisions of humankind, a time when these categories are seen as an elaborate means for claiming place and position, for establishing an advantage, for policing a boundary. It is about encouraging students to catch sight of how culture, race, and nation are used to name the identifiable humanity of a people in ways that, more often than not, justify inequalities. It is to recover the rhetorical force of the categories in fighting against those inequities, in realizing the force of an education—of a language act really—that can shape the world.

Multiculturalism, to return to an opening theme of this essay, certainly forms a critical education site for examining the evolving relations between culture and race among society's more progressive forces.[23]

Multiculturalism gives us a way of recognizing and celebrating difference, but it typically does so without calling the categories or their history into question. It offers much less of an educational program because of that fact, I would argue. It misses out on how multiculturalism, as Henry Louis Gates Jr. points out, "occludes" race (1993, p. 7). The adjective *multicultural* is now used, Gates reminds us, by turning to a time in the early 20th century, when *multiracial* once marked the way ahead in race relations, yet he finds the "shift from race to ethnicity . . . a salutary one, a necessary move away from the essentialist biologizing of a previous era" (p. 7). The embrace of multiculturalism misses the way culture, no less than nationality, ethnicity, and class, can be used to mask how race continues to operate as the real point of division and judgment in the celebration of cultural differences (Goldberg, 1993).

To keep the nature of this shift from race to culture away from students of multiculturalism not only obscures the important social processes that are shaping their education, it also fails to make clear the relation between racial and cultural difference. For these reasons, we need to talk about race in schools as one of the formative principles of public life in the modern era. We need to bring race back into science class in ways that make apparent to students how science first made so much out of race before abandoning the concept (Willinsky, 1998). We need to see how it shapes the way people see the world, especially now that we are prepared to question its biological and cultural status. This means no more, educationally speaking, than learning about the history of difference. Such lessons are intended to prepare students to avoid debating the true nature of differences between people in favor of arguing about how a better job can be made of representing associations and building points of connection between them.

As it stands, the concept of culture too often does the distressing sort of work that race was once used to accomplish, that is, keeping the barbarian at the gate. It happens, for example, when the literary canon is held up as proof of the West's evolution to a higher plane of existence. Yet one can think the world of Shakespeare's poetic accomplishments, I would hope, without necessarily believing that his work testifies to the threat and savagery of other cultures. As thoroughly 19th-century as that fear may seem, it still holds for the likes of such contemporary conservative critics as Roger Kimball. When Kimball writes in the *New Criterion* of the choice facing us today "between culture and barbarism," his critique of multiculturalism is not all that far removed from earlier defenses of race: "Civilization is not a gift, it is an achievement—a fragile achievement that needs constantly to be shored up and defended from besiegers inside and out" (1991, p. 13). This culture represents "civilization," which, in its fragile but subsidized achievements, towers above lesser cultures. It amounts to the best that has been thought and said, in the famous phrase Kimball borrows from Matthew Arnold.[24] Yet it is a culture that Kimball feels is currently under siege from "inside and out" (and who among us knows for sure whether we'd be judged an insider?). The culture that was once strong enough to conquer the world, bestowing the gifts of civilization in its wake, is now fragile and vulnerable, so much so that teachers who entertain debates over the nature of this culture or explore the multicultural dimensions of the planet, according to the implacable Kimball, have "defrauded their students of knowledge" (p. 13).

This confluence of culture and race, however, is not simply a matter of course content; it continues to determine the legal scope of people's lives, as found in two recent decisions of the Supreme Court of Canada. The court has ruled that the fishing rights of this country's aboriginal people (or First Nations peoples, as they refer to themselves) are defined by their culture. One of the judgments stated that "to be an aboriginal right, an activity must be an element of a practice, custom or tradition integral to the distinctive culture of the aboriginal group claiming the right" (Supreme Court, 1996a). The application of this principle resulted in the conviction of Dorothy Marie Van der Peet of the Sto:lo Nation for selling 10 salmon, while Donald and William Gladstone from the Heiltsuk Nation were granted a retrial for selling herring spawn, although none of them had obtained the required license for these activities. The Heiltsuk Nation men won their retrial on the grounds that such commercial trade was, as the court put it, "an integral part of the distinctive culture of the Heiltsuk prior to contact [with the Europeans] and was not incidental to social or ceremonial activities." This was not the case, the court ruled, with the Sto:lo (Supreme Court, 1996b). Restricting the rights of the First Nations peoples to what was once culturally distinct about their lives amounts to a denial of their sovereignty then and now. They were but a culture, in the eyes of the court, and not a nation, although the Heiltsuk and Sto:lo nations did not then sign nor have yet signed treaties that would accede their sovereign rights to the Canadian government. Basing the court ruling on whether the cultural practice in question is integral rather than incidental to a people's distinctiveness only furthers this idea of culture as a boundary that some people are in a position to define.

Although I find troubling the court's use of culture to deny nationhood, the decision was heralded in the press as restricting the government's protection of First Nation fishing rights, which had been under attack by the fishery and tourism industries as racist reverse discrimination. Gordon Gibson, a columnist for the *Toronto Globe and Mail*, for example, accuses the current policy of creating a "racially based fishery" through "racial principles" that are nothing less than "madness" (1996). The courts use culture to contain the rights of the First Nations peoples, ostensibly in the name of protecting those rights, while refusing to acknowledge their aboriginal claim to an unrelinquished national sovereignty. Meanwhile, those who have benefited by centuries of racial discrimination against these peoples appear to feel no shame in now portraying themselves as victims of racism. Thence comes the urgency I feel in helping students to step back from this highly consequential play of categories to see how readily they are worked in resolving disputes and shaping policies that define the nation.

Boas's original success in directing attention away from race and toward culture made a difference in the schools, helping to reduce the damage done to those who were to be educated. Clearly, however, there is no resting on these laurels, especially as the shortcomings of the schools' color-blind stance are made apparent. Moving beyond the legacy of culture, race, and nation does not mean hiding from the force of these ideas in the classroom. The cause of equality among people, of removing the barriers that needlessly constrict people's lives, will always be in need of new strategies that grow out of a firm grip on what the concepts that came before have made of us. These new strategies can emerge, or such is my educational belief, out of a better understanding of how culture, race, and nation have been constructed and how they are related. They can emerge from a better understanding of how these categories continue to be used to maintain a construction of the world that needs to be leveled or perhaps treated as far more fluid than the categories suggest.

Culture after Nation

Fostering an allegiance to the nation lies close to the heart of public schooling. It lies so close to the pride and identification that are to be instilled in each child that I almost shy away from calling nationalism into question in rethinking what has been made of culture. Isn't it enough to take on culture and its continuing association with race? Do I really imagine the neighborhood school chipping away at its own cornerstone as well? Where is the problem with nationalism? Well, James W. Loewen's scathing indictment of history teaching (1995) is directed at the sins committed in the name of nationalism, with textbooks serving students a steady diet of unverified facts and outright falsehoods; they transform everyone into a hero and every event into a step up the stairway to heaven that is America. These stories, selected by state adoption boards and through other screening processes in the bureaucratic expression of democratic education, amount to learning to be stupid, in Loewen's estimation. Still, one might wonder what would be left of the nation if the schools failed to instill flag-waving patriotism in the young. Perhaps, I would hazard, what would be left would be a sense of nationality that was not as closely associated with the triumph of a given culture or race that then defined who belonged to the nation.

It may also seem, at first glance, that nationalism is removed from imperialism and the conceptions of culture and race that have occupied me up to this point. The standard nation-state hypothesis is, after all, that the modern nation was born out of industrialization as an economic unit, with Romanticism rooting the idea of a national identity in blood and soil. Still, Wolfgang Mommsen (1980) and others have argued that European imperialism only extended the expression of nationalism to a colonial empire that played no less a role in national identity.[25] Military, economic, and missionary successes abroad attested to the sterling, bred-in-the-bone character of the nation. Conquest spoke to the triumph of a civilization that was then generously prepared to bequeath aspects of this character to the colonized, who were otherwise without a viable national or cultural identity. It was for want of this civilization and breeding that the colonized were judged unfit for nationhood, with aspects of this attitude lingering to this day, most noticeably in Western media coverage of Africa.

To grasp how a sense of nationality stands today with culture and race, one must appreciate that the nation was regarded during the 19th century as yet another true and natural division of humankind. This is the theme with which Elie Kedourie opens his critical monograph on nationalism:

> Nationalism is a doctrine invented in Europe at the beginning of the nineteenth century. It pretends to supply a criterion for the determination of the unit of population proper to enjoy a government exclusively its own, for the legitimate exercise of power in the state, and for the right organization of a society of states. Briefly, the doctrine holds that humanity is naturally divided into nations, that nations are known by certain characteristics which can be ascertained, and that the only legitimate type of government is national self-government. (1960, p. 9)

The nation, no less than culture and race, becomes the invented meeting ground of nature and politics. The nation may well afford a sense of being at home in the world, and as such identifies an "imagined community," in Benedict Anderson's phrase (1983). But nationality was to become part of the 19th-century conceptual arsenal of imperialism, taking its place alongside the emerging studies of race and culture, as each, in Kedourie's terms, "pretends to supply a criterion for the determination of the unit of population."[26]

And yet whereas everyone was of a race and possessed something of a culture, it took a civilized people to form, maintain, and defend a nation. In France and Germany toward the end of the 19th century, for example, the Jews' lack of a nation and nationality was often singled out as clearly a sign of a flawed "race" (Gilman, 1993, p. 12). The amalgam of race and culture giving a nation its character had been inspired by Romantic visions of blood and soil that help us to see, for example, the Frenchness in Monet and Manet. But we also need to understand the France that treasures the Département des Antiquités Égytpiennes in the Louvre while giving a hard time to Muslim girls who wear *hijabs* to school in Paris. The nation is clearly more than the legal or political manifestation of a single culture, and the mythmaking that suggests otherwise, students need to learn, only diminishes the nation's ability to be a homeland for all who make their home within its borders.

To become educated in the limits and dangers of this nationalism, to see how the nation might be better thought of as a project to determine how we might live together better, rather than a determination of who we are and who we are not, remains an imposing prospect. Nationalism, as Anthony Smith makes very clear, is a continuing force of cultural identification:

> National identity does in fact today exert a more potent and durable influence than other collective cultural identities; and . . . for the reasons I have enumerated—the need for collective immortality and dignity, the power of ethno-history, the role of new class structures and the domination of inter-state systems in the modern world—this type of collective identity is likely to continue to command humanity's allegiances for a long time to come, even when other larger-scale but looser forms of collective identity emerge alongside national ones. (1991, pp. 175–176)

This is why nationalism poses the greatest challenge of the three concepts that I am considering here, and why I would be happy to let it stand unquestioned if it were not that the ethnohistorical question of who is truly French, Australian, or American prevents more than a few students from ever feeling at home in the classroom, and if it did not mislead all of the students about the monocultural nature of that national history. Public schooling has been designed, Smith reminds us, to create "nationals" as well as "citizens" (p. 16).[27]

In the hands of those who look on the changing face of the nation with trepidation, "culture" is a way of naming the nation they nostalgically recall and, by implication, a way of naming those who belong to the nation in the first instance.[28] Where Boas and his colleagues used this new conception of culture to weaken the racial boundaries that were used to set people apart, the term is now being used to fortify national borders. Boas's critique of those who argued that immigration threatened to dilute the race is as timely today in regard to those who currently hold that "our" way of life—our culture—is facing a similar danger. Quebec strengthens its French-language laws in the name of cultural self-preservation. The United States House of Representatives readily passes a bill that would make English the nation's official language. When then Speaker of the House Newt Gringrich made his case for the bill, he appealed to the cultural threat America faced: "It is vital historically to assert and establish that English is the common language at the heart of our civilization." Although the coin of the realm is inscribed with *e pluribus unum* ("out of many, one"), we have to wonder where culture stands with this oneness and plenitude. "Culture" is being worked by both sides in this debate over the necessary plurality and unity of the nation. What educators can contribute, I would hold, are lessons on how this well-worn concept has come to have no equal among recent generations as an educational tool for dividing up the world.

The social-studies curriculum has long used the nation to locate cultures and races in a one-to-one correspondence ("Today we're going to learn about the Chinese") that often contradicts the lives and identities of the students sitting in the classroom. The schools are hardly alone in this pattern of national identification, but as they have worked so hard at helping the young imagine themselves within a world of nations, cultures, and races, they now need to afford the young a place to stand apart from this legacy of divisions and boundaries. Multiculturalists today are struggling to build an alternative curriculum that celebrates the cultural plurality of the nation. This enthusiasm for the tapestry of lives can give rise to its own form of pride and pleasure in a nation that is richly arrayed. I am not asking that we somehow lose our feelings for the nation. What I am asking for here is a considerable loosening of the tie between nation and culture, just as we separate church and state, if reluctantly at times, in order to protect the rights of the young. One can study the long historic influence of Protestantism on America or Australia while still holding that an Islamic citizen is no less a member of the nation than is a Christian.

This shift calls for schools that support the idea of a "civic" nation—civic by virtue of its citizens' adherence to, and democratic participation in, its laws, rather than by virtue of any aspect of their own identity.[29] Teachers can assist students in identifying the curriculum's representation of both an inclusive and an exclusive nation, that is, as both a free political association, in that civic sense, and a line of descent carried through its native sons. Students can thereby gain a vision of where education adds to the history that it presents, a history that they are each participating in through their education. Students can then look around at the textbooks and readers found in their schools and consider what Homi Bhabha terms "the cultural construction of nationness as a form of social and textual affiliation" (1990, p. 292). This approach gives new and educationally valuable meaning to the age-old query, "Hey, why do we have to read this?" Well, we might respond, let's have a look and see why some people have been so insistent that you are schooled in these books.

To introduce such critical self-reflection may seem to display, on my part, a childish and churlish lack of gratitude for a nation that has always protected the rights of those who would criticize it. Certainly, the nation has proven to be a political unit that has given democracy a fair hearing, although one could also look to how well tribal groupings and union organizations have exemplified the concept as well. The spirit of nationalism, moreover, has carried the banner of colonial liberation through its toughest struggles. Allowing for those triumphs of nationalism, however, my concern is still with how forms of ethnic nationalism further divide people by coupling nation with culture and race, and how we may inadvertently teach the young this ready form of nation-culture-race identification in themselves and others.

At this point, the most viable educational alternative to the schools' nationalist tendencies is the movement for global education, which seeks to teach an international perspective on such topics as oil production, forestry products, and human migration. In this way, global education would pave the way for greater international cooperation in the spirit of the United Nations. The global-education model proposed by Barbara Benham Tye and Kenneth A. Tye, for example, pursues the "interconnectedness" of economic, political, cultural, and technological elements while fostering a cross-cultural "perspective-taking" (1992, p. 3). Tye and

Tye are concerned with how schools end up fostering "ethnocentrism" among students in the name of nationalism. Although it is indeed important to stop "regarding one's own race or ethnic group as of supreme importance," as the *Oxford English Dictionary* defines *ethnocentrism*, this does little to call into question the nature of the boundaries that have come to define one's own race or ethnic group. All of which is to say that I am asking for something more than a global perspective as an alternative to the nationalist one that the schools more typically teach.

I can perhaps make my point on this global perspective clearer by turning to the jurisdiction in which I teach in Canada. In an internationalist vein, the Ministry of Education in the province of British Columbia has undertaken a series of "Pacific-Rim Education Initiatives," which stress the importance of connecting with "Asia Pacific" (roughly denoting the Pacific side of Asia), a region that is recognized, although it is now the primary source of immigration in this country, largely for its increasing economic importance: "This friendship and understanding are important to B.C.'s future. The countries of the Asia Pacific region are strong economic and technological forces in the world today" (British Columbia Ministry of Education, 1992, p. 21). The educational stance taken here is still based on the great divide between West and East, which can be bridged by an economically motivated friendship and understanding. Yet, images of neo-imperialism apart, the government's call for a curriculum that reaches across the waters still suggests that culture, race, and nation are aligned in dividing up the world, because it fails to recognize that many Canadians with affiliations on both sides of the Pacific find this appeal to building a friendship with, and achieving an understanding of, Asia Pacific a rather strange request. And although the educational significance of this belated turn to Asia in terms of friendship should not be underestimated, I hope it does not seem small-minded to worry that this government initiative might give a good number of students in Vancouver pause over whether they are of this country or of the befriended and valued part of Asia Pacific. The cultural boundary between that part of the Pacific region known as Asia and that part known as America has already begun to dissolve. Asia is here, where I teach in Vancouver; and there is no there there, as Gertrude Stein might remind us. The government's initiative also fails to take advantage of the educational resource represented by the level of transnationality that already exists within many communities in British Columbia.[30] Taking the lead from their classmates' (if not their own) experience, could students learn to ask whether the materials they study or the media that surround them presume a nation that is a singular homeland of blood-stirring identification or a jurisdiction of political regulation, cooperation, and community?

I want to be cautious, then, of global education initiatives that are still grounded in nationalism. For it was just such a global consciousness that was at the heart of imperialism, and one can hear it in the stirring speeches of that paragon of British imperialism Cecil Rhodes, as he advised his countrymen (and they were men), "Your trade is the world, and your life is the world, and not England," while insisting that they "must deal with these questions of expansion and retention of the world" (cited by Arendt, 1951, p. 12). Today, those American pundits who play on fears of global economic competition can sound much like born-again (Cecil) Rhodesians, intent on keeping the world the proper business of the white race. The schools are once again being called upon, as they were at the turn of the 20th century under the banner of imperialism, to prepare students to join the fight for a greater share of a globalized economy. My interests are in insuring that they sally forth with a decidedly different attitude from that of Rudyard Kipling's classically trained generation of colonial enthusiasts.

Yet it also has to be acknowledged that my postnational approach to education is awfully consistent with what has changed about the global economy since those days of empire. This new era of globalization is not about the cultural or racial affiliations that dominated the last era of imperialism's global economy. The economic reality of the day is that 70 percent of world trade is now carried on by transnational corporations.[31] Empires are again the province of corporations and capital (recall how the East India Company "ran" India in its early years), but this time they operate within what political scientist Richard Rosecrance has recently referred to as "the governing economic culture of the world market," which is "the only global civilization worthy of the name" (1996, p. 45). This development definitely evokes a different sense of culture from the one Boas proposed, one that is no longer about defining the impenetrable lines of understanding that come between people.

The swelling of this global economic intricacy might be better thought of as spreading a transcultural sensibility, which should only make the distribution of inequities and personal suffering all the more apparent. The particular divisions of culture, race, and nation in which we were educated are being displaced by global labor-market reckonings that link together lives in ways such that, for example, large numbers of Vietnamese women make one dollar a day manufacturing hundred-dollar running shoes for Nike. Are we to think of and teach about these inequities as expressions of cultural difference? Is Nike building bridges across a cultural divide? In refusing to do much more than take advantage of the differences at stake, Nike's CEO, Philip Knight, at least, makes it clear that the issue is about dollars rather than history. "We are not here to rewrite economic history," he has claimed in his company's defense.

All of which is to say that an education that addresses Rosecrance's "governing economic culture of the world market" will treat the world as something more than an array of cultures, races, and nations. It will not let these categories stand as the natural divisions of humankind, nor will it treat the inequities that bind us together across the categories as a necessary tale of economic history. Such an education will, perhaps, help us to understand how we arrived at this point and what can be done to support the cause of those who labor 60-hour weeks to clothe us; it will ask what can be done to offer others a greater choice—beyond the categories of culture, race, and nation—in how they live.[32]

Yet when it comes to transnational capital, culture is not bereft of interest. It has merely been transformed, in a technologically enabled marriage of precision marketing and cultural anthropology, into what can sound like, in the hands of Rick Roderick, the near future of sci-fi cyberpunk:

> The world market is now being computer micromapped into consumer zones according to residual cultural factors (i.e., idioms, local traditions, religious affiliations, political ideologies, folk mores, traditional sexual roles, etc.), dominant cultural factors (i.e., typologies of life-styles based on consumption patterns: television ratings, musical tastes, fashion, motion picture and concert attendance, home video rentals, magazine subscriptions, home computer software selection, shopping mall participation, etc.), and emergent cultural factors (i.e., interactive and participatory video, mobile mircomalls equipped with holography and super conductivity, computer interfacing with consumers and robotic services, etc.). (Cited by Dirlik, 1996, p. 33)

This little catalog of surveillance points, just as with Margaret Mead's field note, offers a stunning instructional aid for reminding us how a concept of culture can continue to divide up the world in the service of larger interests than educational concerns.

After Culture, Race, Nation

With culture recast as a tool of residual market analysis, we clearly face serious challenges in working with our students to understand and live within or against this new world order. In closing, let me offer a sampler of postcultural musings that students might want to test against their own experience. Rob Wilson and Wimal Dissanayake have assembled a collection of essays, for example, that speaks to the "transnational imaginary" which they feel defines a new geographical orientation they identify as the "global/local nexus" (1996, p. 3). In their volume, Mitsuhiro Yoshimoto, a professor of film studies, positions a "global image culture" that dominates our lives with its marketing of "image commodities" through films and billboards, and that thereby undermines the look and feel of national cultures (1996, p. 105). Yet Hollywood movies, Yoshimoto insists, are not about creating "hollow replicas of the United States," for "America" is now merely an image commodity or "real virtuality" serving up what people imagine they want of the world (p. 108). It may be, as Frederick Buell observes in his study of the new global system, that "instead of culture unifying us in groups divided from one another, it promises to disaggregate us from those centered unities and interconnect us in more ways than we can easily conceive" (1994, p. 342).

I think it wise to be cautious about this new world order. I think we need to bring the sort of political edge to these transcultural spaces that performance artist Guillermo Gómez-Peña addresses when he speaks on behalf of those who live across borders and within multiple communities, people who possess a "hybridity" driven by a desire "to trespass, bridge, interconnect, reinterpret, remap, and redefine" (1996, p. 12).[33] Finally, Arif Dirlik would have us turn to instances of local action to find an extranational sense of concerned communities intent on remaking the world:

> It would seem by the early nineties that local movements or movements to save and reconstruct local societies have emerged as the primary (if not the only) expressions of resistance to domination: from tree hugging women of the Chipko movement in Northern India to the women workers of the maquiladora industries of the United States–Mexican border, from indigenous people's movements seeking secession from colonial states to the Western Kansas counties that wish to secede from Kansas and the United States because they feel abused by their governments, local movements have emerged as a pervasive phenomenon of the contemporary world. (1996, p. 22)

If the first educational step is to size up one's own experience and education in the face of the changing status of the nation-state, the second is to follow Boas in looking for new ways to challenge the lingering legacy of racism—new ways of pushing the key concepts by which we identify the world to advance the project and possibilities of human equality. From there, we will need to ask after the connections among postcultural themes of the transnational, the hybrid, and the local, and connections that will allow students to work within these themes. This is not about the end of the nation as a political unit, any more than it is about denying differences in how people live. It is about questioning how differences have been cast as the product of fixed and unbridgeable cultures, cultures that operate as extensions of races and nations. It is, above all, about education's conceptual contribution to the ongoing crafting of equality within public forums and private lives, to borrow from the rhetorical project described by Celeste Condit and John Lucaites (1993), even as they tend to place that project in the distinctly nationalist terms of the American experience.

My educational hope in all of this is simple enough. Learning how the divisions of culture, race, and nation have been constructed and maintained seems to me bound to weaken and reform their hold on us, even as it changes the ways in which we envision the world. I still envision the young studying the different ways people live in their social-studies classes, just as they will learn about the rise of the nation-state as a force of both imperialism and postcolonialism, and about the making of race in their science classes. The result is that they will become students of the interplay, overlap, and equivalence of the categories by which we continue to live.

Although I have been no more than suggestive about how we might learn more about a world that is moving beyond culture, race, and nation, resources for educators are beginning to appear.[34] At the very least, the schools' need to address the transnational experience of so many of those who sit in class today means allowing the students' lives and neighborhoods to stand as testimony to how the old divisions have long been a fiction deployed to maintain political and economic differences. To turn to culture, race, and nation in this way is to turn the page on what these concepts have made of the world. It is to allow for greater light to fall among the associations and identifications by which people make their home within the flow of increasingly global economies. In this we should not tire, as obviously Boas did not tire, in imagining and naming ways of overcoming the learned barriers that continue to distance and disadvantage some of us at the expense of us all.

Notes

1 Raymond Williams treats *culture,* in his history of key words, as one of the most complicated words in the English language, noting how it has come to operate in "several distinct intellectual disciplines and incompatible systems of thought" (1976, p. 87). I am concerned here with its anthropological meaning. Gyorgy Markus points to how the etymological roots of *culture,* from the Latin *colere,* stretch from *cult* to *colonial. Culture* came into common parlance during the 19th century when Hegel, Herder, and other German philosophers began to use it to distinguish the particular achievement of a people (1993, p. 11). Although Herder, for example, allowed that culture was, at some basic level, the right and possession of all people, culture still formed a hierarchy: "The difference between the enlightened and unenlightened, cultivated and uncultivated people is therefore not specific, but only a matter of degree" (cited by Markus, p. 21).

2 See Banks and Banks (1995) for the broad spectrum of multicultural educational concerns. Elsewhere, James Banks identifies five dimensions of multicultural education, including content integration, knowledge construction, prejudice reduction, equity pedagogy, and empowerment of school culture and school structure (1995, pp. 318–319). I focus here on the first of these, content integration—the idea that we teach about different cultures—while attempting to provide a lesson in the second, with the knowledge construction of the culture concept.

3 More recently within the academy, culture has outgrown anthropology and sociology, leading to a field known as cultural studies, which has acquired for itself the disciplinary apparatus of job titles, international conferences, and refereed journals. Lawrence Grossberg warns that as a result of its "success" (which he places in scare quotes), cultural studies has become something of a global fantasy, "so that the more we talk about it, the less clear it is what we are talking about" (1993, p. 89). My project on the concept of culture is intended to inform and exemplify what we are talking about with cultural studies.

4 To take but two leading examples, consider bell hooks's call to "allow our pedagogy to be radically changed by our recognition of a multicultural world" (1993, p. 97), and Violet Harris's support for "culturally conscious literature" (1993, p. 177). Hooks and Harris are challenging not the cultural divisions themselves but how the differences are valued and recognized anew.

5 The landmark collection on race and education is McCarthy and Crichlow (1993). In this work Fazal Rizvi, for example, explores how children's "social construction of 'race' articulates with social relations inherent in the broader discourses and practices" of what he describes as "popular racism" in Australia (1993, p. 126). My contribution here is on how the official discourses and practices around this idea of culture are still a way of learning how race matters.

6   This essay arises out of a historical review of imperialism's impact on the educated imagination that I recently conducted (1998). More than once I had to ask myself what distinguishes the schools' approach to culture from the way advocates of imperialism used it (as a concomitant to race and nation) to organize the world between knower and known while always suggesting a difference between civilized and primitive. I began to wonder whether the study of culture in schools and museums, as well as through travel, does not in some way sustain what we should be working to overcome, doing more than necessary to set people apart, shaping the meaning and the very perception of difference. It's no secret that imperialism was a great patron of those who studied the culture of the colonized, with colonial administrators translating ancient Sanskrit legal texts and collecting masks from West Africa. After Edward Said's landmark study *Orientalism* (1978), there can be little doubt about the contribution of scholars to fabricating a lasting imperial vision of the world. And who among us, whether we identify with the once colonizing or colonized, has not been schooled in the sense of cultural differences generated through the photographs, drawings, ethnographies, magazines, novels, films, and museums that were the educational by-products of imperialism?

7   See Linda Alcoff (1994) for an analysis of how the concept of women's culture works within feminism, as well as for a sense of how the study of gender follows the analysis of other cultures: "Man has said that woman can be defined, delineated, captured—understood, explained, and diagnosed—to a level of determination never accorded to man himself, who is conceived as a rational animal with free will" (p. 96).

8   See Cynthia Fuchs Epstein's *Deceptive Distinctions: Sex, Gender, and the Social Order*: "Thus, insights into human nature were skewed by the tendency to perceive separate spheres and separate characteristics and qualities for men and women. Much of the 'research' conducted within these models served to rationalize and justify inequality, and even helped to create it" (1988, p. 1). Although gender is never far removed from assumptions of culture (what are those totems and taboos about otherwise?) and is always part of the configuration of race and nation, this chapter confines itself to culture's relation with race and nation. For gender's place in the postcolonial era, see, for example, Bergmann et al. (1990), Blunt (1994), Schutte (1993), and Spivak (1990).

9   The "possessive individualism" that dominated the political theory of 17th-century England found expression in the study of culture, which offered "a form of wealth (of objects, knowledge, memories, experience)," according to James Clifford's description of the claim to personhood and identity that took hold at that time (1990, p. 143). The theory of possessive individualism, in C. P. Macpherson's words, held that "what makes a man human is freedom from dependence on the wills of others. . . . The individual is essentially the proprietor of his own person and capacities" (1962, p. 263). This effectively excluded the colonized, women, and the unpropertied classes from the very idea of humanity and the right to govern.

10 In the 1930s, Boas's antiracist work ran into considerable opposition from colleagues, with even the sympathetic Harvard professor Earnest Hooton accusing

him of taking "a very extreme point of view on the subject of race, since he is a radical environmentalist and a Jew," and discouraging him from getting involved in the issue because he would be seen as "an interested party" (cited by Barkan, 1992, p. 315).

11 Christopher Herbert points out how the reverse is also true: "If, that is, a 'culture' truly generates its own (even partially) closed system of significance, an outside observer can *never know—or at least never be sure of knowing—what anything means to a man or a woman native to the society under study*" (1991, p. 8; original emphasis). The point is well taken, but I have to ask, what did such internal knowledge afford the native?

12 Malinowski reverts, in *A Diary in the Strict Sense of the Term*, to quoting such desperate phrases as "Exterminate the brutes" (from Conrad's *Heart of Darkness*) and "You'll never fuck them all" as speaking to what he feels and is trying to overcome, just as he also records how, "at moments, I was sorry I was not a savage and could not possess this pretty girl" (1967, p. 256). The sentiments of hostility and desire—or are they one here?—have provided an evincing starting point for those working with a combination of Freudian, feminist, and Foucauldian perspectives on the colonial era. See Torgovnick (1990), Stoler (1995), and Young (1995).

13 See Judith Butler for a Lacanian reading of the force of naming across gender: "The name, which installs gender and kinship [and culture], works as a politically invested and investing performative. To be named is thus inculcated into the law and to be formed, bodily, in accordance with that law" (1993, p. 72).

14 See also Robert J. C. Young: "It was therefore wholly appropriate that sexual exchange, and its miscegenated product, which captures the violent, antagonistic power relations of sexual and cultural diffusion, should become the dominant paradigm through which the passionate economic and political trafficking of colonialism was conceived" (1995, p. 182). Also see Deirdre David, who includes in her analysis of women and empire the gendered tensions expressed by such figures as Maud Diver, who at the turn of the 20th century, through novelistic and nonfiction treatments of the British Raj, played "moral policewoman of the colonizer and moral instructress of the colonized" (1995, p. 163).

15 See Derek Freeman's controversial *Margaret Mead and Samoa* (1983) for a critique of Mead's early reading of this culture.

16 For a recent review of how the biological determinism of race lives on in the social sciences through the work of Arthur Jensen, J. Philippe Rushton, and others, see Lewontin (1996). For an account of the controversy surrounding *The Bell Curve* (Herrnstein & Murray, 1994), the best-selling social-science work that uses IQ to add further weight to race as the determining category of America's future, see Fraser (1995).

17 See Tim Stanley (1995) for a textbook chart of racial characteristics that was used in the public schools of British Columbia in the 1920s. Carl Degler claims that the purging of race in the social sciences took place during the first two decades of

the century, and he includes instances of dramatic conversion among prominent social scientists (1991, pp. 84–104). On cultural deprivation, see Silberman (1964), and for a critique of its racism, Clark (1965). On the color-blind curriculum, see Sleeter (1993), and on the color-blind courts and the Constitution, see Gotanda (1995).

18 See Gerald McMaster and Lee-Ann Martin (1992) for a critique that emerges out of the aboriginal mounting of an exhibition. Charlotte Townsend-Gault (1995) reviews how First Nation artists work "cultural boundaries" by "negotiating the boundaries—their existence, their significance, their permeability" (p. 91), thereby shifting the focus on culture away from the center of a people to the boundaries that they experience as one culture in relation to another.

19 Microsoft's Mungo Park Web site (http://mungopark.msn.com), named after the great imperialist adventurer of the 19th century, featured for October 1997 "Dr. Ruth in the Island of Love" and "Rites of Passage: Stone Age Rituals Survive."

20 See Kwame Anthony Appiah for the case that culture should replace race: "For, where race works . . . it works in an attempt at metonym for culture" (1992, p. 45); and Jayne Chong-Soon Lee (1995) for a critique of Appiah's position in favor of multiple definitions of race.

21 The instability of the categories is demonstrated for Michaels by such examples as the ruling of a Louisiana court in 1985 that "the one-drop rule" (which was all the black blood required to make one black) no longer held because race had lost its scientific validity, whereas what continued to count was the *perception* that someone was black, given that race was now seen as a socially constructed category (1994, pp. 764–766). See Lawrence Wright (1994) for U.S. government conflagrations over multiracial and postracial identities and the design of census forms. See Avery Gordon and Christopher Newfield (1994) for an explicit critique of Michaels's postplural and color-blind liberalism as a "white philosophy" that blames black nationalism for not letting go of race. They insist that those who have traditionally been dishonored and unrecognized have the right to name the basis of their collective identities.

22 As Crenshaw, Gotanda, Peller, and Thomas put it in introducing their sourcebook on critical race theory, "We take racial power to be at stake across the social plane—not merely in the places where people of color are concentrated but also in the institutions where their position is normalized and given legitimation" (1995, p. xxii). For a critique of critical race theory, in its fight against hate speech, see Henry Louis Gates Jr., who sees the attack as both misconstrued and threatening to "the already fragile liberal alliance" (1996, p. 157).

23 See Angela Y. Davis on how multiculturalism can "reproduce the ideologies of racism" through such strategies as "diversity management" in business and can perpetuate patriarchal structures in the name of cultural preservation (1996, p. 44).

24 See Richard J. C. Young for a discussion of how, in Arnold's anthropology, "racism, ethnology and culture slide so easily into each other" (1995, pp. 82–89).

25 If some hold that nationalism can be said to give rise to imperialism, others have proposed the reverse. Historian Frances Yates (1975) presents compelling arguments for imperialism's formative contribution to nationalism, dating back to the joint visions of empire and nation that emerged during the European Renaissance, when the Crown aspired to the title of Lord of the World. The Reformation only enhanced the Protestant nations' assumption of an imperial mission: "It is as successors to the divine imperial power that kings claim the right to throw off papal suzerainty" (p. 39).

26 Conor Cruise O'Brien (1992) is among those who take exception to this 19th-century origin of nationalism, which he traces it back to biblical times, while still keeping it within the realm of the West. On the relation between race and nation, there is Étienne Balibar: "As far as the relation between *nationalism and racism* is concerned at present, the core of meaning contrasts a 'normal' ideology and politics (nationalism) with an 'excessive' ideology and behavior (racism), either to oppose the two or to offer the one as the truth of the other" (1991, p. 46).

27 Among the counterexamples to the inevitability of this strong national identity Smith describes is the Jewish Diaspora. Daniel Boyarin and Jonathan Boyarin (1993) argue that the lack of a nation gave definition to a Jewish identity that managed to transcend racial and national conceptions of a Jewish essence. Opposing culture to race and nation, Boyarin and Boyarin argue that the moral condition of the Jewish people in fact depends on this living out a Diaspora within another's state. Compared to having a hand in the machinations of the modern nation, to be stateless is liberating and ethically secure. They would deny Israel its national mandate in what was once Palestinian territory, while recognizing that the Diaspora has long formed its own tenuous and, at times, deadly state.

28 Among the most notable critiques of multiculturalism and what it can do to the nation are those of Arthur Schlesinger (1992) and Neil Bissoondath (1994).

29 When Michael Ignatieff, in his study of the new nationalism, *Blood and Belonging* (1993), holds up Britain as having achieved elements of a civic state by the mid-18th century with its mix of English, Welsh, Scottish, and Irish peoples, he seems to miss how hard Britain has worked at being identified with a cultural legacy both in building its empire and, now, in sustaining its culture industry. Nor does he pay enough mind, I would say, to how the governing classes ensured that a single English culture was revered and identified with the nation, through the cultural labor force in which teachers stood in the first rank throughout the once and former empire.

30 As Aihwa Ong puts it in his thoroughly postmodern treatment of the "flexible citizenship" exhibited by overseas Chinese, "Their shifting narratives rework global displacements and liminality into a self-inscribed alterity to the Western insistence on a single national identity" (1993, p. 772). Similar points are made by M. Garbutcheon Singh (1995a) in reviewing Australia's current press for "Asia literacy" in the schools, which includes teaching Asian languages and cultures. Singh points out how economic concerns have inspired government efforts at erasing the "negative boundaries between Australia and Asia" after realizing that

"Australia needs Asia more than Asia needs Australia" (p. 599). He sees the challenge in overcoming a national identity that rests on Australians' "rejection of themselves as Asians or as part of Asia" (p. 602). Singh (1995b) also offers a postcolonial curricular approach to Asian studies that would "enable students to reconstruct new social networks, to see themselves as part of new border zones, to engage new types of boundary crossings, and to participate in new global regions" (p. 8). Another important resource is Don T. Nakanishi and Tina Yamano Nishida's collection *The Asian American Educational Experience* (1995).

31 The corporations are best thought of as transcending national boundaries. The *New Internationalist* reports that "there are now 35,000 multinationals with some 150,000 foreign affiliates. The largest 100 manufacturing and service companies accounted for $3.1 trillion of world assets in 1990; about $1.2 trillion of that was outside the multinationals' home countries" ("Going Global," 1993, p. 18). Among the cautionary nationalist notes is James Laxer's *False God: How the Globalization Myth Has Impoverished Canada* (1993), which argues that globalization disguises an effort to further Americanize the Canadian state.

32 One example of how to proceed is found in the work of organized labor and human rights groups, which succeeded in getting President Bill Clinton to secure pledges from Nike and other U.S. clothing manufacturers to work toward decent and humane working conditions.

33 See Edward Said on how "liberation as an intellectual mission, born in the resistance and opposition to the confinements and ravages of imperialism, has now shifted from the settled, established, and domesticated dynamics of culture to its unhoused, decentered, and exilic energies, whose incarnation today is the migrant, and whose consciousness is that of the intellectual and artist in exile" (1993, p. 332). See also *Muæ*, a New York journal of "transcultural production" that "innovatively critiques and re-imagines aspects of asian/diasporic cultures, society, or agency." On hybridity, see Homi Bhabha (1994).

34 See Homi Bhabha for an example of a curriculum that seeks to move beyond "the 'sovereignty' of national cultures" and "the universalism of human culture": "The study of world literature might be the study of the way in which cultures recognize themselves through projections of 'otherness.' Where, once, the transmission of national traditions was the major theme of a world literature, perhaps we can now suggest that transnational histories of migrants, the colonized, or political refugees—these border and frontier conditions—may be the terrains of world literature" (1990, p. 12). In another variation on this pedagogical theme, Germaine Warkentin (1996) announces to her surprised Canadian literature students "that the subject of 'the Canadian identity' is absolutely forbidden in discussion." These approaches still need to be distinguished from my call for attending to the history of the categories themselves. Better in this regard is Stuart Hall's new cultural-studies textbook (1997) that deals with postcolonial and feminist themes of representation, and Gill and Levidow's guide to antiracist science teaching (1987).

References

Alcoff, L. (1994). Cultural feminism versus poststructuralism: The identity crisis in feminist theory. In N. B. Dirks, G. Eley, & S. B. Ortner (Eds.), *Culture/power/history: A reader in contemporary social theory* (pp. 96–122). Princeton, NJ: Princeton University Press.

Anderson, B. (1983). *Imagined communities: Reflections on the origins and spread of nationalism* (Rev. ed.). London: Verso.

Appiah, K. A. (1992). *In my father's house: Africa in the philosophy of culture.* New York: Oxford University Press.

Arendt, H. (1951). *The origins of totalitarianism: Pt. 2. Imperialism.* San Diego: Harcourt Brace Jovanovich.

Asad, T. (Ed.). (1973). *Anthropology and the colonial encounter.* New York: Humanities Press.

Baker, J. R. (1974). *Race.* London: Oxford University Press.

Balibar, E. (1991). Racism and nationalism. In É. Balibar & I. Wallerstein (Eds.), *Race, nation, class: Ambiguous identities* (pp. 27–67). London: Verso.

Banks, J. A. (1995). Modification of students' racial attitudes. In W. D. Hawley & A. W. Jackson (Eds.), *Toward a common destiny: Improving race and ethnic relations in America* (pp. 315–340). San Francisco: Jossey Bass.

Banks, J. A., & Banks, C. A. M. (1995). *Handbook of research on multicultural education.* New York: Macmillan.

Banton, M. (1987). *Racial theories.* Cambridge, UK: Cambridge University Press.

Barkan, E. (1992). *The retreat of scientific racism: Changing concepts of race in Britain and the United States between the world wars.* Cambridge, UK: Cambridge University Press.

Bergmann, E., Greenberg, J., Kirkpatrick, G., Masiello, F., Miller, F., Morello-Frosch, M., Newman, K., & Pratt, M. L. (1990). *Women, culture and politics in Latin America.* Berkeley: University of California Press.

Bhabha, H. K. (1990). DissemiNation: Time, narrative, and the margins of the modern nation. In H. Bhabha (Ed.), *Nation and narration* (pp. 291–322). New York: Routledge.

Bhabha, H. K. (1994). Introduction: Location of culture. In *Location of Culture* (pp. 1–18). New York: Routledge.

Bissoondath, N. (1994). *Selling illusions: The cult of multiculturalism.* Harmondsworth, UK: Penguin.

Blunt, A. (1994). *Travel, gender, and imperialism: Mary Kingsley and West Africa.* New York: Guilford.

Boas, F. (1940). Race and progress. In *Race, language, and culture* (pp. 3–17). Chicago: University of Chicago Press.

Boyarin, D., & Boyarin, J. (1993). Diaspora: Generation and the ground of Jewish identity. *Critical Inquiry, 19,* 693–725.

British Columbia Ministry of Education. (1992). *Pacific Rim education initiatives.* Victoria: British Columbia Ministry of Education.

Buell, F. (1994). *National culture and the new global system.* Baltimore: Johns Hopkins University Press.

Burton, J. W. (1992). Representing Africa: Colonial anthropology revisited. *Journal of Asian and African Studies, 27*(3–4), 181–201.

Butler, J. (1993). *Bodies that matter: On the discursive limits of "sex".* New York: Routledge.

Chase, S. (1948). *The proper study of mankind.* New York: Harper.

Clark, K. (1965). *Dark ghetto: Dilemmas of social power.* New York: Harper & Row.

Clifford, J. (1990). On collecting art and culture. In R. Ferguson, M. Gever, T. T. Minh-Ha, & C. West (Eds.), *Out there: Marginalization and contemporary cultures* (pp. 141–169). Cambridge, MA: Massachusetts Institute of Technology Press.

Columbus, C. (1969). *The four voyages of Christopher Columbus: Being his own log-book, letters, and dispatches with connecting narrative drawn from the Life of the admiral by his son Hernando Colon and other contemporary historians* (J. M. Cohen, Ed. & Trans.). London: Penguin.

Condit, C. M., & Lucaites, J. L. (1993). *Crafting equality: America's Anglo-African word.* Chicago: University of Chicago Press.

Crenshaw, K., Gotanda, N., Peller, G., & Thomas, K. (Eds.). (1995). *Critical race theory: The key writings that formed the movement.* New York: New Press.

David, D. (1995). *Rule Britannia: Women, empire, and Victorian writing.* Ithaca, NY: Cornell University Press.

Davis, A. Y. (1996). Gender, class, and multiculturalism: Rethinking "race" politics. In A. F. Gordon & C. Newfield (Eds.), *Mapping multiculturalism* (pp. 40–48). Minneapolis: University of Minnesota Press.

Degler, C. N. (1991). *In search of human nature: The decline and revival of Darwinism in American social thought.* New York: Oxford University Press.

Dirlik, A. (1996). The global in the local. In R. Wilson & W. Dissanayake (Eds.), *Global/local: Cultural production and the transnational imaginary* (pp. 21–45). Durham, NC: Duke University Press.

Epstein, C. F. (1988). *Deceptive distinctions: Sex, gender, and the social order.* New Haven, CN: Yale University Press.

Foucault, M. (1972). *The archeology of knowledge and the discourse on language* (A. M. Sheridan, Trans.). New York: Harper.

Fraser, S. (Ed.). (1995). *The bell curve wars: Race, intelligence, and the future of America.* New York: Basic Books.

Freeman, D. (1983). *Margaret Mead and Samoa: The making and unmaking of an anthropological myth.* Cambridge: Harvard University Press.

Gates, H. L., Jr. (1993). Beyond the culture wars: Identities in dialogue. *Profession* (Modern Language Association), *93*, 6–11.

Gates, H. L., Jr. (1996). Critical race theory and free speech. In L. Menand (Ed.), *The future of academic freedom* (pp. 117–159). Chicago: University of Chicago Press.

Gibson, G. (1996, August 27). Back to reality on aboriginal rights. *Toronto Globe & Mail,* p. A21.

Gill, D., & Levidow, L. (1987). *Anti-racist science teaching.* London: Free Association.

Gilman, S. L. (1993). *Freud, race, and gender.* Princeton, NJ: Princeton University Press.

Going Global. (1993, August). *New Internationalist,* 246, 18–19.

Goldberg, T. D. (1993). *Racist culture: Philosophy and the politics of meaning.* Oxford: Blackwell.

Gómez-Peña, G. (1996). *The new world border: Prophecies, poems, and loqueras for the end of the century.* San Francisco: City Lights.

Gordon, A., & Newfield, C. (1994). White philosophy. *Critical Inquiry,* 20, 737–757.

Gotanda, N. (1995). A critique of "Our constitution is colorblind." In K. Crenshaw, N. Gotanda, G. Peller, & Thomas, K. (Eds.). *Critical race theory: The key writings that formed the movement* (pp. 257-276). New York: New Press.

Grossberg, L. (1993). Cultural studies and/in new worlds. In C. McCarthy & W. Crichlow (Eds.), *Race, identity, and representation in education* (pp. 89–105). New York: Routledge.

Hall, S. (Ed.). (1997). *Representation: Cultural representations and signifying practices.* London: Sage.

Hannaford, I. (1996). *Race: The history of an idea in the West.* Baltimore: Johns Hopkins University Press.

Harris, V. J. (1993). African American children's literature: The first one hundred years. In T. Perry & J. W. Fraser (Eds.), *Freedom's plow: Teaching in the multicultural classroom* (pp. 167–184). New York: Routledge.

Herbert, C. (1991). *Culture and anomie: Ethnographic imagination in the 19th century.* Chicago: University of Chicago Press.

Herrnstein, R., & Murray, C. (1994). *The bell curve: Intelligence and class structure in American life.* New York: Free Press.

hooks, b. (1993). Transforming pedagogy and multiculturalism. In T. Perry & J. W. Fraser (Eds.), *Freedom's plow: Teaching in the multicultural classroom* (pp. 91–98). New York: Routledge.

Hymes, D. (Ed.). (1974). *Reinventing anthropology.* New York: Vintage.

Ignatieff, M. (1993). *Blood and belonging: Journeys into the new nationalism.* New York: Viking.

Karp, I., & Lavine, S. D. (1991). *Exhibiting cultures: The poetics and politics of museum display.* Washington, DC: Smithsonian Institution Press.

Kedourie, E. (1960). *Nationalism.* London: Hutchinson.

Kimball, R. (1991). Tenured radicals: A postscript. *New Criterion, 9,* 4–13.

Laxer, J. (1993). *False god: How the globalization myth has impoverished Canada.* Toronto: Lester Publishing.

Lee, J. C.-S. (1995). Navigating the topology of race. In K. Crenshaw, N. Gotanda, G. Peller, & K. Thomas (Eds.), *Critical race theory: The key writings that formed the movement* (pp. 441–449). New York: New Press.

Lewontin, Richard. (1996). Of genes and genitals. *Transition, 69,* 178–193.

Loewen, J. W. (1995). *Lies my teacher told me: Everything that your American textbook got wrong.* New York: New Press.

Macpherson, C. P. (1962). *The political theory of possessive individualism: Hobbes to Locke.* Oxford University Press.

Malinowski, B. (1944). *A scientific theory of culture and other essays.* Chapel Hill: University of North Carolina Press.

Malinowski, B. (1967). *A diary in the strict sense of the term* (N. Guterman, Trans.). London: Routledge.

Markus, G. (1993). Culture: The making and the make-up of a concept (an essay in historical semantics). *Dialectical Anthropology, 18*(1), 3–19.

McCarthy, C., & Crichlow, W. (Eds.). (1993). *Race, identity, and representation in education.* New York: Routledge.

McMaster, G., & Martin, L.-A. (Eds.). (1992). Introduction. In *Indigena: Contemporary Native perspectives* (pp. 11–23). Vancouver: Douglas & McIntyre.

Mead, Margaret. (1963). *Sex and temperament.* New York: Viking.

Michaels, W. B. (1993). Race into culture: A critical genealogy of cultural identity. *Critical Inquiry, 18,* 655–685.

Michaels, W. B. (1994). The no-drop rule. *Critical Inquiry, 20,* 758–769.

Mommsen, W. J. (1980). *Theories of imperialism* (P. S. Falla, Trans.). Chicago: University of Chicago Press.

Nakanishi, D. T., & Nishida, T. Y. (1995). *The Asian American educational experience: A source book for teachers and students.* New York: Routledge.

O'Brien, C. C. (1992). Nationalism and democracy. *Queen's Quarterly, 99*(1), 72–83.

Ong, A. (1993). On the edge of empires: Flexible citizenship among Chinese in diaspora. *Positions: East Asia Cultural Critique, 1*(3), 745–779.

Peller, G. (1995). Race-consciousness. In K. Crenshaw, N. Gotanda, G. Peller, & K. Thomas (Eds.), *Critical race theory: The key writings that formed the movement* (pp. 127–158). New York: New Press.

Rizvi, F. (1993). Children and the grammar of popular racism. In C. McCarthy & W. Crichlow (Eds.), *Race, identity, and representation in education* (pp. 126–139). New York: Routledge.

Rorty, R. (1989). *Contingency, Irony and Solidarity.* Cambridge, UK: Cambridge University Press.

Rosecrance, R. (1996). The rise of the virtual state. *Foreign Affairs, 75*(4), 45–61.

Said, E. W. (1978). *Orientalism.* New York: Random House.

Said, E. W. (1993). *Culture and imperialism.* New York: Knopf.

Schlesinger, A. (1992). *The disuniting of America: Reflections on a multicultural society.* New York: Norton.

Schutte, O. (1993). *Cultural identity and social liberation in Latin American thought.* Albany: State University of New York Press.

Silberman, C. (1964). *Crisis in black and white.* New York: Random House.

Singh, M. G. (1995a). Edward Said's critique of orientalism and Australia's "Asia literacy" curriculum. *Journal of Curriculum Studies, 27*(6), 599–620.

Singh, M. G. (1995b). *Translating studies of Asia: A curriculum statement for negotiation in Australian schools* (Occasional paper 6). Melbourne: Australian Curriculum Studies Association.

Sleeter, C. E. (1993). How white teachers construct race. In C. McCarthy & W. Chrichlow (Eds), *Race, identity, and representation in education* (pp. 157–171). New York: Routledge.

Smith, A. D. (1991). *National identity.* Reno: University of Nevada Press.

Spivak, G. C. (1990). *The post-colonial critic: Interviews, strategies, dialogues* (S. Harsym, Ed.). New York: Routledge.

Stanley, T. J. (1995). White supremacy and the rhetoric of educational indoctrination: A Canadian case study. In J. Barman, N. Sutherland, & J. D. Wilson (Eds.), *Children, teachers, and schools in the history of British Columbia* (pp. 39–56). Calgary: Detselig.

Stocking, G. W., Jr. (1982). The scientific reaction against cultural anthropology, 1917–1920. In *Race, culture, and evolution: Essays in the history of anthropology* (2d ed., pp. 270–307). Chicago: University of Chicago Press.

Stoler, A. L. (1995). *Race and the education of desire: Foucault's History of sexuality and the colonial order of things.* Durham, NC: Duke University Press.

Supreme Court of Canada. (1996a, August 23). How to identify an aboriginal right. *Toronto Globe and Mail,* p. A17.

Supreme Court of Canada. (1996b, August 27). When may a government infringe on native rights in Canada? *Toronto Globe and Mail,* p. A21.

Torgovnick, M. (1990). *Gone primitive: Savage intellects, modern lives.* Chicago: University of Chicago Press.

Townsend-Gault, C. (1995). Translation or perversion: Showing First Nations art in Canada. *Cultural Studies, 9*(1), 91–105.

Tye, B. B., & Tye, K. A. (1992). *Global education: A study of school change.* Albany: State University of New York Press.

Warkentin, G. (1996, Sept 27). Canadian identity: Letter to the editor. *Toronto Globe & Mail*, p. A24.

Williams, R. (1976). *Keywords: A vocabulary of culture and society.* New York: Oxford University Press.

Willinsky, J. (1998). *Learning to divide the world: Education at empire's end.* Minneapolis: University of Minnesota Press.

Wilson, R., & Dissanayake, W. (1996). Introduction. In R. Wilson & W. Dissanayake (Eds.), *Global/local: Cultural production and the transnational imaginary* (pp. 21–45). Durham, NC: Duke University Press.

Wright, L. (1994, July 25). One drop of blood. *New Yorker*, 46–55.

Yates, F. (1975). *Astraea: The imperial theme in the 16th century.* London: Pimlico.

Yoshimoto, M. (1996). Real virtuality. In R. Wilson & W. Dissanayake (Eds.), *Global/local: Cultural production and the transnational imaginary* (pp. 107–119). Durham, NC: Duke University Press.

Young, R. J. C. (1995). *Colonial desire: Hybridity in theory, culture, and race.* London: Routledge.

Chapter 6

The Educational Politics of Identity and Category

Simone Weil is one of the 20th century's unlikely French philosopher-heroes. She did not grace the front pages of the Paris newspapers like Simone de Beauvoir and Jean-Paul Sartre who were captured marching through the streets of Paris during the 1968 demonstrations. She suffered no well-publicized arrest of the sort Michel Foucault experienced outside La Santé Prison for, as it turns out, failing to register the copyright of his pamphlets protesting the inhumane treatment of prisoners. Weil's heroics were confined to setting aside a promising career as a scholar for work on the shop floor at a Renault factory, if only for a year of her too-brief life. She left behind the café classes because she believed that the spiritual core of life was to be found in labor. The same understated but intense quality pervades her much-admired writings, all of which were published after her tragic death in 1943 at the age of 33.

That year Weil was among the Jewish refugees working at French headquarters in London. Her already frail health gradually deteriorated as she insisted in restricting her diet to the rations allowed her compatriots in occupied France. She was working at the time on a manuscript that was posthumously published under the title *The Need for Roots* (1952). This final work draws on the experiences of teachers, colonials, police, prostitutes, trade unionists, and surrealists who demonstrate for her the values and ills of collective identity. The book forms an ethical guide to how we are rooted in the world and, as such, it throws considerable light on the current politics of identity and multiculturalism as matters of displacement and rootedness.

"The politics of identity" is certainly a new phrase, coming into postmodern vogue well after Weil's lifetime. But the concept is hardly new, as a century before, in France, identity politics had been at the heart of the Dreyfus affair at the École militaire, just as it is present in the defacing of French synagogues with swastikas. The question is, who can comfortably claim to be fully French? As with the emancipation of Jews and the anti-Semitic backlash in 19th-century France, the politics of identity tends to unearth the root-bound traditions that define people by gender, race, culture, and nation. The politics of identity calls into question how we would be known, and thus regarded and treated. If Jews, for the most part, are no longer seen as a race apart today, the political identity struggle over how people should be known nevertheless continues on other fronts.

So it is that whereas American census developers are currently struggling over how people are to identify their "race," given the instability of the term and the complexity of our genealogies, in some states it still takes only "one drop of blood" to legally constitute an African American before the courts (Wright, 1994). Where once nothing was more obvious than the lines dividing genders, keeping races apart, and distinguishing cultures, we now have a politics of identity that contests the boundary lines and the significance of difference. This sort of politics, to my way of thinking, calls for a corresponding education in the why and wherefore of such divisions. It suggest that we ask, as Edward Said asked in his landmark *Orientalism*, can one "divide human reality, as indeed human reality seems to be genuinely divided, into clearly different cultures, histories, traditions, societies, even races, and survive the consequences humanly?" (1978, p. 45). One approach to this question is to start with the status, or "genuineness" in Said's terms, of the divisions. Although they certainly appear to possess the gravitational force of reality—think of people dragged down by categorical discrimination—there is too much at stake to accept the divisions themselves as a fact of nature. We need an education, I am thus proposing, in the historical dynamics of the categories by which we are divided.

Thus my interest in Weil. The affiliations by which we live are, after all, the subject of her final work. "We owe our respect," Weil states early into *The Need for Roots*, "to a collectivity, of whatever kind—country, family, or any other kind—not for itself, but because it is food for a certain number of human souls" (1952, p. 7). Although talk of the soul may fall beyond where I typically tread in my educational work, I have come to realize in reading Weil that her alignment of food and souls brings home an ethical sensibility that can easily be lost sight of when discussions of identity turn on politics and power, blood and soil. Given that it feeds the soul, a "collectivity" needs to be carefully judged for what it makes of us, and Weil reserves the right to question its particular qualities. Some collectivities "devour souls," she wrote as Nazi Germany continued its march across Europe, whereas other affiliations are simply dead to this world (p. 9). She goes on to identify the qualities of vital, life-affirming collectivities, among which I would single out honor, strange as it may seem at first glance, for the way it directly bears on the current politics of identity (p. 19).

It is undoubtedly true that France's honor was seen to be at stake in the Dreyfus affair, and that a terrible sense of honor was at the root of the Nazis' Aryan vision. But in both cases we can also see precisely how the collectivity plainly failed to honor all of those whom it had a responsibility to respect and protect. The collectivity not only must be willing to honor all of those it harbors, but it also seems to me that, given the lessons of history, it must be willing to honor its past by redeeming the inevitable inequities it has visited on those it has not honored. Weil approaches this idea by focusing on France's treatment of "the subproletariat composed of colonial immigrants and natives" as a particularly dishonorable moment for her country (p. 20). France was failing those from whom it had extracted its imperial due while continuing to demand their loyalty and service. Weil brings her point home by turning to the French schools. All of those lessons on Joan of Arc, she points out, have a way of teaching who belongs to this nation, who is honored by this collectivity: "We now talk about her to the Anamites and the Arabs; but they know very well that here in France we don't allow their heroes and saints to be talked about; therefore the state in which we keep them is an affront to their honor" (p. 20). This sentiment has a familiar ring to it for those who have advocated a multicultural curriculum, as this sort of effrontery has long distinguished national education systems, which typically and shamelessly make the dominant culture of the country the whole of the curriculum. Weil calls France to account for failing to honor those for whom it has assumed responsibility, and her critique makes clear that the nation needs to recognize that honoring the myths of the past is not as important as accepting a responsibility for the present.

In concluding her brief treatment of honor, Weil expresses a concern over "the deprivation of respect reserved for certain categories of human beings" that can go on within a collectivity such as a nation. Her response to this deprivation is to propose, rather idealistically, that "categories of this kind ought not to exist" (p. 20). It is a good instance of how moral visionaries can seem just plain naive at times, and of how helpful that naïveté can prove for the rest of us. Take the designation of "immigrant," which she feels is one of those categories that ought not to exist. Today, more than half a century after Weil wrote about the honor owed a people, immigration from the former colonies of the European empires remains one of the most divisive issues in Europe. I think it safe to say that many of the nations do little honor to themselves with their "fortress Europe" mentality and policies.

Still, to say that "categories of this kind ought not to exist" offers little help in diminishing their hold on our language and minds. This I take to be a large and difficult educational question for the current politics of identity. We have a responsibility to teach about these categories so that they can feed the souls of children in ways that we would stand by. With multicultural educational programs, for example, we are struggling to change the meaning of the categories, to deck out the plurality of cultures, races, and nationalities in glorious and proud colors, to find a place for this plurality within the curriculum and the state. But what if the categories ought not to exist? Is there a place in our philosophies of multiculturalism to question the existence of the categories by which we are known?

As you might gather, I find something of an answer in the life and ideas of Simone Weil. Out of her example, I argue that we would do well to focus on the educational construction of the categories as the most effective contribution educators can make to the current politics of identity. For although Weil certainly spoke about the need for roots, she did not devote her life to such a pursuit. She remained committed to inquiring into the nature of such rooted forms of life. Equally, although she was concerned with the uprootedness that people were made to suffer, in her own case she was little interested in settling down, whether intellectually, spiritually, or physically. She was stretched between her family's Judaism and her own Catholic avocation, between her outstanding academic record in France's finest schools and her factory work at Renault. She relentlessly pursued what it meant to know a place as one's own, a place not determined by geography or genealogy but by contingency, ethics, and thoughtful choice. Weil's desire was not to find her place on the map or within any one collectivity, it was to help think through the need and consequences for such mappings and collectivities in people's lives. It was to judge how well these associations serve human needs. This might seem too intellectual or rational an approach to our deep need for roots, yet it is precisely what makes this a sound educational approach to both the politics of identity and multiculturalism.

To give a quick instance of how Weil might guide us through this politics, consider how Muslim girls in Paris were refused the right to wear a *hijab* to school.[1] Have the students disrupted the school's secular culture, as educational officials have claimed, or has the nation failed to honor these students' religion and history, which have become inextricably bound up with the French nation and the reaches of its former colonial empire? The students are reminded by this act that they are "out of place" in France or in the culture France defines for itself. Yet here is the opportunity for France, in the spirit of Weil, to redeem honorably its own enormous unsettling and uprooting of traditional cultures in the name of imperialism. The nation needs to honor these students and the intersection of histories that have extended the traditional notions of national culture. A France with 3 million Muslims needs to rethink how it honors its citizens' need for roots. The nation is historical, we might say, only as it changes with the times. For it to remain vital, it will need to school succeeding generations of students in the politics of identity, equipping them to read and challenge the changing definition of the nation, no less than the other categories by which they are known. This is the example that can be taken from Weil, and this is the educational approach that needs, I will now argue, to supplement what contemporary advocates and bureaucrats of multiculturalism make of the politics of identity, lest they achieve only a strengthening of these given yet questionable categories. Let me begin with the advocates.

The Philosopher of Recognition

The honoring of roots has more recently received philosophical treatment from Charles Taylor, who has his own story to tell about displacement and rootedness. Taylor grew up in Montreal, the son of a French Canadian mother and English Canadian father, and now teaches at McGill University, an English bastion in the world's second-largest French-speaking city. Amid the separatist and sovereignty politics of Quebec, Taylor identifies "recognition" as a key political issue on a global scale, which bears an obvious relation to Weil's conception of honor. "The politics of recognition," as Taylor phrases it, works "on behalf of minority or 'subaltern' groups, in some forms of feminism, and in what is today called the politics of 'multiculturalism'" (1994, p. 25). Drawing on the psychological commonplace that "our identity is partly shaped by recognition" and on a healthy dose of liberal political theory, Taylor lays out the ethical stance of multiculturalism: "Nonrecognition or misrecognition can inflict harm, can be a form of oppression, imprisoning someone in a false, distorted, and reduced mode of being" (p. 25).

Multiculturalism's mission, then, might be characterized as freeing the prisoners of misrecognition. The recognition of cultural plurality will allow the distorted and the reduced to be who they are, fully, completely. But what it is to be fully oneself is no easy question, and one that I will return to, after allowing Taylor to extend his argument about modes of being into the larger political sphere of democracy. He holds that "democracy has ushered in a politics of equal recognition" whose principal project is to encompass at every point the "equal status of cultures and genders" (p. 27). Yet this reasonable and common position creates its own politics of identity that I think undermines Taylor's position while pointing, after Weil, to what needs to be taught about culture and other collectivities within a democracy. The lesson here is about the fundamental tension within democracy between individual and collective rights.

Whereas Taylor stands his case for multiculturalism on a foundation of individualism that he sees lying at the heart of modern Western notions of morality and authenticity (p. 28), I think the politics of identity brings a new realism to a sense of individual-versus-collective. Consider how democracy, for all of its celebration of the individual, has made its progress toward a universal franchise through a series of strictly categorical extensions of the franchise to the propertyless, women, and colonial natives. The arguments in favor of extending that right to the disenfranchised assumed that such people were now ready, as a group, to participate in self-governance. The "universal rights of man" celebrated by European democrats were never quite universal, never quite about individuals; they were most certainly about how categories of people were recognized and treated accordingly.

In this sense, democracy's politics of recognition is not about ending the "nonrecognition or misrecognition" of certain categories of people, as Taylor has cast it; it is about changing the meaning and significance of the categories. Those in power felt compelled to redefine the political status of women, for example, after being persuaded by the suffragettes that refusing women the vote was unacceptable democratic practice. Had men misrecognized women as their equals? That may be one way of putting it, but I think it fair to consider how men had constituted, by the powers of the state invested in them, the legal status of the category "woman." They didn't misrecognize the category. Consider how, when it came to articulating the category of woman, writers from Plato onward in the West sought to recognize every plausible and implausible shortcoming as constituting the category. To say that they got women wrong is to treat the divisions as given and fixed, if terribly misconstrued. This misses the point that the category itself is largely man-made. The category was constituted by those in power, who shaped it in their own image of "woman" and had to be convinced to change the meaning of the category.[2] Which is only to say that the extension of democratic rights has been about reducing the political effectiveness of the categories as tools of exclusion and instruments of power.

This is why I feel that the political issue here, as well as the educational one, is the ongoing construction of the category. Taylor suggests, with his philosophy of recognition, that there is a truth to the category that needs only be finally recognized, as the scales of prejudice fall from our eyes. Taylor does not take issue with the categories themselves, at least not directly. When he denounces "imprisoning someone in a false, distorted, and reduced mode of being," he directs our moral and political energies toward liberating the true, accurate, and expanded mode of a person's being. My fear is that this does too little to dissuade us from believing that, if it were not for this tradition of misrecognition, we would see each other's (true) nature and accurately grasp the qualities currently clouded over by social forces. Thus, although I welcome Taylor's interest in expanded modes of being, I can't help feeling that the political and educational work that needs our immediate attention is addressing how the categories by which we know and name each other have been shaped, categories that give every indication of continuing to serve, within the politics of identity, as a means of differentiating the distribution of power in this society.

Whereas I want students to attend more to all that goes into the making of the categories (Donna Haraway's "scientific discourse and other social practices" [1991, p. 155]), Taylor feels that the best hope for education is "comparative cultural study," which will permit us to identify "the relative worth of different cultures." He feels that this approach will curtail ethnocentrism or "displace our horizons in the resulting fusions"; it is also intended to check "inauthentic judgments of equal value" in assessing other cultures (p. 73). By all means, I would respond, there is nothing wrong with studying how other people live, becoming discerning and critical students of the world's subtle arts and crafts. Yet I question Taylor's antirelativist insistence that *we refine our ability in order to* compare the relative worth of cultures. What is Taylor referring to, I wonder, when he speaks of the "ultimate horizon from which the relative worth of different cultures might be evident" (p. 73)? It brings to mind the excitement felt in climbing the steps of the British Museum. Here one is about to enter into the presence of the cultural wonders of the world, yet at some level such venerable institutions as the British Museum could be characterized as the horizon-dominating repositories of the West's ultimate vantage point in comparing cultures. On a simpler level, it suggests those protomulticultural efforts to teach the young how Native Americans gave corn, potatoes, tomatoes, and tobacco to the West, as if a people's worth were to be gleaned from their contribution to our own table and well-being.³

The relative worth of different cultures stands humbled before the achievement of the West and before its power to assemble and judge them as part of its greater educational function. For my part, I ask that we become students of the distinctions that this educational disposition has done much to construct through museum displays and social-studies textbooks—students, for example, of how the West created the Orient as a category, further constituting itself in the process (Said, 1978). The politics of recognition I'm advocating here is about recognizing and contesting the historical fabrication of categories that identify us as, say, female and French but obscure who we are on another level as complete human beings.⁴

Taylor does distinguish between private and public spheres of recognition, but he also conflates the two when he speaks of a "politics of difference" in which "what we are asked to recognize is the unique identity of this individual or group, their distinctness from everyone else" (p. 38). To speak of a group's unique identity, as if that identity formed like a snowflake, with no two alike, misses how that identity forms within the forceful social relations that shape just how one grows up female and French. Taylor acknowledges social influences on both individual and group, but he does not see them, as I do, at the very core of the politics of recognition. What is political about recognition is the contest around how a group is constituted by social influences and how the group is named and placed in the larger social structure. As such, this process warrants educational attention.

This is only to say that the politics of recognition should not draw us into trying somehow to recognize who anyone "really" is, especially given postmodern renderings of just how partial and fragmented what we take to be the self may be. An education for the politics of recognition would do far better to focus on the science of race that arose in the 19th century and continued through the 20th. It should examine immigration policies and the treatment of women in the media. It should pause over the language laws in Quebec that restrict the use of English on public signs. It should consider how the idea of "nation" aligns with "race," and how "culture" has come to mediate between the two terms in dividing the world among us.

Such an educational effort is bound to affect how I recognize myself and others, even as it works more directly on my understanding of the process of recognition itself. Yet because the politics of recognition, as Taylor describes it, underlies the spirit of multicultural initiatives in the schools, I next need to consider how an attention to the construction of the categories, in the spirit of Weil's initial urge to understand and act on the obligations that bind us, might sit with multiculturalism, that progressive public concept, as well as with its harshest critics.

Multiculturalism in Action

Canada offers an excellent starting point for considering multiculturalism in action. Although there is a resurgence of right-wing criticism, the country is still duly proud of the official policy, which was adopted as a national policy in 1971 and grew into the Canadian Multiculturalism Act of 1987. The government now engages in active sponsorship of cultural community groups, ethnic events, and related school programs (supported in 1996, for example, by an $18.5 million budget). This legislative act is intended to ensure that people have the "freedom . . . to preserve, enhance, and share [Canada's] cultural heritages" (*Multiculturalism*, 1987, p. 18). In what has struck some as a patronizing manner, the act recognizes a hyphenated mode of being among the nation's citizenry as not simply an enriching addition but a defining element: "Multiculturalism is a fundamental characteristic of the Canadian heritage and identity and . . . provides an invaluable resource in the shaping of Canada's future" (p. 18). After a century of racially restrictive immigration policies, this could truly stand, Taylor might note, as a political step toward improved recognition. And the act has certainly had an impact on education.

Heritage Language programs have been initiated in a number of Canadian communities after sometimes tempestuous struggles over providing public support for languages other than English and French (Cummins, 1989). After years of trial programs, British Columbia now allows students to study Punjabi, Mandarin, or Japanese for high school graduation. In literature classes, a new generation of anthologies are being used that extend the Anglo–North American traditions of English literature to a new range of voices and experiences.[5] In science and mathematics, which sometimes claim exemption from multicultural interests, lessons are now being offered on non-European inventors, scientists, and mathematicians (Price, 1992, p. 31). In these ways, educators have sought to broaden the school's representation of who constitutes the nation in the name of multiculturalism.

A second, more recent educational approach to the politics of identity in Canadian schools has been to confront the scourge of racism head-on through antiracist programs. Provincial ministries of education in Canada that have attempted to implement antiracist programs have followed two directions. One seeks to help students deal with the racism they encounter in school and community. The Ministry of Education in British Columbia, for example, advises high school teachers to seek ways of "explicitly addressing and providing intervention strategies to eliminate stereotyping, prejudice, discrimination, and racism" (British Columbia Ministry of Education, 1992, p. 47). It calls for forms of assertiveness training that will enable students "to intervene in cases of racial and cultural harassment" (p. 47). Given that racism is more than the work of louts and bullies, a second tack has emerged, one that seeks to identify how systemic racism has long shaped policies and practices in immigration, housing, employment, and education.

Pursuing this second line, the Ministry of Education and Training in Ontario has issued the statement *Antiracism and Ethnocultural Equity in School Boards*, which calls for a curriculum that not only recognizes diversity but takes on its own educational tradition of ethnocentrism:

> Antiracist curriculum provides a balance of perspectives. It enables all students to see themselves reflected in the curriculum and provides each student with the knowledge, skills, attitudes, and behaviors needed to live in a complex and diverse world. It consciously examines and challenges the Eurocentric nature of the curriculum and of the society in which young people are growing up. (Ontario Ministry of Education and Training, 1993, p. 13)[6]

Notice how recognition works in both directions here. The curriculum opens up to a greater diversity of experience while also turning a critical eye on its own closed tradition.

The move from multicultural to antiracist education seems a promising step in pursuit of how collectivities are constructed. Yet it is still not the whole of the matter for me. To see how a map offered a Eurocentric projection of an imperial fantasy that saw civilization radiating out from a European center is one thing, but the map also needs to be turned into a lesson on not only how the West looked out at the world as if it were its own, but also how it named first the Other and then itself as if assuming that the differences were a reflection of nature rather than taking their meaning from history. Still to come, then, in multicultural, antiracist education is the history of the learned investment in the significance of the differences and divides among humankind. I am asking that students gain some sense of how the world came to be divided in just this way. This seems crucial to appreciating, critiquing, and unraveling the political play of identity in today's world.

I am hardly the only one asking for this addition to the multicultural and antiracist educational agenda. For example, James Banks, a long-time leader in American multicultural education, shares this determination to focus on the formation of the categories by which we are identified: "Students should be given opportunities to investigate and determine how cultural assumptions, frames of reference, perspectives, and biases within a discipline influence the ways the knowledge is constructed" (1993, p. 11).[7] Banks goes on in a later article (1995) to propose that students learn how the changing meaning of race reflects a struggle over the construction of difference. He is seeking not a multicultural celebration of diversity but a transformation of the way in which students understand the categories that divide. He focuses on how African American "race reconstructionists," as he names Kelly Miller, W. E. B. Du Bois, and others, wrested the meaning of the concept away from the exclusive hold of a genteel and educated yet deeply racist society (1995, pp. 17–18). He seeks to inspire students, through this engagement with the past, with the continuing reconstruction of race as a process in which they are able to participate:

> Students should examine the ways in which the construction of race reflects the social context, the historical times, and the economic structure of society. *Students should also understand that the concept of race is still in the process of change and reconstruction.* (1995, p. 23; original emphasis)

The educational issue for Banks, and clearly for me as well, is to make the political history of difference part of the school program. Students need some insight into the long, learned process by which culture, race, and nation (even as they overlap and map onto each other) continue to be invested with meaningful differences. These conceptual interests need not undermine the importance of learning about the cultural diversity that continues to reshape the North American continent. I am only asking that we go warily into the politics of recognition and difference, asking after the formation of the categories by which we declare ourselves. We have only to ask students to put aside the idea that there is a truth, essence, or core to any given category; we are not, by field trip or interactive multimedia, about to uncover the truth that lies beneath the labels.

But then many students are already into rewriting the categories. They are pursuing another sort of politics of identity and recognition, or so I began to suspect during a variety night at a Vancouver high school. What proved to be the most exhilarating moment of the evening for this audience of students and their families came when a student-formed and directed group of Bhangara dancers rushed onto the stage in their handmade costumes and performed this East Indian pop-music form. This wasn't multicultural folk dancing; it wasn't about the preservation of a distant culture. It was, as far as I could tell amid the cheers, about the affirmation and invention that were a part of these students' lives. It forms a very real and heartfelt statement in response to the question "Where is here?" in the sense of who is honored and what can be recognized in a school auditorium. The Bhangara dancing was followed by rap music and soul acts in a cultural cross-dressing that might be taken, had the appropriate critical-theory pundits been in attendance that evening, as defining "the postmodern transgressive chic . . . the overlay of codes" that, for Peter McLaren, distinguish the "border identities" of the age (1994, p. 74).[8] This auditorium full of exuberantly grooving students may be regarded by some as a weak force in the politics of identity, but they were synthesizing and sampling their way into a new set of cultural roots. They performed the possibilities of redefining and reworking the categories. I want only to complement their artful work with supporting lessons in geography, history, literature, and science classes on the making of the differences they are playing with and against. But the politics of identity has heated up with a conservative backlash against multiculturalism, a development that also lends weight to the need for the sort of lessons on category construction that I am calling for here.

The Multiculturalism Backlash: Bissoondath and Schlesinger

If advocates of multiculturalism seek a politics of recognition based on respecting difference, they are not far removed from their best critics. Those who would have none of multiculturalism argue for respecting differences by preserving and protecting those jdifferences which they believe define the nation. Conservative critics of multiculturalism have become increasingly intent on rescuing and redeeming the nation in jeopardy. In just this vein, the novelist Neil Bissoondath and the historian Arthur Schlesinger have written books warning of the fragmentation that will befall the multicultural state. In *Selling Illusions: The Cult of Multiculturalism in Canada* (1994), Bissoondath makes it clear that he is tired of the triteness of it all. The annual Caribbean festival in Toronto leaves him cold. He rejects the subsidization of cultural ghettos. He pokes fun at the "the excesses of sensitivity" that have found their way into government and universities and complains that under such sponsorship, "culture becomes an object for display rather than the heart and soul of the individuals formed by it" (p. 88). He aptly shows, as I earlier tried to do with Charles Taylor's work, that multiculturalism cannot possibly "accommodate the complex reality" of people's lives, to which he adds that "cultural heritage is not always a pretty thing" (pp. 87–88). It is also easy to see that government intervention in culture is bound to rob it of at least some of its spontaneous and authentic expression.

Yet in launching this critique, Bissoondath plays his own politics of identity. In the words of a back-cover blurb on his book, he has "refused the role of ethnic and sought to avoid the burden of hyphenation—a burden that would label him an East Indian–Trinidadian–Canadian living in Quebec." He seems determined to make apparent the categories only to refuse them. Here is that voluntary and individualist element that Taylor held in the sense of a dialogue. Can you declaim the hyphenation when you and your publisher recognize how much your race-bound identity adds to the public's interest in your critique of what is intended to protect your interests? Using a provocative comparison, Bissoondath would rule his identity out of bounds of the government and the politics of recognition: "My sex life is my own, we say, for instance. Yet so many of us seem to depend on the state for the sense of self that comes from official recognition of our cultural background" (p. 213). This is fine for straight people to say, some would point out. However, the Canadian experience has meant, among various forms of public intervention, having gay literature confiscated by customs officials at the Canadian border. The state is deeply engaged in educating, if not policing, the politics of identity by which we live. Can we refuse that politics by unilaterally declaring the independence of the self?

Bissoondath directs his appeals toward the imaginary and unified nation of yesteryear that is now threatened by multiculturalism: "In eradicating the center, in evoking uncertainty as to what and who is Canadian, it has diminished all sense of Canadian values, of what is a Canadian"

(p. 71). He readily acknowledges that what is a Canadian has always been a hodgepodge of conjectures, typically around order, good government, and respect for Mounties. He counters, however, that multiculturalism can only make matters of national self-definition worse.

If multiculturalism has made the question of identity worse, that only makes it better, as I see it, because uncertainty about who is Canadian means a good deal less posturing about who is truly of this land. Now is the time to recognize that the nation is constituted by all it contains, and not just by those at an imaginary center or origin; the nation is a political organization of space, not a quality of character that need only be properly recognized.[9] We should be past the era when pundits and scholars prided themselves in how adroitly they could name the character of a nation by way of race and culture. And as for Bissoondath's fear of a "diminished . . . sense of Canadian values," could those be the same values that kept the vote from women, Chinese Canadians, and First Nations peoples; that refused to recognize women as persons under the law; and that continue to contest the land claims of First Nations peoples?[10] Changes to those values over the years were consistently resisted in the name of preserving what was Canadian. We need to honor those who have suffered this history by calling the making of the nation into question, rather than looking to see how well each of us holds to some sort of national center.

This fear that the center cannot hold has its American counterpart in the well-received critique of multiculturalism *The Disuniting of America* (1992), by the dean of American historians, Arthur Schlesinger. So alarmed by this perceived threat to the American fabric is Schlesinger that he sees his best hope in reviving the powerful association of race and nation. He takes his lead from J. Hector St. John de Crèvecoeur, whose *Letters from an American Farmer* was published at the time of the American Revolution (reprinted 1963). "Here individuals of all nations," Crèvecoeur wrote, "are melted into a new race of men" (cited by Schlesinger, p. 12).[11] Schlesinger pursues this theme of a "new race," bolstered by Emerson's "Smelting Pot" and Gunnar Myrdal's "American Creed." He mounts a relentless attack on what he terms the "cult of ethnicity," which "rejects the unifying vision of individuals from all nations melted into a new race" (p. 15).[12] The race-and-nation myth is redoubled in Schlesinger's book. He assumes, in the first instance, that identity is a matter of choice, by virtue of being in America: "Most American-born members of minority groups, white and nonwhite, while they may cherish particular heritages, still see themselves primarily as Americans and not primarily as Irish or Hungarians or Jews or Africans or Asians" (p. 19).

This new-world myth of a fresh identity has proven a powerful literary theme, from *Native Son* to *The Joy Luck Club*. Those who chose, or were chosen by, America have had to learn the terms on which they would be admitted to the fold. Schlesinger reinforces this idea when, without discounting the contributions of other cultures, he names the common ground: "The Anglo-Saxon Protestant tradition was for two centuries—and in crucial respects still is—the dominant influence on American culture and society" (p. 28). And the carriers of that influence? "Our public schools in particular," he points out, "have been great instruments of assimilation and great means of forming an American identity" (p. 17). How can Schlesinger imagine that American identity is anything but divided? The schools have always taught the young to trace the lines that will divide them as Americans, not least of all by gender, race, culture, and class.[13]

Yet the schools are now really failing America, Schlesinger points out in his sometimes cranky and exasperated attack, when they introduce Afrocentric programs that focus on the civilizations and accomplishments of the African continent.[14] He has little patience with programs that "deny the essentially European origins of American culture" and thereby, in his estimation, "falsify history" (p. 136). His tone with regard to Afrocentric and multicultural programs is "let's get one thing straight":

> Whatever the particular crimes of Europe, that continent is also the source—the *unique* source—of those liberating ideas of individual liberty, political democracy, the rule of law, human rights, and cultural freedom that constitute our most precious legacy and to which most of the world today aspires. These are *European* ideas, not Asian, nor African, nor Middle Eastern ideas, except by adoption. (p. 127; original emphasis)

Schlesinger's certainty about the exclusivity of ideas—"*European* ideas, not Asian"—is unsettling, given the traffic in ideas over the centuries. So is his seeming historical obliviousness not to "particular crimes of Europe" but to how its "liberating ideas" were often used to perpetuate injustices. This continent's achievement was underwritten by the skillfully argued denial of "individual liberty, political democracy, the rule of law, human rights, and cultural freedom" to a good number of people. Schlesinger is celebrating the ideals of the victors while failing to realize that the struggle to extend these ideals to the whole of the nation was an intellectual battle that many people who form part of "the *unique* source" fought long and hard against. This does not mean that we need reject the accomplishments of European culture. But we could stand to benefit by a little more of that troubling historical perspective on the course of those liberating ideas.

When all is said and done, Schlesinger's argument comes down to the most basic of allegiances: "Nationalism remains, after two centuries, the most vital political emotion in the world" (p. 47).[15] That the nation doesn't appear to love all of its citizens and has forced a hyphenated self on so many of them would seem readily apparent to a historian. One might be equally disappointed to find Schlesinger accusing those who fail to love the dominant influences on American culture of being a threat to democracy. Although nationalism has certainly had its liberating, anticolonial moments, the dangers of ethnic versions of nationalism have never been more apparent. And basing nationalism on the founding of a new race—"still the best hope," as Schlesinger puts it (p. 138)—would only set America under the spell of that tired parade of nationalism led by the British and French races through the 19th century.[16]

To use the metaphor of race in calling for a unification of the nation under one God does little to honor the history of a nation tragically built out of racial divisions. The politics of identity becomes, in Schlesinger's hands, a demand that people identify with the dominant culture and honor its history and historians by submerging themselves in what is cast as the authentic and essential identity of the nation. It may well seem that Schlesinger fears for both the nation and the domination. Yet his case rests on the confusion that Taylor did so little to clarify, a confusion which allows the hard-earned, authentic identity of the individual to become the soul of the collective. Although I take exception to Bissoondath's and Schlesinger's dismissal of multicultural initiatives as harmful to the health of the nation, my purpose here has not been to defend the necessary and ethical recognition of the plurality of our communities. The educational corrective, for me, still lies in pursuing what I take to be Simone Weil's probing of the human interests served by collectives.

For Weil, the need for roots draws us into judging our identifications and testing their affirmation of life and liberty, their powers of exclusion and inclusion. This critical engagement with our identity amounts to its own way of being rooted in this world. In France today, another of the country's leading intellectuals, Julia Kristeva, has been led by a reconsideration of the nationality question to realize that we are all, at some level, "strangers to ourselves" (1991). She describes an inner dynamic that gives rise to this experience of self-estrangement: "The foreigner comes in when the consciousness of my difference arises, and he disappears when we all acknowledge ourselves as foreigners, unamenable to bonds and communities" (p. 1). Rather than a security of place, Kristeva is led to a postnational sensibility that she finds succinctly stated in the words of Meleager of Gadara, from the first century B.C.E.: "The only homeland, foreigner, is the world we live in; a single Chaos has given birth to all mortals" (cited by Kristeva, p. 56). Kristeva is not ready, as it turns out, to give up on the distinctions of nationhood and her adopted France, but she has at least come to question how foreigner and community are constituted.[17]

To make a study of the divisions by which we live is a risky education. No longer can it leave one unthinkingly at home with one's self or place. Such was the example of Weil's own life, as she was both at one with her country, writing of the need for patriotism, and forced into exile as a Jew, while the Vichy government of France collaborated with the conquering Nazis. I would hold that education has no less of an interest in getting a distance on one's own life and on what we call home. We are, at once, subject to the named collectivities of our existence and in possession of the possibility of turning them into objects of study that are always forms of self-inquiry which can give rise to thoughtful and creative expression. We have always lived within a politics of recognition and identity. We have now to become wiser students of how this politics operates, even if this requires that we step away from ourselves into a larger unbound world, if only for a moment or two, in order to look back on how we have been cast and how we have cast others. That we are strangers to ourselves, with the world our only homeland, seems a proper tonic for rethinking the divisions by which we have for so long set ourselves apart from others.

Notes

1. On the banning of the *hijab* by students in the schools of France and Quebec, see Narsulla (1994).

2. Donna Haraway critiques what science has made of "woman." She writes that when it comes to a critical analysis of gender, "there is not even such a state as 'being' female, itself a highly complex category constructed in contested sexual scientific discourse and other social practices" (1991, p. 155).

3. This is not to discount the contribution of Native Americans. See Jack Weatherford (1988) for an extensive review of "how the Indians of the Americas transformed the world."

4. Maxine Hong Kingston presents a wonderful instance of recognition's complexity in speaking to hyphenated readers about the parts of her that are Chinese: "Chinese-Americans, when you try to understand what things in you are Chinese, how do you separate what is peculiar to childhood, to poverty, insanities, one family, your mother who marked your growing with stories, from what is Chinese?" (1975, pp. 5–6). The Otherness is manifest, ascribed, confused, proudly held. One can simply stare into the mirror and wonder, or one can expect a little more from the schools in understanding how these identity questions are moments of both personal and larger political histories.

5. See Borovilos (1990) for an example and Greenlaw (1993) for critique. Diana Brydon warns that "we face the danger that the new vogue for 'third world,' 'minority' or 'marginalized literatures,' as they have variously been called, will merely introduce more subtle versions of 'incorporated disparity' instead of challenging an organization of discourse that justifies the status quo" (1989, p. 91).

6. George Sefa Dei, at the Ontario Institute for Studies in Education, speaks of the need "to problematize Eurocentric, white male privilege and supremacy, and the consequent social inequalities in our pluralistic society" (1993, p. 37). He places an emphasis on history in his antiracist approach: "The effectiveness of antiracist work in the schools will depend on the clear historical understanding of the institutional structures, factors, and issues that have contributed to discriminatory and ethnocentric education within the school system" (p. 39). For a review and application of multicultural, antiracist, and postcolonial curriculum programs in the English classrooms of Ontario, see Greenlaw (1993).

7. For a survey of multicultural education in America and beyond, see James Banks and Cherry McGee Banks (1995).

8. McLaren argues that "students need to be provided with opportunities to construct border identities . . . intersubjective spaces of cultural translation—linguistically multivalenced spaces of intercultural dialogue" (1994, p. 65). Many students already have done the construction work; what we educators can provide are opportunities for further insights into their schoolwork and other aspects of identity formation.

9   Bissoondath's concluding note, calling for "blending [differences] into a new vision of Canadianness . . . where inherent differences meld easily . . . and every individual is a Canadian, undiluted and undivided," seems to long for a transcending metaphysical and apolitical sense of nationality (1994, p. 224).

10 See Alison Prentice et al. (1982).

11 It may be worth noting that Crèvecoeur (1963) had to flee his new homeland and fellow Americans for failing to take a stand during the American Revolution, a decision that cost him his wife and children.

12 This sense of forging a new race is found in Israel Zangwill's turn-of-the-century play *The Melting Pot*, which betrays its dated and naive reading of race: "America is God's crucible, the great melting pot where all the races of Europe are melting and reforming" (cited by Shipman, 1994, p. 123).

13 See, for example, the McCarthy and Crichlow collection (1993).

14 Molefi Kete Asante characterizes the Afrocentrist approach as holding that "all knowledge results from an occasion of encounter in place. . . . The Afrocentrist seeks to uncover and use codes paradigms, symbols, motifs, myths, and circles of discussion that reinforce the centrality of African ideals and values as a valid frame of reference for acquiring and examining data" (1990, pp. 5–6). George Dei speaks to the challenge of teaching the place of Africa in the world after so many years of misrepresentation (1993, pp. 43–46). That African and Semitic influences on the West through the culture of the ancient Greeks were deliberately obscured in the 20th century by scholars is found in Martin Bernal (1987). On the other hand, Henry Louis Gates Jr. (1993) names "demagogues and pseudo-scholars" among the Afrocentrist advocates. The most notorious of the proposals Gates attacks is the Portland, Oregon, "African-American Baseline Essays," available from Portland Public Schools; see Hughes (1993, pp. 130–151). For more favorable reviews of Afrocentric curriculum ventures, see Murrell (1993) and Perry (1993).

15 For a brief survey of the work that connects Schlesinger and E. D. Hirsch, Jr. through educational historian Dianne Ravitch, see Seixas (1993, pp. 236–237).

16 It is interesting to note that geneticist Theodosius Dobzhansky speaks of how new races are in the process of forming, with Europe "well on the way to fusion into a single race" (1962, p. 279) in what appears to be a common blurring of the figurative and literal (scientific) language of race and culture.

17 Salman Rushdie also pursues the theme of being at home with a sense of distance, reminding us that the dislocated writer's powers are not just a matter of the fiction that is written. In his essay on "imaginary homelands" (1991), Rushdie invokes the memories of such productive and provocative "foreigners" as Swift, Conrad, and Marx, while praising his own Bombay-born and England-bound "plural and partial" identity. He can see the profit in a distancing that helps in the literary "business of finding new angles at which to enter reality" (p. 15).

References

Asante, M. K. (1990). *Kemet, Afrocentricity, and knowledge.* Trenton, NJ: Africa World Press.

Banks, J. A. (1993). The canon debate, knowledge construction, and multicultural education. *Educational Researcher, 22*(5), 4–14.

Banks, J. A. (1995). The historical reconstruction of knowledge about race: Implications for transformative teaching. *Educational Researcher, 24*(2), 15–25.

Banks, J. A., & Banks, C. A. M. (Eds.). (1995). *Handbook of research on multicultural education.* New York: Macmillan.

Bernal, M. (1987). *Black Athena: The Afroasiatic roots of classical civilization: Vol. 1. The fabrication of ancient Greece, 1785–1985.* Baltimore: Johns Hopkins University Press.

Bissoondath, N. (1994). *Selling illusions: The cult of multiculturalism in Canada.* Harmondsworth, UK: Penguin.

Borovilos, J. (1990). *Breaking through: A Canadian literary mosaic.* Scarborough, ON: Prentice Hall.

British Columbia Ministry of Education. (1992). *The graduation program working paper: Partnerships for learners.* Victoria: British Columbia Ministry of Education.

Brydon, D. (1989). New approaches to the new literatures in English: Are we in danger of incorporating disparity? In H. Maes-Jelinek, K. H. Petersen, & A. Rutherford (Eds.), *A shaping of connections: Commonwealth literature studies—then and now* (pp. 88–99). Sydney: Dangaroo.

Crèvecoeur, J. H. St. J. de. (1963). *Letters from an American farmer; and, Sketches of 18th-century America: More letters from an American farmer.* Toronto: New American Library.

Cummins, J. (1989). Heritage language teaching and the student: Fact and friction. In J. H. Esling (Ed.), *Multicultural education and policy: ESL in the 1990s: A tribute to Mary Ashworth* (pp. 3–17). Toronto: OISE Press.

Dei, G. J. S. (1993). The challenge of anti-racist education in Canada. *Canadian Ethnic Studies, 25*(2), 36–51.

Dobzhansky, T. (1962). *Mankind evolving: The evolution of the human species.* New York: Bantam.

Gates, H. L., Jr. (1993). Beyond the culture wars: Identities in dialogue. *Profession* (Modern Language Association), *93*, 6–11.

Greenlaw, J. (1993). *The postcolonial conception of the high school multicultural literature curriculum.* Unpublished dissertation, University of British Columbia, Vancouver.

Haraway, D. (1991). *Simians, cyborgs, and women: The reinvention of nature.* New York: Routledge.

Hughes, R. (1993). *Culture complaint: The fraying of America.* New York: Oxford University Press.

Kingston, M. H. (1975). *The woman warrior: Memoirs of a girlhood among ghosts.* New York: Vintage.

Kristeva, J. (1991). *Strangers to ourselves* (L. S. Roudiez, Trans.). New York: Columbia University Press.

McCarthy, C., & Crichlow, W. (Eds.). (1993). *Race, identity, and representation in education.* New York: Routledge.

McLaren, P. (1994). White terror and oppositional agency: Towards a critical multiculturalism. In D. T. Goldberg (Ed.), *Multiculturalism: A critical reader* (pp. 45–74). Oxford: Blackwell.

Multiculturalism . . . Being Canadian. (1987). Ottawa: Ministry of Supplies and Services Canada.

Murrell, P. (1993). Afrocentric immersion: Academic and personal development of African American males in public schools. In T. Perry & J. W. Fraser (Eds.), *Freedom's plow: Teaching in the multicultural classroom* (pp. 231–260). New York: Routledge.

Narsulla, A. (1994, December 13). Educators outside Quebec mystified by hijab ban. *Toronto Globe & Mail,* pp. A1, A4.

Ontario Ministry of Education and Training. (1993). *Antiracism and ethnocultural equity in school boards: Guidelines for policy development and implementation.* Toronto: Ontario Ministry of Education and Training.

Perry, T. (1993). "I am still thirsty": A theorization on authority and cultural location of Afrocentism. In T. Perry & J. W. Fraser (Eds.), *Freedom's plow: Teaching in the multicultural classroom* (pp. 261-270). New York: Routledge.

Prentice, A., Biurne, P., Brandt, G., Light, B., Mitchinson, W., & Black, N. (1982). *Canadian women: A history.* Toronto: Harcourt Brace Jovanovich.

Price, M. (1992). An anti-racist generation: A challenge for education. *Education Today, 4,* 8-11, 30-31.

Rushdie, S. (1991). Imaginary homelands. In *Imaginary homelands: Essays and criticism, 1981-1991* (pp. 9-21). London: Granta Books.

Said, E. W. (1978). *Orientalism.* New York: Random House.

Schlesinger, A. (1992). *The disuniting of America: Reflections on a multicultural society.* New York: Norton.

Seixas, P. (1993). Parallel crises: History and the social studies curriculum in the USA. *Journal of Curriculum Studies, 25*(3), 235-250.

Shipman, P. (1994). *The evolution of racism: Human differences and the use and abuse of science.* New York: Simon & Schuster.

Taylor, C. (1994). *Multiculturalism: Examining the politics of recognition.* Princeton, NJ: Princeton University Press.

Weatherford, J. (1988). *Indian givers: How the Indians of the Americas transformed the world.* New York: Fawcett Columbine.

Weil, S. (1952). *The need for roots* (A. Wills, Trans.). Boston: Beacon.

Wright, L. (1994, July 25). One drop of blood. *New Yorker,* 46-55.

PART THREE
AUTHORITATIVE

Chapter 7

Cutting English on the Bias: Five Lexicographers in Pursuit of the New

> Ideally, the linguist should be able to observe all linguistic events. Every human utterance should come under his scrutiny. At present no one has the time, machinery, or qualified assistants to record or store or analyze on such an ideal scale.
>
> —Philip Gove

Realistically, the lexicographer about to observe the language faces close to a billion people engaged in linguistic events in English each day (McCrum, Cran, and MacNeil 1986, 3). Only by dint of the sparsest sampling procedures can the lexicographer hope to turn away from the cacophony of utterance long enough to fashion a dictionary. Such highly selective attention both permits and determines the dictionary. Yet insofar as the discretionary process is buried from view in the editorial offices of the publisher, the user of the dictionary is tempted to imagine the sort of comprehensiveness the legendary lexicographer Philip Gove addresses in the epigraph. I suspect that the authoritativeness of the dictionary may unduly rest on this imagined comprehensiveness. To know exactly which utterances are attended to—though most of them are not so much uttered as published—is not only to realize the claim of the dictionary on the language but also to perceive the manner in which the language's continuing development is monitored and recognized, if not always sanctioned.

This inquiry attempts to meet the mythical comprehensiveness of the dictionary with a description of the realistic limitations of actual lexicographical practice. To portray the current state of that practice, I have conducted interviews with the senior lexicographical staff of five publishers of English-language dictionaries in the United States, England, and Canada.[1] The reading and marking programs at Houghton Mifflin, Merriam-Webster, Random House, Oxford University Press, and Gage make it clear that because lexicographers cannot possibly scrutinize everything, they have learned to trust certain sources, to seek systems and standards, and to exclude some sources categorically while tripping onto others, each in their own search and in their own way. To report on these ways is not to knock over the screen hiding the Wizard of Oz anxiously working the levers and wires of his apparent greatness. As Gove's comment suggests, many lexicographers would gladly have their work more realistically portrayed and appreciated. However, in spite of this interest in realism, some slip at times into the rhetoric of the authoritative and the comprehensive. The temptation is understandable. Readers and writers may also find it difficult to face the displacement of authority that emerges from a description of the human dimensions in this project of ascertaining the new in the language.

Though lexicographers describe their culling habits in the small print of the introductory passages and prefaces to their dictionaries, they can be singularly vague about the nature and selection of their sources. The documentation so helpfully provided in the *Oxford English Dictionary (OED)* tells us only where the word was first found (and where it has been found in each subsequent century or, in the *Supplement,* each decade). Yet we know not from among which sources and in what fashion these citations are drawn out of the linguistic events that populate the language. Even with the Oxford dictionaries, the reading program receives little prefatory attention. The senior editor of the recently completed *Supplement*, Robert Burchfield, omits the reading program from his seven-level triangle representing "the editorial process" in his introduction to the first volume (Burchfield 1972, xvi). He refers in the second volume to the use of "long runs of regional American and Canadian newspapers" and "the principal publications of the United Kingdom" (1976, vii); yet the *New York Times* and the *New Yorker* alone receive specific mention. To state only these two obvious choices, it would seem, is to beg the actual scope of such terms as *principal* and *regional*; it is to raise the specter of what has been included and excluded, though Oxford is hardly alone in this tendency to imply an exhaustive coverage of the language.[2]

To pursue this instance of Oxford, Burchfield does, in the preface to the third volume, concede changes in "emphasis or detail here and there" due to "research interests of scholars in various subjects, and the vicissitudes of the *OED* Department and of my own life" (1982, v), just as he qualifies the search for first appearance as one necessarily limited by "the printed sources read for the Supplement" (1972, xv). But, that much frankly stated, he can be given, on occasion, to the rhetoric of the authoritative, sensitive, and exhaustive record of the language. He has suggested recently that his predecessor James Murray fell only two words short of Gove's mythological ideal, and those two words were not overlooked so much as overstepped: "There were no exclusion zones, no censorings, no blindfoldings, except for the absence of two famous four letter (sexual) words. Dr. Murray, his colleagues, and his contributors had drudged up the whole of the accessible vocabulary of English (two words apart) and had done their best to record them systematically in the *OED*" (Burchfield 1986, 23-24).[3] Over the course of my conversations with the editors of the five dictionaries of my sample, I occasionally found this sort of lexicographical mythos both belabored and betrayed. Although the editors sought system and method in their search, nonetheless disquieting exclusion zones became apparent. Elements of serendipity also proved a pervasive factor in determining the ground covered in this search. Bias itself is not surprising; every step of the editor's craft is marked by the application of a delicate sensibility and years of educated subjectivity. Yet even as editors' lexicographical practices are "perfectly sensible," as one editor termed them, that sensibility is shaped by the culture which that language embodies. And the first step in lexicography, this initial selection process, has to be regarded as the strongest moment of editorial omission in the process, even as it continues to receive the slightest attention.

As if to emphasize that the selection of sources is the principal entry point of editorial discretion, once the results of the initial search are in hand, lexicographers are careful to stress the impartial nature of the next step in their work. As an anonymous editor at Merriam-Webster has put it: "The definitions, then, are based not on an editor's idea of what words ought to mean but rather on their meanings actually given to words by the speakers and writers of English who use them" (*Nine Thousand Words* 1983, 17a).[4] If that is the case, then this matter of the lexicographers' procedure for selecting the "words by speakers and writers"—the nature of the sources they turn to in order to find these gems—becomes the crucial point of their influence and authority over the language. It is not, then, the editors' ideas about what words mean that determine the lexicographical contribution to the shape of the language, but rather their ideas about where it is best to spend their limited resources looking for this language.

To cover the principal publications in the language systematically, lexicographers draw on four constituencies: an internal reading program led by the editors; an external reading program directed by the editors and consisting of part-time readers from across the English-speaking world; a systematic check of other lexicographical sources; and, finally, the unsolicited but welcomed contributions of interested readers of the dictionary. In addition to these methods, which represent an extension of 18th- and 19th-century lexicographical techniques, a radically new method has appeared on the block. Thoroughly modern lexicographers have begun electronic searches of commercial on-line databases that contain the full texts of major newspapers and magazines; in this way they fly through several billion words at the speed of light, turning up sources, citations, and frequency counts of new linguistic events (Shapiro 1986; Sedelow 1985; Paikeday 1983). As will become clear in my report, this technique holds both promise and problems that have only begun to be explored among the publishers with whom I consulted.

As I discovered in investigating these different methods with the five firms, a shift since Samuel Johnson's day has been seen not only in the techniques of the search but also in the texts picked up for the search. Johnson set the standard for the hunt by drawing on the authority of the language's "polite authors," turning aside from them, with apologies, only when certain arcane topics demanded it. Today, with its eye still on published sources, lexicography has embraced the immediacy of these periodical times, principally, as will be seen, at literature's expense. The press, especially what might be termed the "polite" press, has altered its pre-20th-century status of *verbum non grate* to become the standard lexicographical source.[5] Along with selection, a second issue is the degree of attention paid to a given source. As will be seen, some sources are read regularly without lapse, some sporadically sampled, and others happened upon, whereas most are unavoidably lost to view.

In visiting the five publishing houses, I found different mixtures of the old and the new in the reading programs. Yet I would have to conclude that the older habits of the publisher's reading club, whether working in-house or drawing from readers abroad, still dominate the lexicographical process. The electronic search is, at best, employed as a supplement to what is still essentially a language traced by readers. The temptation of high-speed, systematic searches has proven slow to take among those cautiously practicing what remains essentially a personal craft in the language. This craft bears a history of prejudices and comforts, and it behooves those who would turn to the dictionary to understand that history better. Though common threads link the practices of the five publishing houses, I offer separate descriptions of their individual reading programs in 1986. In this manner, one can begin to gain a sense of the different ways in which the language is currently being monitored, even as the approach may do little to support the concept of a single lexicographical standard.[6]

Houghton Mifflin

The internal reading program at Houghton Mifflin Company in Boston is staffed by the seven editors of the reference department. Anne Soukhanov, then executive editor of the department, explained that those editors read and mark for "designated periods of time," generating, through a wide variety of sources, more than 2,000 citations a month from which to draw their definitions for the dictionary. To supplement the internal program, Houghton Mifflin currently employs one experienced freelance editor. Soukhanov described in some detail the substance of the program, which consists chiefly of magazines (from *Academic American* to *Vanity Fair*), newspapers, and books. Soukhanov made reference to "first-class" writers as one guiding light in the staff's quest for both quotable citations and a "sound backing" for existing usage notes and potentially new ones. Among the list of source titles she provided me (though hardly a scientific measure), periodicals were dominant, running from 43 magazines and 8 newspapers to 11 books.

As with the other American publishers in this study, one of Houghton Mifflin's day-to-day mainstays of this search is the *New York Times*. At Houghton Mifflin, this is supplemented by the *Christian Science Monitor* and the *Wall Street Journal,* both of which have proven to be productive sources of what Soukhanov referred to as "excellent cites." In a new effort to extend the publisher's national coverage of the language, Soukhanov has also begun to subscribe to various regional papers from such cities as Charleston, South Carolina, and Richmond, Virginia, and plans to rotate similar regional subscriptions about the nation. Previously, regional coverage tended to be more sporadic and spotty. The airport reading done by an editor caught on a stopover was mentioned as one effective source of regional items. Other editors I spoke with lent their support to the suggestion that long layovers make traveling lexicographically broadening. Along with regional coverage, another area of increasing interest at Houghton Mifflin is the growth in scientific terminology; closer attention is now being paid to the science-and-technology end of the magazine rack and bookshelf.

The *American Heritage Dictionary* ad campaign was then running on the slogan, "when you need to be right." Though I am not naive enough to imagine that marketing strategies dictate editorial policies, the lexicographers stressed that I not mistake the commercial imperative of their publishing enterprise. However, the editors of the forthcoming *New Oxford English Dictionary* must be troubled by the current Oxford campaign claiming that the new 16-volume *OED* is "the last word from the ultimate arbiter." And with Houghton Mifflin, Soukhanov described a number of principles guiding her reading program that would provide this authoritative support–this sense of being right–to purchasers of the dictionary. She spoke, for example, of a concern with "good taste," which did not emerge in my discussions with the other lexicographers. She added, in our postinterview correspondence, that "while we strive to include quoted illustrations reflecting the work of respected writers, we do not try to superimpose vague, biased ideas of 'taste'–good or bad–on the content of the dictionary."

In matters of authority, Soukhanov follows the discretionary path of Philip Gove, senior editor of *Webster's Third International Dictionary,* under whom she was trained at Merriam-Webster. His policy proscribed poetry, drama, ghostwritten material, headlines, and advertising from a regular role in the reading program. Such sources might still be marked for "internal use," Soukhanov explained, being excluded as illustrative quotes yet allowed "as indicators of word occurrence." But essentially, these areas do not receive coverage comparable to that given to the other areas in the language. Poetry and drama would seem, by this act, cordoned off into a literary ghetto, whereas in the case of advertising, the policy reflects a linguistic suspicion of some of the best-paid and most widely read writers, even if they write somewhat anonymously. "The main reason for such exclusion," Soukhanov explained, "is that the language of poetry, drama, headlines, and advertising copy often tends to be contrived for special effect."

However, in this scheme of things, fiction is still read and marked. Though not all of it can be cited, all of it counts: "Fictional dialogue also falls into this category [of the proscribed], but we mark it for the sake of word occurrence." To give some indication of the range of fiction consulted, Soukhanov listed as "some of the more productive sources of cites" John Fowles's *A Maggot,* John le Carré's *A Perfect* Spy, Margaret

Atwood's *The Handmaid's Tale,* Jimmy Breslin's *Table Money,* Garrison Keillor's *Lake Wobegon Days,* Robertson Davies's *What's Bred in the Bone,* and John Updike's *The Witches of Eastwick*—a list which suggests that only the most reputable of fiction was read for the dictionary.

In other areas of language development, the citation of oral language has a place in the Houghton Mifflin program, with television mentioned as one of the strong contributors of the spoken word to the files. The staff has also begun to conduct electronic searches through such on-line sources as the *New York Times,* the *Los Angeles Times*, and the *Congressional Record* to rapidly accumulate citations for new or changed terms. No stranger to the field of computers, the company for a number of years has employed the Brown Corpus and other frequency studies for quick editorial reference in developing adult and student dictionaries. Margery S. Berube, then vice president and director of editorial operations, reported that "we have developed a program for electronic scanning of database streams for quick accrual of a wide variety of citations." Yet Soukhanov was careful to point out the risks of relying solely on the computer to generate citations providing definitions or citations deemed quotable: "After all, the editors—not the computers—have sound judgment and good taste."

The program at Houghton Mifflin also circulates a "watch list" among the editors, drawing their attention to stigmatized terms, such as *snuck* or *irregardless,* which may be on their way to greater respectability. To alter the conservative editorial position of Houghton Mifflin on any given shibboleth, according to Soukhanov, the editors must find "sustained usage in a broad spectrum of contexts by a wide group of educated native English speakers." She summed up her own policy as being guided by a sense of what publishers will accept. Certainly an aspiring writer is well served by such a policy, though it does suggest a certain circularity in the process, if one then imagines other editors of publishing houses reaching for the dictionary to find the standard they are expected to set.

But this concern with publishable correctness in the program should not be taken as representing a closed mind at Houghton Mifflin toward linguistic change or inventiveness. Even as this editorial policy deliberately played to the right side of the street, Soukhanov expressed a certain fascination with such lexically improper areas as rock and roll and art, citing as instances *garage rock* and *art runner.* The lexicographical attraction to these fresh sources of the new suggests that even if the linguistically conservative want to be right, they don't necessarily want to be left behind. This interest in the bold and lexically inventive at Houghton Mifflin recently found an outlet in "Word Watch," Anne Soukhanov's new column in the *Atlantic*. In the February 1987 issue, the words ranged from *bazuka* (a highly addictive brown powder) to *zone* (a level of mental concentration), with full citations from the *Boston Globe* and the *New York Times*. These and the other words listed, the column was careful to note, are so far only candidates for the dictionary: "A new word that exhibits sustained use over time may eventually make its way into the dictionary." Soukhanov expects that the column will draw supporting citations from readers, a development that would seem likely to boost the fate of words chosen to instruct and delight the readers of the *Atlantic*. Though the influence of this new venue for the reading program is difficult to determine and slight at best, it reflects another of the contributing aspects in the search for the new in the language. It suggests how the program at Houghton Mifflin can move energetically between two poles in its attempt to offer readers an authority on the side of propriety while keeping them in touch with those who would dare to run ahead of lexical approval.

Merriam-Webster

Merriam-Webster of Springfield, Massachusetts, maintains a strong internal reading program as part of the daily office routine of the editorial staff. In 1986, Frederick Mish, editorial director, stated that his staff spent an hour a day, possibly two, reading and marking; the program also includes an hour of broadcast television and radio, which is monitored to build the publisher's record of pronunciation patterns rather than its citations for the vocabulary files. Merriam-Webster does not employ an external program of readers. This disinclination is part of a desire for self-contained editorial efficiency and independence—in the spirit of Noah Webster, one might suppose—of which the publishing house is understandably proud; it also appears to be less inclined to consult outside authorities on the regular basis that other houses suggest they do as part of their editorial practice.

Mish described the reading and marking program as taking four principal directions: a search for new words, the current state of compounds and capitalizations, good illustrative quotations, and instances of "semantic instability," referring to new senses of established words, a term borrowed from his predecessor at Merriam-Webster, Philip Gove. Mish is interested in sources that are "likely to produce," and the program does generate from 10,000 to 11,000 citations a month. The productive literature proves to be principally periodical; an editor might expect around 100 citations from a good magazine. Periodical sources in both professional and hobby areas are sampled through occasional copies or over the period of a subscription, with, say, *Sports Illustrated* being read for one year and then another sports magazine being picked up for the next. Mish pointed out that "single-subject" magazines have a specialized vocabulary that can be exhausted within a number of issues; these magazines are left and returned to sometime later when they might again prove productive sources.

The only specialized sources considered to be consistently productive enough to warrant unflagging attention by the editorial team are *Science* and *Nature*. The *New York Times* is also an editorial constant, while other metropolitan dailies, such as the *Los Angeles Times,* provide a more balanced national coverage. And for those areas in between, every three or four years, and more recently with even greater frequency, Mish explained, the editorial team reaches out into the hinterlands for regional and small-town papers to supplement its regular big-city diet. Along with the maintenance and rotation of subscriptions for the reading program, there is the influence of incidental reading, such as restaurant menus and mail-order catalogs. One example of the influence of the incidental which emerged in our discussion was *TV Guide.* Because it is required for the daily monitoring of television programs by the pronunciation editor, it receives a regular reading, whereas otherwise the team might have subscribed to it only "occasionally," as Mish put it.

The contribution of the book in Merriam-Webster's search of the language is considerably less vital than that of the periodical. Mish described the selection of books as somewhat "haphazard," with the influence of the editors' interests having greater play than with periodicals. In discussing the coverage of literary language, Mish described the editorial policy as being guided by the pursuit of good expository prose of the sort which John McPhee writes so well in the pages of the *New Yorker.* One inadvertent result of this preference is to set the book reviews of John Updike above his fiction, not to mention his poetry. As Mish explained in our later correspondence, "I would mark [book reviews] because they do not pose the kinds of special problems for the lexicographer that are posed by fictional and dramatic dialogue (to what extent can such dialogue, being artificial, be taken as equivalent to actual speech?) or poetry (with its often deliberately wrenched syntax)." The lexicographer reflects a certain displacement of literature's contribution to language and culture in our time. "Poetry and drama are not excluded," he explained, "though they are handled with great care and are read much less often than ordinary prose" and must show "good reason for inclusion." This fact reflects part of the mark Philip Gove left on American lexicography; he believed that by establishing such policy he ensured sources in which "the native language is genuinely at work" (1967, 2).

Random House

The editor in chief of the reference division at Random House, Stuart Berg Flexner, described three sorts of readers employed in the publisher's reading program: internal, external, and consultant. As part of the internal program, members of the reference division are expected to read and mark an hour or two per day. Flexner explained that the reading might well be completed in commuting to and from the publisher's office in mid-Manhattan. The key to the internal program is a system of title rotation among the staff of 25. Popular magazines are read for three or four months by one editor, until they lose something of their freshness for the reader and are traded off; the editors also have their own subject specializations, such as pathology, theater, or football, for which they maintain an ongoing responsibility.

To supplement this active internal reading program, Random House also employs 12 to 15 external readers of general publications, who are paid at an hourly rate. At one time these readers were selected on a regional basis, but that was found to be little guarantee of productivity; the external readers now tend to be retired employees and others connected with the study of the language, though some concern is still given to regional representation. Random House provides subscriptions for the newspapers and magazines the editors want the readers to search. Here again the editors play on the readers' special interests, along with maintaining a policy of rotating titles. To provide coverage of developments in technical language, Random House has contracted the occasional services of 80 to 90 consultants in various professions and academic disciplines. Flexner gave the instance of one productive professional in the area of dentistry, who had recently sent in half a shoebox full of citation slips covering a six-month period. The object among the consultants is to find words that are basic to their field or on the verge of entering the highbrow world of the scholarly journal. The importance of terms that might be crossing over from restricted to general use was stressed by Flexner, who feels that to be literate means increasingly to be versed in specialized lexicons.

As with the other American publishers consulted, the emphasis at Random House is on periodical literature ("By the time most new words or uses appear in textbooks, popular books, etcetera, Random House hopes to have already found several previous cites from the periodicals"). The *New York Times* and *Time* magazine lead the list of regulars. But, to give some sense of the range of titles read, Flexner also mentioned the *Village*

Voice, Gourmet, Playboy, Seventeen, Rolling Stone, Chess, and *Mother Jones*. For a more specialized and technical language, "the journals considered the leaders in each field" are read by the special consultants. To better systematize the search for general vocabulary, Flexner consults magazine circulation figures to limit his coverage toward the most widely read sources; he also suggested that it is important to watch for new developments on the newsstands—computers, bodybuilding, and aerobics, for example. In this way, Flexner gives the impression of a keen journalist always on the lookout for the fast-breaking lexical story. Where once, in search of general vocabulary, he tried to live by the "rule of fives" in lexicography—a word must appear in five cities in five sources over five years to be considered standard—he has since learned to turn to his staff, his consultants, and his own sense of what stands a good chance of finding a permanent place in the language and what will prove useful to those who would turn to the dictionary.

Flexner described a heightened sensitivity on the lexicographer's part to the usefulness of the dictionary to such groups as those learning English. This sensitivity suggests a shift in lexicography from an authority based on the dictionary's claim to being a record of the standard to an authority based on providing a specific service to those who most need its help in the language. As part of this policy of greater utility, Flexner asks his general readers to read periodicals from cover to cover, including the ads and letters to the editors, as potential users of the dictionary are often drawn from the central text to the marginal areas; he also puts a special stress on the personal ads as well as the classifieds, citing the instance of a recent want-ad acronym, *mfh* (indicating, he pointed out, "male, female, and handicapped"). Flexner feels that this sort of inclusion is particularly useful for the increasing number of non-native speakers who are turning to the dictionary, though it speaks as well to the newsworthy: *mfh* is not unfamiliar to newcomers alone, and it does represent an expanded social awareness (even as it would seem to sexually denigrate and segregate the handicapped).

Popular literature of a slightly less periodic sort is also sampled, if not as heavily read and marked. As a rule—Flexner again seeking system in his coverage—half the titles from the *New York Times* best-seller list are distributed among the readers. Paperbacks, both serious books and "cheapies," are also frequently employed as strong sources of the new. One convenience of disposable paperbacks, Flexner explained, is the trick of cutting them horizontally across the middle to concentrate the attention of the apprentice lexicographer on the words and away from the absorbing story. Except for "the work of well-known authors," other sorts of literature of a more serious, less popular type are left to receive coverage incidentally on the basis of the editors' reading habits and any reading time that might survive the rather strenuous program at Random House. Poetry and drama are "very seldom" read. There is no editor in charge of the literary, and the "little magazine," which serves the aspiring and the accomplished writer, is not covered. Scholarly journals with critical treatments of poetry and other forms of literature are more likely to receive the attention of the reading program.

Flexner also reported that, to supplement the publisher's scrutiny of the written word, "we listen for new common vocabulary terms in movies, on radio and television, popular records, etcetera." He pointed out that "most of the original citations for the new drug use of the word *crack* were oral ones." The creative lexical force of the street and the spoken word is not completely lost to Random House. As Flexner went on to explain, the street can receive another sort of lexical attention in the editors' quest of written support for the oral citation: "In fact, our first 'written' citation was a photograph of the term 'crack is a wack' taken from graffiti on an outdoor wall." This represents a rare instance of what might be termed a cultural shortcutting of the normal channels of lexicographical legitimation, reminding us of the norm even as it refreshingly transgresses that norm.

To further supplement the Random House reading, watching, and listening program, Flexner stated that the reference division has begun to experiment with the employment of commercial databases to check the occurrence of new words and usages. Random House was an early leader in computerized lexicography, beginning with the original plans for *The Random House Dictionary* in 1958 (Urdang 1967, 6). Its dictionary is now part of a number of spelling programs for microcomputers. As part of its reading program, the reference department has begun to explore commercial on-line services. But at this point the primary problem Flexner's editors have found in consulting commercial databases, such as Lexis-Nexis, is the plethora of data generated. "Effective accessing" of the databases, to use the appropriate term, demands a great deal of human vigilance and expertise if one is to take full advantage of searching the last few years of the *New York Times* and a dozen other papers at the speed of light for how frequently a word was used and with what spelling. Though it has yet to happen at Random House, Flexner has concluded that inevitably the editorial staff will arrive at some sort of daily check of the databases as one more way of keeping on top of developments in the language.

Oxford University Press

Though Oxford has not set aside regular office hours for an internal reading program, it is well into its second century of employing a most active and productive set of external readers. John Simpson, senior editor of the *Supplement* and coeditor of the *New Oxford English Dictionary,* feels that a reading and marking program by his staff is something needed but impossible at the moment; the 15 to 20 readers in the field generate more than enough citations to keep his staff busy each day. The external reading program Oxford employs today is based on the one James Murray managed during the 19th century while editing the original *OED*; it is legendary both in Murray's manner of managing it and in its productivity. According to his granddaughter and biographer Elizabeth Murray, the program involved about 1,200 readers—"many very intelligent ladies, lonely widows or spinsters living at home"—who produced about a million slips (1977, 178, 185). Remuneration was modest ("If Readers will send a note of their postage, Dr. Murray will be glad to repay them in stamps" [384]), and a number of the books distributed for reading were either lost, read for just a single letter, or came back carefully cut up into citations (175–77).

Only traces of such thriftiness and inefficiency remain with the program today. Readers are often sent to their local library with no more than a list of books from which to choose their reading; few free books are to be had for reviewing, unlike the case with the American publishing houses. Readers are now paid in cash rather than stamps. Simpson expressed a certain patience with the understandable inefficiencies of amateur lexicographers working about the countryside. Though these readers are not as systematic or careful as they might be in gathering citations, the external reading program remains a mainstay, and there are no plans to curtail its size now that the four-volume supplement to the *OED* has been finished. The continuing productivity of the external readers is graciously acknowledged by Robert Burchfield in the preface to each of the four supplements. For the second volume alone, a Miss Laski and a Mr. Chowdharay-Best are each given credit for 30,000 slips covering such interest areas as detective fiction and politics (1976, p. x).

Simpson estimated the current rate of productivity for his department to be approximately 120,000 citations a year, or 10,000 a month, 10 to 20 percent of these comprising unsolicited contributions from what can best be described as interested readers. Reflecting its stature as a respected institution in the language, the *OED* has also attracted substantial donations of materials from the public, who provide it with a rich, if somewhat odd, assortment of resources. Simpson described, for example, the contribution of Professor A. Hench's large collection of the *Baltimore Sun* and other American newspapers from the 1930s and 1940s, and Dr. H. Orsman's extensive citation slips of New Zealand English. Serendipity in the sampling process seems to lie behind Burchfield's comment, in the preface to the second volume of the *Supplement,* that "we have given somewhat more attention in this volume than in the last to the special vocabulary of the West Indies and, nearer home, of Scotland" (1976, vii–viii). This swing in attention for the benefit of the letters *H–N* is taken in stride as part of the lexicographers' function, as "marshallers of words," "to form a permanent record of the language of our time" (viii).

One result of the current computerization of the *New Oxford English Dictionary* will be an end to the cyclical nature of the revision process in which the reading program tends to fade away between major revisions and supplements (the reading program was effectively shut down between 1933 and 1957) and which has always done an injustice to the initial letters in the alphabet. By publishing these letters early in both the original edition and the supplement, this process effectively skews the results, dating the entries under *A* (1965) and privileging those under *Z* (1985). Simpson has pointed out a wonderful circularity that marries the two letters in the first entry for the *Supplement,* which is "A. Add: from A to Z: see Z 3" (Simpson 1986, 1). With the advent of the electronic dictionary, revisions and additions (though not deletions, as a rule) can be entered on a continuous basis and across the alphabet. The effect will be that this mirror of the language, as Burchfield has referred to the *OED,* will lose some of its previous distortions.

Among the sources consulted by Oxford, books seem to play a larger part in relation to periodical literature than I found among the American publishers. In the reading list for March 1986, for example, there were 42 book titles and a dozen periodicals. Simpson pointed out that some of the periodical titles represented several issues; an effort was made to balance the two forms. But not only in this effort at balance did the policies at Oxford differ from the American standard, set perhaps most sharply by Philip Gove. Robert Burchfield, as editor of the *Supplement,* lent considerable weight to the serious literary figure. It was one of the few areas, Simpson found, that he had favored to the extent of allowing a single literary citation to swing a term into the *Supplement.*[7] Burchfield describes the range of literature in the introduction to the *Supplement*: "The sources included all important literary works (in both prose and verse) of' the period, a wide range of scientific books and journals, and large numbers of newspapers and periodicals, ranging from *The Times* to publications which emanate from the so-called 'underground'" (1972, xii). One can note the resolute tone toward the literary—"all important literary works"—and the patronizing aspersions cast on the underground press by employing "so-called" and setting *underground* in quotation marks. Burchfield's faith in the language is ultimately Johnsonian: "It can be used with majesty and power, free of all fault, by our greatest writers" (1982, vi).

Among the books on the Oxford reading list for March 1986, 11 were fiction, dating from 1979 and including Anita Brookner's Booker Prize winner *Hotel du Lac* (which, a note adds, had been "previously read only for adverbs") and Jeffery Archer's best-seller *First among Equals,* suggesting that prizes and sales figures contribute to one form of screening among the literate and the popular. Besides fiction, other categories included squash, opera, computing, and psychiatry; the list also referred to a continued reading of the 1985 *Sears Catalogue.* Among the periodicals consulted during the month were *Modern Railways,* the *New Yorker, Barnhart Dictionary Companion, Here's Health,* and the *Pertnysaver* from Waterloo, Ontario, which is the site of the new database-management system for the electronic version of the dictionary.

Though a "camera script" from the British Broadcasting Corporation appeared on the reading list, strictly oral citations are still excluded from this mirror of the language, because, as Simpson described it, there is no way of properly documenting the citation. In rigorously pursuing this matter of verification, the *OED* has gone so far as to retain the services of freelance researchers at the Bodleian Library at Oxford, the British Library at the British Museum in London, and the Library of Congress in Washington. This dedication to verification and documentation takes considerable editorial and support-staff energy. Yet a passion for the earliest citation is one area in which the computer search has proven worthwhile; it is part of the daily routine in the editorial offices of the dictionary division to check the frequency of occurrence and the earliest use in the American and British periodicals that are part of the Lexis-Nexis, Dialog, and World Reporter databases. The press also works in close association with the Oxford Centre for Computing in the Humanities, which has produced more than 50 concordances of major works in English history and literature.

As the most advanced user of commercial on-line services in my survey, Oxford has realized much of the promise and many of the shortcomings of the electronic database. The publisher's century-old commitment to the full documentation and historical verification of entries made the electronic database singularly useful. Yet the search still begins with what the reader finds in the language; the computer serves as merely a supplement in ascertaining the earliest use and most frequent form of spelling. This function of the computer is especially crucial with nominalizations and new compounds; the instance Simpson showed me was *file management,* for which the database turned up more than 700 uses versus rather skimpy results for 20 other *file* collocations. He also reported, however, that the technology is still severely limited by the inability to make semantic and syntactic distinctions in the search, which prevents it from identifying certain meanings of a word. Another problem has emerged in the tendency of the database companies to promote their own standardization of the language by allowing only a single spelling for terms in its word index. Finally, the electronic search is still an expensive procedure, especially in light of having to support it with manual searches of original documents for such traditional matters of documentation as the page number, which is omitted and rather irrelevant on the database. Yet, with time, Simpson concluded, the lexicographical importance of the database can only increase as it naturally accumulates greater historical depth in its files.

Gage

The *Dictionary of Canadian English* series published by the Gage Educational Publishing Company is available at three levels–junior, intermediate, and senior–corresponding to the three divisions employed in the schools of Ontario. The trade version, the *Gage Canadian Dictionary,* is marketed in bookstores as "the only Canadian dictionary," based on the claim that competitors sell Canadianized versions of American dictionaries. The *Gage Canadian* is a repackaging of the *Gage Senior Dictionary.* Stripped of its telltale school level, it has yet to lose what might be termed its scholastic aptitude and it still sells well in senior high schools. Although I wish to deal with the educational place of the dictionary at another time, the school turns out to be central in the case of a country of 24 million people sustaining some manner of national distinction in its book of lexical record. Tim Hendrie, the current editor of the dictionaries at Gage, estimated that school orders outnumber trade sales by a factor of almost a hundred. In fact, he explained that there would simply be no dictionary of Canadian English if it were not for the patriotic patronage of the school system. The sense of a national standard, as defined by the

Gage Canadian Dictionary, exists by virtue of what might be termed a scholastic artifact.

But in terms of editorial policy, Gage also consigns the sense and substance of this national language to the demands of the school textbook market, specifically to the need to receive approval from the provincial departments of education. Hendrie pointed out that the one explicit demand he had faced from the government departments was for a "balanced view of sex roles and the like." Otherwise, there has been no direct editorial interference. But rarely are things that clear-cut. As Hendrie explained, "If we do want to meet the requirements of students, we have to make choices that do result in a book that thus is less suitable in some ways for a general adult readership." Especially with the intermediate and junior levels, the reading program at Gage encompasses the school curriculum; a good number of provincially approved textbooks have become a major source for setting these editions of the national standard. Of the oddities that this process is capable of producing over many years, Hendrie reported that in one recent revision of the junior dictionary, he discovered that the various anatomical terms for human genitalia covered only males. He assured me that this imbalance in representation had been righted. I found on checking the entries that a certain androcentrism had been borrowed from the senior edition (including definitions in terms of sex for males and in terms of birth for females), though progress had been made.

Although I may seem to be stressing the less sophisticated aspects of this national dictionary, there remains another side to the operations at Gage that exceeds the work of the American and British publishers I visited. Listed among the editors on the dictionaries' title pages, from the junior edition to the senior edition, are three of Canada's most distinguished linguists: Walter Avis, Matthew Scargill, and R. J. Gregg. Among other scholarly endeavors, they are responsible for a number of sensitive studies of regional linguistic forms and forms common to the country as a whole. Bringing their research to bear in these dictionaries represents a remarkable degree of direct cooperation between academic and commercial pursuits. These scholarly linguists were not brought in as consultants but exercised extensive editorial control in the making of the *Gage Canadian Dictionary.*

As I discovered in visiting the different publishers, many lexicographers have a strong academic background, yet their training is, for the most part, in literature and the humanities rather than in the science of the language, linguistics. Only at Gage has there been the opposite tradition; Hendrie continues it with his graduate degree in linguistics. Even so, since the time of the initial work of the academic editors on the Gage series, the high degree of academic involvement has waned, and most of the editorial work and responsibility now fall on the in-house editors.

There were six external readers in 1980 reading and marking for Gage; however, the budget for external readers was cut in 1982. Currently, without a dictionary project on the go, Hendrie is carrying on his editorial work in other educational areas. He assumes that when the next project arises, "there will be some effort put into lexicographical research," though he is not certain that it could represent the level of effort and expertise demonstrated by Walter Avis and company. However, as part of the remaining reading program, Hendrie reported that Gage maintains subscriptions to 10 Canadian periodicals, including *Maclean's, Saturday Night,* and the *Imperial Oil Review.* Another distinguishing feature of Hendrie's editorial practice is the attention he pays to the radio, a source which did not emerge as important in my discussions with the other editors. The state-sponsored Canadian Broadcasting Corporation (CBC) is Hendrie's favorite source; it tends to play a special role of bringing national awareness to the educated commuter in Canada. Moreover, the CBC helps alleviate another special problem for the national lexicographer searching out the new: a good deal of the news published in Canadian newspapers comes over wire services that are edited in the United States.

This wire-service problem, in conjunction with his limited budget, has contributed to Hendrie's reluctance to employ commercial databases, though a number of Canadian newspapers are available on them. As Hendrie summed it up, "If you want to use original Canadian sources, beware of copy that has been produced and edited outside of the country." Equally telling, he has found that publishing houses in Canada have house styles that do not differ from their American counterparts, of which they are often enough subsidiaries. In the search for the national tongue, Hendrie pointed out, we have to recognize that "the greater part of Canadian vocabulary is the same as spoken anywhere in the world." The lexicographical result is that "very little vocabulary is peculiar to Canada, but it is the minor differences that distinguish our dialect, and our main 'Canadian' task is to define them in Canadian terms and in the Canadian idiom." The lexicographical struggle for Hendrie is to provide a word-hoard that is not provincial in its nationalism but that does offer some reassurance of national distinction, and to provide it in a manner that will continue to sell well to the schools.

Conclusion

The five reading programs described here provide a pattern of response to the flood of linguistic events in the English language. The pattern suggests certain standards and preferences among the various publishing houses; it points to historical continuities and a few radical breaks with the lexical past. Though these five publishers do not exhaust the instances, they certainly represent modern practice, and on the basis of that practice I am led to believe that the dictionary has at the center of its quest a fairly narrow circle of sources. A coterie of writers, guided by an even smaller number of editors, have their every word counted in this stocktaking of the language. A much greater number of writers are sampled and happened upon in one fashion or another, and the vast majority of writers and speakers in the language go unheeded. Perhaps it is only reasonable that most of the language, even most of the language sanctioned by publication, falls beyond the lexicographers' reach. As I learned in this study, they are only human.

Still, I would tender the proposition that the "polite press," with the *New York Times* at its pinnacle (even Oxford turns to it daily) is currently the single most powerful influence in constituting the record of the English lexicon. That the relative, though still large, handful of people who contribute to the *Times* play this powerful role in the language may well be a surprise to them, as it may seem to the lexicographers to whom, in part, I am making this case. Yet it seems clear to me that the degree of representation the *Times* receives in this limited search determines its paramount position. It is not an unlikely solution to the lexicographer's dilemma. The *Times* may be a regional paper in more than title, but it is often taken as a standard in journalism, because its regionalism represents a standard in culture. Many who turn to the dictionary gladly trust and unabashedly emulate the *Times*. (The other lexicographical regulars I ran into in my discussions, such as the *New Yorker,* the *Wall Street Journal,* and *Time,* serve more to confirm the relative narrowness constituting this core than to expand it.)

The sources to which lexicographers turn before any other do not represent a disservice or a deception for the purchaser of the dictionary. But over the long road to a more descriptive, dispassionate lexicography, this continuing degree of magnification of a core of sources deserves recognition. At the other end of the spectrum, or perhaps more accurately at the broad base of this pyramid of linguistic resources, the influence of the fortuitous and the incidental has also to be acknowledged. The West Indian contribution to the letters *H–M,* the large donations of odd materials to Oxford, the airport anecdotes from Houghton Mifflin and Random House, the *TV Guide* coverage at Merriam-Webster—all extended the lexicographical reach of the system, but in thoroughly random ways. Of course, between these two extremes of concentrated and incidental attention, the lexicographical system of sampling—the use of circulation figures, best-sellers, and prize winners, the rotation of titles, the reaching into the hinterlands, and the keenness for fresh sources–indicates a relative thoroughness in monitoring the language. However, the lexicographical quest is still marked by zones of exclusion. Only snatches of oral language have reached the earshot of many lexicographers, most often through the officiating channels of television. Though the oral instance still suffers documentation problems at Oxford, it provides a strong national source at Gage. Things are uneven in other linguistic zones as well. While the "so-called 'underground' press" has been welcomed into the offices of Oxford and snapshots of graffiti are in the citation files at Random House, the scripts of Sam Shepard and the poetry of Elizabeth Bishop have been marginalized by the reading programs of at least two major American publishing houses. (Bishop seems the appropriate poet to cite because of the credit she gives lexicography in reading poetry: "Use the dictionary. It's better than the critics" [cited by Gora 1986, 92].) Even at the other houses poetry and drama fare little better. At Random House, I was told that such works are seldom read; and at Oxford, with the literary imperative of Burchfield and Murray still in the air, poetry did not make the fairly extensive March 1986 reading list.

Philip Gove downgraded the lexicographical importance of poetry and drama by constructing what I find to be an unfortunate distinction between "contrived" language and language "genuinely at work" (1961, p. 5). Ironically, this distinction has taken root at Merriam-Webster, known for its breakthrough in descriptive fidelity, and at Houghton Mifflin, with its regard for propriety. Both instances may accurately reflect the 20th century's marginalization of literature as a linguistic and cultural force. One need only recall the major part the poet played in shaping the *Oxford English Dictionary* a century ago—in which Shakespeare has 2,000 first citations (Schäfer 1980)—and before that with Samuel Johnson's dictionary, in which poets Dryden, Shakespeare, and Milton account for 30 percent of the citations (Osselton 1983). Likewise, a similar second-class regard for advertising, equally a part of this policy, would seem to under estimate the pervasiveness and influence of this creative force on the language. This attitude may be, perhaps, an instance of a puritan linguistic work ethic, but it is certainly a subject for further documentation and theoretical discussion about the nature of literature, language, and culture.

The limited loss of literature's influence was the strongest break I noted between current lexicography and its traditions. It was not the break I had predicted. I had expected that modern lexicography would have turned away from the reading program in favor of an automated on-line search of the language. However, I discovered only a tentative employment of this lexicographical possibility, limited by a certain measure of conservative caution combined with the current restrictions of a relatively primitive search technology. At this point, the professional and the amateur reader, under editorial direction, remains the "technology" of discrimination and choice in scouring the language for the new; it seems a fair loop in that the general reader, if not the reader of poetry, is the one whom the dictionary still serves. Though my earlier apprehensions over the possible impact of the electronic search on the language (1984) now appear thoroughly premature, I still believe that this new method–above all else promising greater method–shows signs of initial acceptance and is bound to play an increasing role in the lexicography of the future.

This stocktaking of the lexicographical quest has meant challenging the claims of comprehensiveness and systematic coverage in the dictionary. These claims continue to underwrite the dictionary's authority, but it is an authority divided by a tension in our language attitudes. Ronald Wells, in his seminal study *Dictionaries and the Authoritarian Tradition* (1973), has described how this tension runs between "an urge toward propriety and certainty in the language, and an equally strong resistance to this urge, a resistance which centuries ago foiled efforts to establish an English-language academy and which currently underwrites the descriptive stand of lexicography."[8] This tension continues to pervade the reading programs of the publishers I visited. The need for a certain authority in the marketplace makes it difficult for lexicographers to speak in terms of limitation and discrimination. Yet the strong sense of professionalism that I met at every turn brought to our discussion of these factors a real interest on the publishers' part for the linguistic implications of their work.

The lexicographers need to continue to take stock if we are to have a more accurate understanding of the factors that determine the patterns of proliferation in the English language, patterns of standardization and legitimation, of circulation and currency. This study has examined a number of the features in current reading programs; it needs to be followed by a more systematic analysis of editorial practices to provide a measure of what is read, what is cited, and what finally receives a place in the book of record. Perhaps the strongest indication of the importance of this analysis comes from a recent dictionary whose editors I failed to visit and whose dictionary is a direct response to the process of discretionary selection among lexicographers. Cheris Kramarae and Paula Treichler's entry for the word *dictionary* in *A Feminist Dictionary* defines the issue at stake in recording the language: "A dictionary is a collection of somebody's words in somebody's book. Whose words are collected and who collects them influence what kind of book a given dictionary turns out to be, and in turn, whose purposes it can best serve" (1985, 119). This study of five lexicographers has begun to describe whose words are collected. In order to understand better the pattern of recognition in language development and the purposes served by this necessarily selective culling, the next step is a more exact assessment of the process.

Notes

1. This study began with visits to the five lexicographers, with our discussions together followed by written inquiries on specific questions. Finally, my reports on each of the editorial programs were returned to the interviewees for annotation, correction, and comment. The lexicographers demonstrated a graciousness and concern that have made this work both informative and pleasurable, and for which I publicly express my gratitude. This study was supported by a grant from the Social Sciences and Humanities Council of Canada.

2. To give two other important instances: Merriam-Webster describes its reading program as one in which "the editorial staff regularly reads a variety of periodicals as well as fiction and nonfiction books in many fields" (*Nine Thousand Words* 1983, 17a); Clarence Barnhart is only somewhat more helpful when he refers to his own program covering "a balanced sampling of published material" and "publications of wide currency read chiefly by the general public" and "works of recent standard fiction" (1970, 107). But there lingers about these specifications a certain caginess that I believe exaggerates the sense of comprehensiveness, a caginess that fuels our faith in the dictionary through suggestive terms like "balanced," "general public," and "standard."

3. Not surprisingly, Samuel Johnson was more direct, if overly principled, about his choices, at least as cited by Thomas Tyers in 1784: "When I published my Dictionary, I might have quoted Hobbes as an authority in language, as well as many other writers of his time; but I scorned, sir, to quote him at all; because I did not like his principles" (Tyers 1952, p. iii).

4. Samuel Johnson notwithstanding, Merriam-Webster suggests a standard not much changed from Ephram Chambers's admonition in 1728: "The Dictionarist is not supposed to have any hand in the Thing he relates; he is no more concerned to make improvements, or establish the Significations, than, the Historian to achieve the Transactions he relates" (cited by Read 1986, 33).

5. As late as the 1880s, the delegates overseeing the original publication of the *OED* expressed their objections to the citing of the newspaper (Murray 1977, 223). Hyde Clark first broke lexicographical ground for the press in his *New and Comprehensive Dictionary of the English Language as Spoken and Written*, published in 1855. He argued for the importance of both the oral and the periodical source against certain literary snobberies: "It is the growth of the periodical press which has given this importance to the English oral language, the influences of which cannot be long neglected. While the lexicographer is hesitating, weighing, suspending, harshly rejecting, or tardily admitting, a language is being worked out, which will react upon our literature. The periodical press, hardly dignified with the name, much less with the honors of literature, though it embodies some of the most classical compositions in our times, is not accepted as an academic authority, and yet the *Times* ought to be as eligible an authority as

some book long since defunct, and only known by its epitaph on the title on its coffin plate" (cited by Read 1986, 42–43). Though oral language has yet to receive the due Clark claimed for it, his veneration of the press and his dismissal of literature has, to a degree, been realized.

6   On the question of to what degree the publishing houses actually diverge, we have Robert Ramsey's calculation that "nearly all college dictionaries agree close to 90 per cent of the time upon choice of words" (cited by Barnhart 1967, 162). This rough estimate suggests that we might expect up to 10 percent of the dictionary to arise from differences in the practices of the publishing houses.

7   As Burchfield declares about his literary policy, "I have been as much concerned about the unparalleled intransitive use of the verb *unleave* ('to lose or shed leaves') in G. M. Hopkins' line 'Margaret, are you grieving / over the Goldengrove unleaving' as Murray was to record Milton's unparalleled use of the word *unlibidinous*" (1986, 24).

8   In the face of this history, Wells would set the record straight by declaring it a "fiction" that the dictionary "establishes the standard of usage for the language" (1973, 7). Yet a fiction so widely held takes on the forcefulness of reality. In this case, in spite of lexicographers' methods and declarations, the fiction serves, in fact, to establish as it embodies the concept of a standard. As Samuel Johnson discovered two centuries ago, though the dictionary will neither fix nor embalm the language, it can serve as an ersatz academy shoring up, both in specific instances and in concept, a standard in the language. Harold Whitehall (1962, xxii) reports that in 1880 a bill was thrown out of the British Parliament because one of the words used in it was not in "the Dictionary," referring, of course, to Johnson's dictionary.

References

Barnhart, C. L. (1967). Problems in editing commercial monolingual dictionaries. In F. E. W. Householder and S. Saporta (Eds). *Problems in lexicography* (pp.161–181). (2d ed). Bloomington: Indiana University Research Center in Anthropology, Folklore, and Linguistics.

Barnhart, C. L. (1970). Of matters lexicographical: keeping a record of new English, 1963–1972. *American Speech 45,* 98–107.

Burchfield, R. W. (1986). *The Oxford English Dictionary.* In R. Ilson (Ed.), *Lexicography: An emerging international profession* (pp. 17-27). Manchester: Manchester University Press.

Burchfield, R. W. (Ed). (1972, 1976, 1982). *A Supplement to the Oxford English Dictionary* (Vols. 1–3). Oxford: Clarendon.

Gora, D. (1986, September 15). Studying with Miss Bishop. *New Yorker,* 90–101.

Gove, P. B. (1961). Linguistic advances and lexicography. *Word Study, 37,* 3–8.

Gove, P. B. (1967). The making of the dictionary. *Language Arts News, 31,* 1–2.

Kramarae, C. and Treichler, P. A. (1985). *A feminist dictionary.* Boston: Pandora.

McCrum, R., Cran, W. and MacNeil, R. (1986). *The story of English.* New York: Viking.

Murray, E. K. M. (1977). *Caught in the web of words: James Murray and the Oxford English Dictionary.* New Haven: Yale University Press.

Nine thousand words: A supplement to Webster's third new international dictionary. (1983). Springfield, MA: Merriam-Webster.

Osselton, N. E. (1983). On the history of dictionaries. In R. R. K. Hartmann (Ed.), *Lexicography: Principles and practices* (pp. 13-22). London: Academic.

Paikeday, T. M. (1983, December). The joy of lex. *Creative Computing,* 240–45.

Read, A. W. (1986). The history of lexicography. In R. Ilson (Ed.), *Lexicography: An emerging international profession* (pp. 28–50). Manchester: Manchester University Press.

Schäfer, J. (1980). *Documentation in the O. E. D.: Shakespeare and Nashe as test cases.* Oxford: Clarendon.

Sedelow, S. Y. (1985). Computational lexicography. *Computers and the Humanities, 19,* 97–101.

Shapiro, F. R. (1986). Yuppies, yumpies, yaps, and computer-assisted lexicography. *American Speech, 61,* 139–46.

Simpson, J. (1986). The New *OED* Project. *Proceedings of the first annual Conference of the New Oxford English Dictionary Centre* (pp. 1-6). Waterloo, ON: UW Centre For the New *OED.*

Soukhanov, A. (1987, February). Word watch. *Atlantic Monthly.*

Tyers, T (1952). *A Biographical sketch of Dr. Samuel Johnson* (Original 1785). Los Angeles, University of California: William Andrew Clark Memorial Library.

Urdang, L. (1967). The making of the dictionary. *Language Arts News, 31,* 1–8.

Wells, R. A. (1973). *Dictionaries and the authoritarian tradition: A study in English usage and lexicography.* The Hague: Mouton.

Whitehall, H. (1962). The English language. In *Webster's New World Dictionary* (pp. xv–xxiv). Toronto: Nelson, Foster and Scott.

Willinsky, J. M. (1984). The computer and the language. *Queen's Quarterly, 91,* 898–906.

Chapter 8

Learning the Language of Difference: The Dictionary in the High School

The place of gender in language is in the representation of difference. Gender is spoken in the contrast between the feminine and masculine. The sources of this telling, this speaking of gender, begin for children with the talk of parents. It is part of the literary world these children will go on to discover; they will hear it in the talk of their teachers and their television sets. It travels through both what is said and what is omitted, through the words and the silences. This play of language and silence about gender has an air of authoritativeness about it, as it seems both to explain and to move the world. Although all of this talk seems marked by an unwritten veracity, assumed and hidden, some of the contexts in this use of language imbue the words with greater certainty than others.

The school is one source of that greater certainty, as it provides a public sense of the importance of difference, of distinctions in language. The dictionary, in turn, might be thought of as the textual embodiment of the school's authority to define the nature of differences in meaning. The dictionary engages in a form of representation that is authoritative in the extreme with its authorless definitions seemingly descended from on high. During their earliest years of schooling, students learn to turn to the dictionary for precision and propriety in the language. In terms of presence, it has replaced the Bible as the commonplace source of meaning in many homes and classrooms. Clearly, English educators, as part of their craft, need to understand the nature of its construction and representation of the language. With English, for example, the dictionary takes on an added importance in that our culture lacks an officiating body to rule over the language, such as the Académie française that serves the French. Instead, we have the unofficial dictionary with its aura of exhaustive comprehensiveness and certainty, which the schools do a great deal to bring home to the students.

The dictionary's representation of language in the high school can work to bring both definition and silence to the terms of gender and difference. The representation of sexual difference in the dictionary takes on a certain urgency in the exploration of gender and self for the English educator, as the English classroom is dedicated to looking deeply into the nature of language and literature. In that looking, for example, students may happen upon Dickens's Mr. Gradgrind, a schoolmaster of realities: "Girl number twenty possessed of no facts, in reference to one of the commonest animals! Some boy's definition of a horse. Bitzer, yours." Then, too, students may also come across Thackeray's Becky Sharp, who, on being given a copy of Johnson's dictionary as a parting gift from the school ("You mustn't leave us without that"), "actually flung the book back into the garden." The definition and the dictionary in the schoolroom signify a great more than the simple meanings of words.

On this question of signifying gender, H. Lee Gershuny (1977) has documented one element of sexism in the modern dictionary. Limiting her search to the illustrative sentences provided in *The Random House Dictionary*, published in 1966, she has found that masculine references outnumber feminine ones 3 to 1 in her sample of 2,000 sentences. The masculine pronoun is generic and stereotypical ("Each doctor posted his office hours" [p. 145]), and the limited representation given to women tends toward denigration, as in "She romanticized her role as editor" and "She always wears a crazy hat" (pp. 146–147). Gershuny also points out, for example, that women and men appear together in the sentences only in the context of marriage and family life Furthermore, men are often represented in terms of assertiveness, strength, rationality, and courage, whereas when female assertiveness emerges among the illustrative sentences, it is likely to be expressed as a specific dominance over males. In this incidental manner, the dictionary serves to define gender through such models of language in use.

The Discovery of Difference by Definition

In this chapter I wish to report on another instance of the dictionary's power to misrepresent gender. Specifically, I will concern myself with the wording of the definitions of reproductive organs, which subtly encodes the dominant ideology of gender. This discovery of misrepresentation arose out of a study of lexicographical practices that I have been conducting among publishing houses responsible for a number of the major English-language dictionaries (1987). The lexicographers whom I interviewed expressed the importance of equal representation of the sexes in such areas as illustrative sentences and illustrations, along with a concern for ethnic balances, for it seems that such balances are now necessary before various school districts will approve the purchase of dictionaries. In this case, it would seem that the work of Gershuny and other concerned parties has pricked the conscience of education officials.

However, one lexicographer I spoke with used a rather unusual example to emphasize the importance of this revision for the dictionary. Working with an earlier edition of his junior-level dictionary, he had discovered an extremely unequal representation of female and male genitalia—the book had simply excluded this aspect of female anatomy from the language. He assured me that he had righted this imbalance in the subsequent edition. I thought it a remarkably interesting, though not atypical, example of omission in the education of the young. Only later did I happen to check on what righting this imbalance might mean by way of constructing a definition of sexual difference.

On looking up the different terms for the sexual organs in this lexicographer's dictionary, I did find that the complete omission of female parts had been rectified. But I was struck by the startling difference in wording, especially having learned from lexicographers how much care goes into the making of a definition. The male organ is marked by a sexuality that the female appears to be denied. The fact that this was a school dictionary seemed especially significant, as curious students might well turn to the book for some definition of the mysteries of their own bodies. As they pass through their formative years with regard to their sexual identity, many children find and develop their public selves within the educational setting. Schools in many jurisdictions are also playing a more active role in furthering children's understanding of human sexuality. The classroom dictionary would seem capable of playing a large part in these processes.

Shortly after stumbling across what I felt was still a considerable discrepancy in representation in one dictionary, I found myself among the publishers' displays at the annual conference of the National Council of Teachers of English. I realized that I had the unique opportunity to compare this issue of representation across the latest editions of the leading high school dictionaries. I decided to go with the junior and senior high school dictionary (roughly grades 7 to 12), rather than the original middle school level (grades 4 to 6). The case seemed slightly stronger and less easily deniable for the urgency of equitable representation in students' adolescence, during periods in which the high school dictionary is omnipresent in classroom after classroom.

As a methodological aside, I would add that in the midst of a busy book exhibit, it was rather an uncomfortable task to ask the publishers' representatives whether I might examine a copy of their high school dictionary and then surreptitiously copy out the definitions of sexual difference. Some exhibitors suspected that I was engaged in a comparative check on either key terms or dirty words for my state's program before making a major purchase. Two helpful exhibitors quickly assured me in my search that theirs was a "clean dictionary," and yet another suggested that the publisher had a long list of words the lexicographers were not allowed to define, all of which I took to mean that their dictionary would not undermine the shared authority of classroom and dictionary in favor of propriety. To one persistent and curious exhibitor, I owned up rather sheepishly to the nature of my study, and to the credit of Simon and Schuster, the publisher of *Webster's New World Dictionary*, its representative expressed an interest in following up on the disparities I found.

The selection of words with which to work was an initial problem, and though I began my check with five words from among the terms covering the reproductive organs, I finally arrived at three—*clitoris, penis,* and *vagina*—that seem of primary importance in defining the structure and function, to use the classic biological framework, of biology as destiny. The definitions for these three terms proved to be more than sufficient for reading how gender is constructed and defined in the context of the dictionary. Each of these words has also gained a symbolic significance that extends beyond anatomical description; they also have meaning within, for example, Freudian psychology and literary theory. But most importantly, they have become caught up in the long struggle for women's right to define and defend their own sexuality.

The Definitions of Difference

In order to present and organize the definitions of the terms *clitoris, penis,* and *vagina* as they appeared in the original sample of six American dictionaries, to which I added two Canadian dictionaries, I have summarized the key words used to define the terms, in the order in which they appear, in Table 1 (for which I would ask forbearance from turning it into a bad bit of found poetry).[1]

Table 1 Summary of Definitions Found in High School Dictionaries

High School Dictionary	clitoris	penis	vagina
1. American Heritage	or/vul/pen	or/cop/ver/ur/mam	pas/mam
2. Canadian Dictionary(a)		or/ur/sex	can/mam
3. (Macmillan) Dictionary		or/ur/cop	an/can
4. Gage Canadian	or/vul/pen(b)	or/ur/sex	can/mam
5. School Dictionary		an/sex/or/mam/ur	can/birth
6. Scott Foresman Advanced	or/mam/vul/pen	or/cop/mam/ur	mam/can
7. Webster's High School	or/vul/pen	or/cop	can
8. Webster's New World	sex/or/vul	or/sex/mam/ur	mam/can

Code: *an*imal, *birth*, *can*al, *cop*ulation, *mam*mal, *or*gan, *pas*sage, *pen*is, *sex*/*sex*ual, *ur*ine/*ur*ination, *ver*tebrates, *vul*va. Bibliographical information on the individual dictionaries is located at the end of the chapter.
(a) Described as a junior high school dictionary.
(b) Entry is omitted from the *Gage Canadian Intermediate* (junior high school) edition.

In this tabling of the definitions, the points of omission are the natural starting point for discussion. The absence of *clitoris* from three of the dictionaries begins the act of lexicographical misrepresentation, of sexual imbalance, in favor of the masculine. Yet it is an absence with a history. The significance of the missing clitoris from the language has to be understood in the context of the key figure in our understanding of sexuality in the 20th century. Freud created a psychology of women on the basis of this absence, as their own sexuality seemed hidden, *rien à voir* ("nothing to be seen"), invisible to the gaze of men (Moi, 1985, pp. 132-135). Freud's concern with the mystery of women—"What does Woman want?"—was met with the apparent absence of a sexual organ, a penis. The clitoris was posited as the original site and source of penis envy and castration fear—the Oedipal struggle—in young girls. For the implications of such absence of meaning, consider that Freud felt this fear to be part of a troubled developmental history often resulting in weak superegos and a deficient moral sense in women (Gardiner, 1985, p. 117).

Understandably distressed by this act of misrepresentation, modern feminist theory has turned this fear and envy back on Freud, describing it as a projection of men's own phallic obsessions (Moi, 1985, pp. 133); the missing representation of the clitoris can be taken as an avoidance of that deep masculine fear. It marks a larger tendency to deny the sexuality of women as something of their own making and control. Even among the dictionaries that have an entry for *clitoris*, sexuality is referred to only in *Webster's New World*—"a small, sensitive, sexual organ at the upper end of the vulva." Otherwise, the dictionaries I examined represented a denial of female sexuality that can be read across the definitions of both *clitoris* and *vagina*.

Such denial or deletion has been present in our culture for a long time, as Luce Irigaray has pointed out: "It was admitted already in Greek statuary that this 'nothing to be seen' must be excluded from such a scene of representation. Women's sexual organs are simply absent from this scene: they are masked and her 'slit' is sewn up" (cited in Moi, 1985, p. 144). What might be taken as the unimportance of this center of sexual experience in women—or the anxiety about its representation—is part of the masculine objectification of women. The sexual object is but a source of masculine pleasure and not a subjectivity in itself.

Three of the dictionaries in my sample, two of them Canadian, lend their authority, however inadvertently, to the idea of the threatening sexuality of women. They contribute in their own way to this sexual deletion in the education of young women and men learning the ways of the language and the world. I realize that it may seem a little bold to claim so much from so little, from a sin of omission among only a portion of my sample; yet I would have this deletion from the lexicon witnessed in its accord with an androcentric perspective influencing such powerful instruments in the language as lexicography and education. For the silence of this omission contributes to the lessons the dictionary has to teach about the representation of difference in language and society.

This denial of sexuality does not occur with the term *penis*. Reference to sexuality is present in all of the definitions, including "male organ of copulation" *(Webster's High School)* and "a male animal's sex organ and, in most mammals, the organ for urination" *(School Dictionary)*. This is the visible moment of a phallocentrism that feminist theory has named and described, and about which the dictionaries in my sample are clear: the penis inscribes sexuality. In fact, in five of the dictionaries, the reference to sexuality precedes that of urination in the definition of the term. One lexicographical principle in the ordering of meanings in an entry is frequency of use. In this instance, however, the majority of dictionaries suggest another principle: the power of signification.

In this set of English definitions, the penis becomes the exclusive organ of copulation, and what it unites with is not named in the dictionary. To point to one indication of the importance of this claimed potency, an importance that reaches from the definition of the word to the entire realm of literature, consider the opening question in Sandra Gilbert and

Susan Gubar's study *The Madwoman in the Attic: The Woman Writer and the 19th-Century Literary Imagination*: "Is a pen a metaphorical penis?" (1979, p. 3). A good part of the early project in feminist literary criticism was to expose and address this veiled yet central assumption, reflected in such phallic declarations as Gerard Manley Hopkins: "The male quality is the creative gift" (cited by Gilbert & Gubar, 1979, p. 3).

As can also be seen in Table 1, the penis often serves in the definition of *clitoris,* when the latter term appears at all; in each case the expression of relation was described as "homologous to the penis." My college edition of *Webster's New World* defines *homologous* as "matching in structure, position, character" and "deriving from a common primitive origin." But in the dictionary entries I examined, this state of homology between clitoris and penis is not reciprocal; it is as if the one is a primitive form of the other, the original one, the known one, the one that serves to define. And for all of that, this process of definition continues to mask the sexual role of the clitoris in all but one of the dictionaries by failing to name the point of homology. What students realize time and again in turning to the dictionary is that a definition, an understanding of meaning, works by already half knowing what is meant, by drawing on that circular support which sustains our hold on the language. Though it is simple enough to leave this web unraveled and unquestioned, with a little scrutiny the manner of its construction begins to show.

Finally, in the definition of *vagina*, there is also a sense of feminine absence. The vagina is described in most instances as a canal, such as "the canal extending from the uterus to the external genital opening in female animals" (Macmillan's *Dictionary*), and twice as a passage, as in "the passage leading from the external genital orifice to the uterus in female mammals" *(American Heritage)*. It is not an organ and is not related to copulation; in fact, there is something of a mystery with regard to its function. In one case it is related to birth—"through which the fetus passes at birth" *(School Dictionary)*—but more generally the definition declares the vagina to be no more than a transportation site of some mystery. In an intriguing gesture, lexicographers have felt compelled to give this canal a direction, yet a direction they cannot seem to agree on. The dictionaries under study are evenly divided: "from the uterus to the external genital organs" appears in four of them, and "from the vulva to the uterus" in the other four. Which way is it? The question is absurd, yet it is perpetuated in the apparent tendency of lexicographers to borrow from established dictionaries to make "new" ones, a form of plagiarism which Robert Burchfield has examined in some detail (1984). The result, in this case, has been a masculine oblivion to the inadequacy in this definition of *vagina*.

The History of Difference and Definition

My modest search for the common source of the definition of *vagina* has led to the *Oxford English Dictionary (OED),* which took shape under the guidance of that eminent Victorian lexicographer Sir James Murray. Both Samuel Johnson and Noah Webster had decided that *vagina*, along with the other two terms under consideration in this chapter, was not in need of definition in their dictionaries. I did find all three included in John Kersey's earlier dictionary of 1708, with *vagina* defined as "the Neck of the Womb" (1708/1969). Yet it is the *OED* which appears to give *vagina* its initial definition as a one-way canal ("the membranous canal leading to the vulva from the uterus in women and female animals"), possibly based on the first citation provided, from Thomas Gibson's *Anatomy of Human Bodies Epitomized,* of 1682: "It has passages . . . for the neck of the Bladder, and in Women for the vagina of the Womb." Gibson would seem the perfect source for Kersey's definition, if not Murray's. Still, the subsequent supporting citations in the *OED* for this definition, running up to 1896, make no reference to canals or passages. The definition is unlike the citations enough to leave me suspicious that there is some other lexicographical source I've yet to come across. Burchfield (1984) is strangely silent about the plagiarized "genealogy" of the *OED,* for which he has completed editing the *Supplement.*

The other source of definition, besides published usage (which does not seem to have been employed with *vagina*), is definition by expert, in all likelihood by an anonymous medical expert in this instance. With *clitoris*, one can also find the lead in the *OED* for the homologous definition I found in four of the dictionaries I studied: "A homologue of the male penis present as a rudimentary organ, in females of the higher vertebrate." The reference to "rudimentary," it should be noted, has been dropped in the later versions of the definition represented by my sample, but then so has the distinction made with "vagina" between women and animals cited in the preceding paragraph.[2]

The definitions form a pattern of 19th-century representation that has been sustained, with some minor modifications, well into the 21st century. Its denial of the subjective sexuality of women is no more than the etymology, the root of meaning, that the language continues to carry.

But before arguing for a language still in touch with its roots, we must consider just how far this objectification can go in dominating language and experience. What difference can such acts of representation make? The effect can be found, for example, in the degree to which women have traditionally felt compelled to take on the masculine "view" of themselves. John Berger has explored this process historically through the world of artistic representation in his *Ways of Seeing*:

> Men look at women. Women watch themselves being looked at. This determines not only most relations between men and women but also the relation of women to themselves. The surveyor of women in herself is male: surveyed female. Thus she turns herself into an object—and most particularly an object of vision: a sight. (1972, p. 42)

But this objectification has also been noted as part of the educational process in the language, in learning how to read the dominant modes of literature from the dominant masculine perspective, as testified to in the work of Judith Fetterly (1978). Elaine Showalter has summed up the woman's undergraduate experience in literature: "She would be learning, in fact, how to think like a man" (1971, p. 858). This particular education in the invisibility of women's subjectivity through difference begins in the very words of our language and has found its support in English education and the reference books that guide it—in this case, through the high school.

An Alternative View of Difference and Definition

What it might take to break this pattern of 19th-century representation in the dictionaries dominating the classroom and home has been suggested by the *A Feminist Dictionary,* edited by Cheris Kramarae and Paula Treichler (1985). Kramarae and Treichler realize that defining the language is an ideological act and proceed to rewrite the language in their own terms, exposing along the way the masked androcentrism of the lexicographical tradition. They arrive at some of the same observations I discovered in examining the high school dictionary, and they directly address this bias in their definitions. Consider the opening of the definition for *vagina,* which speaks to other definitions as well as the greater significance of the word:

> From Latin *vagina,* "sheath." Traditional dictionary definitions: "a sheath or sheathlike structure"; "the canal leading from the vulva to the uterus." Compare definitions for penis as the "organ of copulation." According to psychoanalytic

and medical literature of the first half of the twentieth century, the vagina was the site of orgasm for "mature" women, and vaginal orgasm was yoked to maternal instinct, marriage fidelity, domesticity and theories of female masochism. There was evidence to the contrary: Alfred Kinsey's research, for example . . .

Also part of the radical break with lexicographical tradition in *A Feminist Dictionary* is the fresh semantic web it spins for a circle of definitions that bring to the fore the overlooked significance of the words. The cross-references listed for *vagina,* for example, represent the spectrum of contested meanings in female sexuality: "clitoris, myth of vaginal orgasm, penetration, penis, pleasure, sexuality, vaginal orgasm." This dictionary is also subversively playful in its lexicographical citations—the penis is "a vestigial clitoris which has lost much of its sensitivity"—and daring in its scholarly challenge to the subtleties of difference:

> A Greek formulation with *kleit-* in it always receives a strong vowel from scholars. It is significant that in this one word *[clitoris],* however, the imperishable rules of scholarship gave way to a more irresistible psychological need: that of suppressing the pronunciatory gusto of an organ which never did quite fit in with women's subordinate role in society.

What might it mean to redefine the language in this fashion? When Ludwig Wittgenstein asks us to imagine different sorts of language in his *Philosophical Investigations,* he reminds us that "to imagine a language is to imagine a form of life" (1958, p. 8e). Here, we are considering gender and difference as constituting a form of life and meaning, one not simply imagined in the language but defined as such. The new process of definition Wittgenstein arrived at is one that turns away from fixed representations: "The meaning of a word is its use in the language" (p. 20e). Although lexicographers may claim as much as they consult their recent citations—clipped from such spots as the *New York Times*—in drawing up definitions of new words, it becomes obvious that the high school dictionary is not yet a healthy source through which to imagine a new form of life, a new world in the representation of gender.

In looking up these three terms as students well might, what I have found in high school dictionaries is another representation of silence about the experience of women, a silence and absence that for too long have marked the history of women's participation in the structures of discourse. Such silencing, of course, has always been employed by dominant groups to mute the experience of subordinate bodies, whether the discrimination has been based on origin, culture, or gender.

In English classrooms, the silencing has been realized in the classic literary anthologies, and alternatives have appeared full of fresh voices. The dictionary, on the other hand, has been spared the close scrutiny reserved for literature. Yet in the space of this particular silence, the feminine continues to be defined in terms of the masculine, both in its gaze and in its blindness. Because words give meaning to our experience, the dictionary continues to indicate that a woman remains the Other. Or to use the language of Simone de Beauvoir in *The Second Sex*: "She is defined and differentiated with reference to man and not he with reference to her; she is the incidental, the inessential as opposed to essential. He is the subject, the absolute—she is the Other" (1961, p. xvi).

Although it is hardly surprising that the dictionary would represent the language patterns of the predominate language users, it seems incumbent on the lexicographer and the educator to realize the limitations of their principal reference work. It does not represent the full range of use and significance but, in these instances, tends toward a definition of the masculine gaze. As part of the revision project, as part of that ongoing work that keeps the dictionary as a useful tool in the language—especially in an education in the language—lexicographers need to rethink what they have taken for granted. They will have to maintain a watchful eye, not only for the neologisms and semantic instabilities of the computer age but also for the burden of bias embodied in definitions carried forward from the 19th century.

If Gershuny's work more than two decades ago on the decided bias of the dictionary's illustrative sentences has contributed to a greater awareness and some measure of correction, then taking this trouble of looking up terms of misrepresentation may well be worth the effort. The lesson for the schools in the meantime, as we wait for this revision process to slowly creep over the high school record of the language, is that the dictionary should be taught and read as a cultural artifact of its times. It should be turned to in a critical and curious spirit, not just for the fascinating history of words but also for the construction of meanings and of silences, in the book's power to select and define.

Without presuming the courage of teachers to break the silence in the classroom with the three terms discussed in this chapter, educators can at least begin to critically explore with their students the dictionary's hold on the language. For its assumption of authority rests on the reader's respectful silence, just as Sissy Jupe, girl number 20 in Mr. Gradgrind's school, was soon silenced about what she actually knew of horses in favor of "some boy's definition." Resistance to that silence, to being defined by the book, is a matter of listening to the fullness of the language and speaking out on behalf of those who have not been heard by such sources of certainty and authority. Tossing the dictionary out the window, as Becky Sharp did in *Vanity Fair,* is an easy shot but a short-lived victory. Better that, we should turn to the dictionary and the language it contains with renewed interest, attending directly to the meanings and uses that otherwise remain conveniently overlooked.

The Dictionaries

Avis, W., Druysdal, P., Gregg, R., Neufeldt, V., & Scargill, M. (Eds.). (1983). *Gage Canadian dictionary*. Toronto: Gage.

Guralnik, D. (Ed.). (1983). *Webster's new world dictionary* (student ed.). New York: Simon & Schuster.

Halsey, W. (Ed.). (1987). *Dictionary*. New York: Macmillan.

Haskett, L. (Ed.). (1981). *Canadian dictionary for schools*. Toronto: Collier Macmillan.

Morris, W. (Ed.). (1982). *American heritage dictionary of the English language* (high school ed.). Boston: Houghton Mifflin.

School dictionary (1985). New York: Harcourt Brace Jovanovich.

Thorndike, E., & Barnhart, C. (Eds.). (1979). *Scott Foresman advanced dictionary*. New York: Scott Foresman.

Webster's high school dictionary. (1986). New York: Globe Book Company.

Notes

1. On the question of how the definitions in these dictionaries compared with those in the adult versions, *American Heritage, Webster's New World,* and *Webster's High School* did not differ from the adult versions. The Gage senior high school edition is marketed as the publisher's adult trade dictionary; the *Scott Foresman Advanced,* Macmillan's *Dictionary, Canadian Dictionary,* and *School Dictionary* are not published in a trade or adult edition.

2. In the updating of the *OED* in the *Supplement,* completed in 1986, there are the following relevant additions: *clitoridectomy,* supported by citations from 1866 ("as a cure for hysteria will not prove of permanent value") and 1960 ("performed on thousands of children"); *penis-envy* ("postulated by Freud to occur in girls and possibly resulting in a castration complex"), supported by a sole citation from 1972 ("you'll find penis-envy in a peach"); and *vagina dentata,* which culminates in this citation from 1983: "the heroes fight against being fed into the all-consuming mouth . . . of a nightmarish gigantic vagina dentata."

References

Beauvoir, S. de. (1961). *The second sex.* New York: Bantam.

Berger, J. (1972). *Ways of seeing.* Harmondsworth, UK: Penguin.

Burchfield, R. (1984). Dictionaries, new and old: Who plagiarizes whom, why, and when. *Encounter, 67,* 10-19.

Fetterly, J. (1978). *The resisting reader: A feminist approach to American fiction.* Bloomington: Indiana University Press.

Gardiner, J. (1985). Mind mother: Psychoanalysis and feminism. In G. Greene & C. Kahn (Eds.), *Making a difference: Feminist literary criticism.* London: Methuen.

Gershuny, H. L. (1977). Sexism in dictionaries and texts: Omissions and commissions. In A. Nilsen, H. Bosmaijan, H. Gershuny, & J. R. Stanley (Eds.), *Sexism and language.* Urbana, IL: National Council of Teachers of English.

Gilbert, S., & Gubar, S. (1979). *The madwoman in the attic: The woman writer and the 19th-century literary imagination.* New Haven: Yale University Press.

Kersey, J. (1969). *Dictionarium Anglo-Britannicum.* Merton, UK: Scholars Press. (Original work published 1708.)

Kramarae, C., & Treichler, P. (1985). *A feminist dictionary.* Boston: Pandora.

Moi, T. (1985). *Sexual/textual politics: Feminist literary theory.* London: Methuen.

Showalter, E. (1971). Women and the literary curriculum. *College English, 32,* 855-862.

Willinsky, J. (1987). *Cutting English on the bias: Five lexicographers in pursuit of the new* (Research Report no. 490-86-1001). Ottawa: Social Sciences and Humanities Research Council.

Wittgenstein, L. (1958). *Philosophical investigations* (3d ed., G. Anscombe, Trans.). New York: Macmillan.

Chapter 9

Wittgenstein's Dictionary

> The earlier Wittgenstein, whom I knew intimately, was a man addicted to passionately intense thinking, profoundly aware of difficult problems of which I, like him, felt the importance, and possessed (or at least so I thought) true philosophical genius. The later Wittgenstein, on the contrary, seems to have grown tired of serious thinking and to have invented a doctrine which would make such an activity unnecessary. I do not for one moment believe that the doctrine which has lazy consequences is true. I realize, however, that I have an overpoweringly strong bias against it, for, if it is true, philosophy is, at best, a slight help to lexicographers, and at worst, an idle tea-table amusement.
> —Bertrand Russell, *My Philosophical Development*

Poor Bertrand Russell. Ludwig Wittgenstein had obviously disappointed him. The "earlier Wittgenstein" had played a crucial role in Russell's philosophical development, not least of all by convincing Russell that he was wrong, shortly after Russell had befriended the young engineering student from Vienna. Wittgenstein had arrived in Cambridge in 1911, leaving behind his aeronautical research in Manchester, drawn by the sheer intellectual verve of Russell and Whitehead's *Principia Mathematica*. The great German logician Gottlob Frege had brought the book to Wittgenstein's attention and he was positively fascinated by this bold project of determining a foundation for number and logic. It opened the box for Wittgenstein on the most profound of philosophical puzzles, for which he gladly left behind the slide rule and graph paper of his engineering career.

At 22 years of age, Wittgenstein took up the study of philosophy in earnest at Cambridge, and within a few years, he was telling his then close friend Bertrand Russell that the distinguished professor was not at all on the right track in thinking that his application of mathematical logic to the logic of mathematics would lead to a true knowledge of the external world. The proper path, Wittgenstein argued, lay through the thicket of language. What must it have been like for this newfound philosophy student to have gradually dissuaded Russell from pursuing his logical analysis of knowledge, to convince him to walk away from his entire attempt to find the source of the epistemological Nile, the origins of knowledge?

Now, at a much safer distance from Russell than Wittgenstein stood, I want to suggest that the later Russell was also wrong in his discrimination between the earlier and later Wittgenstein (1959, pp. 216-217), wrong both philosophically and lexicographically, although I remain grateful for the rarely made conjunction between the two. For I want to consider, with this chapter, the philosophical impossibility of the dictionary. I want to imagine a Wittgensteinean dictionary that stands to all other dictionaries as antimatter stands to matter. The later Wittgenstein, after all, went to considerable trouble to refute the earlier version of himself that he had carefully set out in *Tractatus Logico-Philosophicus* (1961b). In a substantial body of manuscripts, notes, and remarks (albeit almost none of them published during his lifetime), the later Wittgenstein devoted himself to disentangling his ideas from what he came to regard as an earlier bewitchment by language. Out of the ashes of this refutation arises not an invented doctrine, as Russell disdainfully claims, but a far-ranging and unsettling inquiry that lays bare our understanding of language, meaning, and world just as a sharp whiff of vinegar can clear the sinuses. Although Wittgenstein's early work has its allies and expounders—and there are those who refuse the notion of a divide in his work—it is his later philosophical work that has been most thoroughly taken up as both true and more than tea-table amusement, to use Russell's measures, by succeeding generations of analytic, pragmatist, and poststructuralist philosophers.

On the second, lexicographical point, I find, contrary to Russell, that the earlier Wittgenstein is surely the true consolation of the dictionary maker. I realize Russell felt justified in throwing in the dig about lexicography because of the attention the later Wittgenstein paid to how it is that words mean what they do. Yet it was the singular fruit of that earlier genius of the *Tractatus* that provides a thorough, and perhaps final, philosophical defense of what a dictionary makes of meaning. In his survey of modern language theory, Allen Thiher calls the *Tractatus* "the last serious attempt to view language in much the same way that classic metaphysics did, as a mirror to the world" (1984, p. 9). The later Wittgenstein, as I will argue, is actually lexicography's, as well as modernity's, philosophical nemesis.

As for Russell's other petulant charges, the later Wittgenstein did, in a sense, take himself and his trade less seriously than he had done in those first heady days at Cambridge. That's understandable in itself, but

Wittgenstein's change also came from taking the language of those who did not practice philosophy thoroughly to heart. What Russell disparages as Wittgenstein's mental laziness, I would hold, reflects his hard thinking about the world that he had encountered during his years as a soldier and a schoolteacher. Wittgenstein was refusing to treat the world as philosophy's oyster, thought to contain (to confound my metaphors) a gritty chess problem in search of a necessary and sufficient solution.

The turning point came with Wittgenstein's realization that philosophy solves nothing. At its best–as in the hands of the later Wittgenstein–philosophy catches sight of how we live, by grasping, in this case, the indeterminacy of meaning in language. Wittgenstein's insight into language's relation to meaning, which I will treat in more detail, reveals how the dictionary can serve as a misleading guide to meaning. The dictionary's careful fixing of words to definitions, like butterflies pinned under glass, can suggest that this is how language works. The definitions can seem to ensure and fix the meaning of words, just as the gold standard can back a country's currency. What Wittgenstein found in the circulation of ordinary language, however, was a free-floating currency of meaning. The value of each word arises out of the exchange. The lexicographer abstracts a meaning from that exchange, which is then set within the conventions of the dictionary definition.

Now, lexicographers are not oblivious to the troubles that Wittgenstein raises for their work, even if they are unsure of how best to respond. Robert Burchfield, who edited the *Supplement to the Oxford English Dictionary*, respectfully accedes that "one must pay all due regard to such primary statements of philosophical belief as those of Wittgenstein and Strawson," but he makes that the end of it: "Once accepted such statements recede into a kind of black hole. We know they exist but we are not quite sure how they help interpret the cruel asymmetrical facts of a given language" (1989, p. 46). Wittgenstein's philosophical black hole tends to draw in more lexicographical light and matter than Burchfield perhaps realizes. But to appreciate the extent of this slight help, we must, like Alice, follow this elusive philosopher down the receding warren of primary statements that I find to be very much about interpreting the cruel, asymmetrical facts of a given language.

I have worked elsewhere with the clutter of dictionary's editorial offices and publishing houses, with their stacks of citation files and clippings (1988; 1994), but I leave those behind here to pursue another element in the making of the dictionary. Although the dictionary is undoubtedly a work of editorial labor and craft, it is also a metaphysical treatise on meaning. Johnson might well have titled his dictionary *The Social Contract*; Webster could have named his *An American Inquiry into Verbal Understanding*; and James Murray might have added the subtitle *Thus Spake Literature* to the *Oxford English Dictionary (OED)*. Even without leaving its place on the bookshelf, the dictionary contributes in the subtlest of ways, I would argue, to our perception of language in what must be taken as a philosophical sense. In what other instances do we have the scope of a language's potential for meaning assembled in one place? Where do we turn when in doubt about language and meaning?

The dictionary appears to be a ready guide to the word's relationship to thought and world; it makes apparent the limits of our language in the proportion of words that we carry at the ready. Those limits are not simply philosophical in a remote sense. They are something we feel, in the frustrating reach for the right words during times of intimacy and caring as well as consternation and anger. Against this sense of being failed by the words we need, the dictionary speaks to the immense capacity of language for distinction and precision. Yet it is not so easy to consider the philosophical presumption of this unassuming reference tool, this court of last appeal in the languages. Philosophers have shown a traditional shyness around public sites, such as the dictionary, where language is forged into prosaic forms. Certainly, Plato, in the *Phaedrus*, touched on the threat that writing words down posed to memory and wisdom, suggesting that an extended conversation on the streets of Athens was the surer road to knowing. More recently, Jacques Derrida has swung by Plato's "pharmacy" to substitute a concept of intertextuality for what we have treated as the presence of the writer's voice, especially as that voice gives a text its authority (1981).[1] But despite the relevance of literacy and intertextuality to the dictionary's project, who among philosophers, from Plato to Derrida, has looked at what we have done with our birthright and mother tongue by ordering words from A to Z in the dictionary?

Not Wittgenstein, certainly. He did not pay much mind to the dictionary. His references to it are few amid his many pages on meaning and definition. Yet I believe that Wittgenstein and lexicography illuminate each other's project. In Wittgenstein's manner of attending so closely to the nature of meaning, I find a hold on language that is at once a comfort and a threat to the dictionary. Despite his disregard of the dictionary and the lexicographer's uncertainty about what to do with him, this lone philosopher makes a perfect foil to the dictionary industry, At the very least, he is a match for Dr. Johnson, as the philosophical archetype versus the literary celebrity, in the prevailing forms of self-cultivated genius. Wittgenstein, from within the displaced, romantic pose of his portraits, looking a little gaunt with his shock of dark hair and ever intense eyes, tore away at the metaphysics of language while working in the hut that he built by a Norwegian fjord or in his cottage by the rugged Irish coastline. Yet he did this solitary, remote work by reaching into the public domain of language's chaotic energy and carefully examining what was said, taking down in his notebooks snippets of an imagined conversation, each in its own entry, accompanied by its own analysis, as per the dictionary, that reveals its nugget of significance. He both defers to how others carry on in the language and takes charge of what others would make of it. He occupies, in that sense, the same ground as the good lexicographer Johnson. Yet his work raises a number of challenges to the public enterprise of building a house of language out of a host of cards each of which cites an instance of how a word is used in print.

Wittgenstein's assault on meaning must seem an unlikely outcome for a promising engineering student, born in 1889 into one of Vienna's wealthiest industrialist families, the youngest of seven children. But his life has a sense of unexpected turns, driven as he was by what one recent biographer has called "the duty of genius" (Monk, 1990). He was drawn into a form of ascetic withdrawal from the world that took him to the Austrian Alps, Norway, and Ireland. It was a life driven by an intensely moral sensibility, even as he kept his philosophizing rigorously stripped of such judgments. He wanted only to see, as did Russell and the philosophical world of the day, how far he could go in getting to the root of things. Wittgenstein found inadequate the Cartesian starting point of *cogito, ergo sum*—I think, therefore I am—which had served as Western philosophy's fertile acorn for the previous three centuries. Rather than turning within, Wittgenstein built his philosophical inquiry on the *meeting* of minds through a language that in its public nature constituted "all that we can ever claim by way of knowledge," to borrow David Bloor's characterization of the Wittgensteinian project (1983, p. 2).

When Wittgenstein returned to Austria in 1914 to serve in the army of his homeland after those initial three years of studying philosophy at Cambridge with Bertrand Russell and G. E. Moore, his own thinking about the foundation of meaning was well under way. He was already formulating a rebuttal to not only Russell's work but Frege's foundational work on logic and language. It is easy to paint a rather picturesque scene of the young philosopher in a military uniform with shiny leather boots, filling in notebooks with a stubby pencil between patrols through the trenches. The record does reveal that he fought bravely and wrote strenuously, so that by the time he ended up a prisoner of the Italians in the final months of World War I, he had completed the *Tractatus*. "I believe I solved all our problems," he blithely wrote to Russell about the book from the prison camp in 1919 (1974, p. 67).

The war was the beginning of the end for an age of European imperialism, unsettling the civilized sensibilities and claims of more than one generation of Europeans; it forms a striking backdrop for Wittgenstein's initial and equally delimiting philosophical work. With remarkable precision, the *Tractatus* stripped away foundational pretensions of philosophy in a logical critique of language, moving from the entirety of the world to the unspeakable realm of silence in 60 axiom-filled pages. The book opens by dramatically setting on the table the pieces of a reality that language was destined to fit, hand in glove:

1   The world is all the case.
1.1   The world is the totality of facts, not things.
1.11   The world is determined by the facts, and by their being *all* the facts . . .
1.2   The world divides into facts. (1961b)

These initial axioms reveal a line of reasoning that can seem, with hindsight, to stretch from Russell's earlier Wittgenstein to what he found in the disappointing later one.[2] It is a line roughly described by a move from the aspirations of positivism to the acquiescence of pragmatism. A positivist reading of these axioms would hold that we can bring language into careful alignment with the world by pursuing the totality of facts, or what is known of the world. Knowledge of the world can be built, proposition by proposition, on this foundation of ascertainable assertions, which describe "the existence of states of affairs" (1961b, §2). The logical analysis of language becomes a guide not only to thinking but to the building blocks of the world, with each sentence operating as "a logical picture of facts" (§3). Bringing to language this concern for the precision of the parts and the care with which they are fitted together speaks to the very inspiration of lexicographers. As is made clear by the tone of these opening lines, Wittgenstein was intent on stripping language down to its significant properties, to what can be surely said about the natural world (although he went on to make it clear, outside of the book, that he drew these limits in order to demarcate the "sphere of the ethical," which lies beyond the knowable, or that which can be spoken).[3]

These opening lines can also suggest how the world is known in a pragmatic sense, because what counts as a "fact" is a consequence of language. It need not be that we are born or die by the word, although that can happen, but that birth and death are linguistic designations; they are ways of dividing up the world into facts that are named in language. The grammar and logic of language is all about the designation of facts. Within that grammar, "I" am and so is "the world": "I am my world" (§5.63). The *Tractatus*, in pressing the neopositivist model to its limits, came close to transcending its original project, which is precisely what the author advises in the book's concluding points: "He [the reader] must transcend these propositions, and then he will see the world aright" (§6.64).

Setting the limits to the known world is the task Wittgenstein sets out in the preface to the *Tractatus*: "The aim of the book is to draw a limit to thought, or rather—not to thought, but to the expression of thoughts" (1961b, p. 3). The notion of such limits forms a constant theme for the book; perhaps its best-known aphorism is, "The limits of my language mean the limits of my world" (§5.6). This speaks to the virtue of the dictionary's efforts at expanding the world for those who look into its word-hoard, even as it presumes to encompass the limits of possible worlds within a given language. James Murray claimed to be only two (rather undesirable) words short of covering the entire English language with the *OED*. The dictionary becomes our best guide to the world's limits. But we might stop and ask whether it is the number of carefully defined words that designate the whole of the world for us. Wittgenstein's limits-of-language equation has, unfortunately, found its equivalent in educational and anthropological circles, which amount to circumscribing the lives and worlds of others by passing judgments on the limits of *their* language.[4]

After the war and the publication of the *Tractatus*, Wittgenstein closed the book on this philosophical chapter in his life. Without ceremony, he relinquished his claim on the family fortune and his studies in philosophy, retreating from the semi-aristocratic academy of Cambridge and the intense cosmopolitanism of Vienna. At a time when the postwar hopes of school reform were a source of some intellectual excitement in Austria, Wittgenstein attended a teachers' training college in Vienna and soon secured work in an isolated elementary school in the Austrian Alps. While working there, his interest in building the children's vocabulary led to his publication of a "wordbook" for students. There was always a question about Wittgenstein fitting into the mountain communities, and after six years of teaching, some of the parents unsuccessfully instigated legal action against the seeming severity of his teaching methods. Still, it was enough to send him back to the world of philosophy, first with the antimetaphysicians from the Vienna circle and then back to Cambridge to begin anew. In 1929, he submitted the *Tractatus* for his doctorate with Russell's support, although they had fallen out as friends by that point. Wittgenstein was then elected a fellow of Trinity College, and he began to develop, through his teaching and notebooks, a radical rewriting of his original position just as it was beginning to have a profound influence on the analytical movement in British philosophy as well as in Vienna (Ayer, 1985). The resulting reconstruction of language and meaning that he was to effect would come to shake again the foundations of modern thought decades later, when it would lay bare the roots of the lexicographical project.

The starting point for Wittgenstein's second model of language might be thought to lie in the question he posed at the opening of his 1933 philosophy class, which he held in his rooms at the top of the stairs in Whewell's Court, Cambridge. Looking up from the notebook, opened on the card table that served as his lectern, at the dozen or so students sitting on deck chairs, he asked, "What is the meaning of a word?" (1958a, p. 1). It must have seemed an innocent, preliminary ruse to the undergraduates there to learn philosophy at the feet of a man with a reputation for being "addicted to passionately intense thinking," as Russell put it. It was a trick question, surely, to occupy the class as the students brought their minds around to the subject at hand. Yet Wittgenstein was not to answer the question in that class session or until well into lectures, and only then in the form of veiled references and other questions, like the much-promised great trick that the magician keeps postponing to build the performance to its proper climax and culmination. Only in the posthumous *Philosophical Investigations* (1958b) does the philosophical wizard come clean and answer the question directly.

But before getting to Wittgenstein's answer, it pays to think about the question for another moment. There is an oddness to "What is the meaning of a word?" that gives pause, even as it sets the tone for the remainder of Wittgenstein's philosophical journey. The question's gem-like hardness has none of the dreamy melancholy of "What is the meaning of life?" nor the Platonic weightiness of "How do we determine the Good?" With disarming modesty, Wittgenstein asks after no more than a word's meaning. Although I first came across the question in the transcribed lectures published as *The Blue and Brown Books* (1958a) during my undergraduate days, far from Cambridge, in the SCM Bookstore down the street from my student digs in Toronto, I still recall being drawn into this intriguing manner of philosophizing. I read on for pages without getting a straight answer. Yet the series of questions that unfolded in turn were equally appealing for the way they, simply in the posing, asked so much. The questions have the power to edge up the ante on what can be asked of the language by which we live. There is a perverse pleasure in how they produce what Wittgenstein terms "a mental cramp" (1958a, p. 1). One can sense in these lecture questions Wittgenstein's earnestness, his unapologetic abruptness in setting off these small firecrackers. As he put it, in the grammar of a single word, in the ascription of meaning, hangs the sensibility of the world, a special version of which the dictionary manages to embody.

Surely, a few of Wittgenstein's students gave his opening question a try in their minds, during the famous silences that punctuated Wittgenstein's time in class. Some must have figured that obviously the meaning of a word is the thing that the word refers to, as *swans* referred to those birds drifting along the river Cam; others might figure that, of course, the meaning of a word is exactly what you find when you look it up in the dictionary (where, for example, *word* is given 45 definitions through six centuries of citations in the *OED*). Foreseeing the commonsense responses to the question, Wittgenstein allows in that first lecture that we may well point at something as a form of ostensive definition, but how can we be sure, even in a simple case such as pointing to a pencil and saying a word, that we are indicating with that word the pencil, or its roundness, woodenness, or some other quality? Equally so, to define a word's meaning with a careful explanation only leads to more words and not, seemingly, to the realm of what a word's meaning is. Meaning cannot easily be taken as the gesture of pointing nor as the act of explaining.

In the course of the lectures, Wittgenstein offers the example of *wishing*, for which he describes various cases of wishing, before concluding that "someone" might well say, "Surely this is not all that one calls 'wishing'":

> We should answer, "certainly not, but you can build up more complicated cases if you like." And after all there is not one definite class of features which characterize all cases of wishing (at least as the word is commonly used). If on the other hand you wish to give a definition of wishing, i.e., to draw a sharp boundary, then, you are free to draw it as you like; and this boundary will never entirely coincide with the actual usage, as this usage has no sharp boundary. (1958a, p. 19)

The meaning's hem begins to unravel. That a word possesses one or more fixed meanings is well represented in the dictionary; *wishing* has definitions (a) through (d) in the *OED*. Wittgenstein's point that "usage has no sharp boundary" gives the lie, or at least the limits, to such definitions. Even in the case of proper nouns, it does not work to say that the meaning of the name is simply the person the name refers to. In the *Investigations*, Wittgenstein takes up the meaning of Moses' name. After a quick review of biblical incidents, he argues that "'Moses,' can be defined by means of various descriptions." This leads to the telling question, "Has the name 'Moses' got a fixed and unequivocal use for me in all possible cases?" Once more, Wittgenstein arrives at the conclusion that, even with a proper noun, we happily use the word "without a *fixed* meaning" (1958b, §79). The meaning is not so much the gull that rises from the undisturbed surface of the sea as it is the ripples that spread out when the bird takes wing. Meaning suggests a point of departure.

What is the meaning of a word? A promising question. A good opening gambit for a philosophy class, sweeping aside typical assumptions of meaning, showing how they do not really stand on their own merits. In seeking the answers to these questions of meaning, Wittgenstein defers to the philosophically innocent speaker. He appeals to language's common stock as evidence: "We may say . . . "; "I could have said . . . "(1958a, p. 2). His notebooks often carry on in conversational form, complete with quotation marks and interjections: "'I know that this is a hand.'—And what is a hand?—'Well, *this*, for example'" (1969, §268). In his lectures, Wittgenstein insists that whatever the dilemma posed by questions of meaning, there is only one place to turn: "The thing to do in such cases is always to look at how the words in such cases *are actually used in our language*" (1958a, p. 56). This, of course, is the lexicographer's motto. This is why the *OED* has a reading program devoted to endlessly clipping and saving examples of how each word is used in books, newspapers, and magazines. Such citations are a guide for writing definitions. Yet such searching, as Wittgenstein would have it, also reveals the ultimate and lasting impossibility of actually arriving at a definitive sense of a word's meaning. At best, uses are sampled and compiled for consultation by philosophers and lexicographers, without any hope of grasping the whole of what is represented by words as they are "actually used in our language."

Such is the consequence of accepting that the limits of our world are found in the workings of ordinary language. Yet to have more than two millennia of philosophical refinement arrive at this embrace of the ordinary language of bus stops and pubs must have surprised the brightest and the best gathered in Wittgenstein's room at the top of the stairs. "But ordinary language is all right," he reassured the class, adding with perhaps some recollection of his schoolteacher frustrations, "as though we could improve on ordinary language" (1958a, p. 28). The aim of improving ordinary language had been his original philosophical project, at least as Bertrand Russell refers to it in his introduction to Wittgenstein's *Tractatus* (1961b). But then, it had been part of what Russell and other logical positivists during that period had earnestly sought as well.

By the time Wittgenstein came to preparing a preface to what was to be the *Philosophical Investigations,* in 1945, he spoke frankly of "the grave mistakes in what I wrote in that first book" (1958b, p. vi). He had stopped seeking the conditions of a "logically perfect language," to use Russell's term, and had become absorbed in pinning down the conditions of the existing one, as if language, rather than the world, were all that is the case, to turn the tables on the opening of the *Tractatus.* In rather direct opposition to the well-known exhortation of Marx, Wittgenstein declared that the point of philosophy is not to change the world nor explain the whole of it, but only to describe aspects of it. Philosophy will never be that simple, but at this point it is important to appreciate the philosopher's original intent.[5]

For my purposes, it only takes a handful of Wittgensteinian descriptions to expose the cracks in the lexicographical project. Of course, the dictionary follows this philosopher in his belief that ordinary language is all right, at least ordinary language as, in large measure, it is edited and published. Lexicographers go a lot further in verifying how words are actually used, rather than relying on imaginary speakers as Wittgenstein does. They also "improve" ordinary usage by adding precision to meaning, resolving ambiguities, standardizing spelling, and ruling on the bounds of propriety. The dictionary's descriptive function becomes a point of improvement, in setting a standard for the language. The Wittgensteinian rub is that there is something in the very ameliorative spirit of the dictionary that runs contrary to the nature of language.

The dictionary's manner of fencing language in may well be a minor act against nature, like Robert Frost's line "Something there is that doesn't love a wall, / That wants it down," from "The Mending Wall." Could it be running contrary to language's basic operating system? Wittgenstein spoke of concepts with blurred edges as "often exactly what we need," as if that fluidity not only made the concepts operational but also kept the language game open to participation (1958b, §71). The dictionary remains a small part of that opening into the language. My point is not to write it off as simply a tool or guidebook, but to understand its double function of science and technology, of describing and improving the language. The dictionary carries deep within its columns this double sense as its persistent Enlightenment heritage of reason's mastery over untamed words. It begins, innocently enough, with a representational theory of meaning that finds its perfect likeness in a child's first illustrated "pictionary." Taken to its logical extreme, this representational theory was the position pursued by the earlier Wittgenstein in the *Tractatus* so admired by Russell.

The later Wittgenstein came to attack the picture theory of word and meaning in the *Philosophical Investigations* (1958b). The book opens with an incident from Augustine's *Confessions*, as if Wittgenstein returned to the very roots of his error. Augustine recounts, in what amounts to an archetypal description of language acquisition, how he paid careful attention to the language of others: "Thus, as I heard words repeatedly used in their proper places in various sentences, I gradually learnt to understand what objects they signified; and after I had trained my mouth to form these signs, I used them to express my own desires" (cited by Wittgenstein, 1958b, §1). This is an interesting passage with its own psychological insights about the crucial role of sentences in establishing meaning and the relationship between desire and expression. But as Wittgenstein points out, it describes a very restricted picture of language, limited to nouns for the most part. It also seems to assume that the child somehow already understands how language operates, or as he puts it, "as if the child came into a strange country and did not understand the language of the country" (§32).

Although Wittgenstein's point is not without its critics,[6] it does seem reasonable to side with him in suspecting that the superbly levelheaded thinking of Augustinian childhood is unlikely to be achievable prior to the acquisition of language: "Does a child learn only to talk, or also to think? Does it learn a sense of multiplication before—or after it learns multiplication?" (1967, p. 60e). The child fumbles with the words well before clarifying a discrete sense of objects, desires, and actions. Talking is regarded, after all, as a form of thoughtful activity. But, Wittgenstein points out, it is not that we put thoughts into words, filling each word to the top with thought while selecting each word through some form of metalanguage that matches thought to word. Rather, it makes more sense to imagine that we pull together the words that will pass as an idea, a request, an observation. Words are tools with which we do this thing that counts as thinking: "When I think in language, there aren't 'meanings' going through my mind in addition to the verbal expressions: the language itself is the vehicle" (1958b, §329). There are still elements of nonlinguistic judgment and intuition called into play in this conception of language-in-use, but the words we assemble through habit and craft still give rise to what seems thoughtful rather than operating as a translation of that thoughtfulness into words.

To stay with the instance of the child's acquisition of language for another moment, Wittgenstein speculates in the *Investigations* on how a child learns the name for pain: "A child has hurt himself and he cries; and then adults talk to him and teach him exclamations and, later, sentences. They teach the child new pain-behavior" (1958b, §244). We attribute meaning and thinking to our use of language, and although the philosopher does not want to deny us this attribution, it is his duty and pleasure to circumscribe what it entails. Language is but a game, to call on one of Wittgenstein's key metaphors: "Here the term 'language-*game*' is meant to bring into prominence the fact that the *speaking* of language is part of an activity, or a form of life" (§23). He proclaims his wonder at what he refers to as "the multiplicity of language games": "There are . . . countless different kinds of use for what we call 'symbols,' 'words,' 'sentences'" (§23). By taking up the play of words within these various language games—ordering, obeying, describing, reporting, speculating, constructing, singing, translating (§23)—the child has more or less the very process of thinking and meaning at hand. To this variety of form and function I would add *context*, as language games encompass courtrooms, classrooms, operating rooms, and countless other settings.

In one of his rare references to the dictionary, Wittgenstein refers to "the power language has to make everything look the same, which is most glaringly evident in the *dictionary*" (1980, p. 22e). Does he have this analysis right? On one level, the dictionary bristles with the distinctions among words, with etymology, part of speech, and definition. Yet each word is accorded its exact equivalent, as if defining *the, love,* and *pencil* called on the same order of meaning. He wishes to turn our attention from the simplified and ordered sense that we have made of language and direct our eyes and ears to the actual wording of our lives. And he makes his case with more than childish instances and games, by taking us to the grocery store. When a shopkeeper is given a slip marked "five red apples," to use the example that follows immediately on the heels of the child Augustine in the *Investigations*, Wittgenstein points out how unlikely it is that the grocer stands before the bins, matching up the words with mental images or meanings of *five, red,* and *apples* (1958b, §1). This definitional process implies that language is made up of a large series of words that the speaker matches, as required, to an even larger assortment of meanings that are carried in the mind. Wittgenstein challenges the notion of a separate but equal status for a word and its meaning; he would delimit the emphasis we place on meaning apart from word:

> You say: the point isn't the word, but its meaning, and you think of the meaning as a thing of the same kind as the word, though also different from the word. Here the word, there the meaning. The money and the cow that you can buy with it. (But contrast: money and its use.) (1958b, §120)

If meaning is not the cow, neither is it, except secondarily, the stuff of dictionaries. What meaning *is* brings us, finally, to Wittgenstein's direct answer to the question "What is the meaning of a word?" Augustine's childhood and the trip to the shopkeeper clear the ground for his decidedly short answer to the original query: "For a *large* class of cases though not for all—in which we employ the word 'meaning' it can be defined thus: The meaning of a word is its use in the language" (1958b, §43).

The point is both apparent and elusive. The first thing to note is the double play on *use*. Wittgenstein is speaking of how the word *meaning* is used, rather than speaking of meaning in itself. He is practicing his point to make it. And still this sense of meaning-as-use is said to hold for only a large class of cases. Thus, Wittgenstein offers an additional point of reference, less often quoted, to this famous 43d entry in the *Investigations*: "And the *meaning* of a name is sometimes explained by pointing to its *bearer*." With that "sometimes," Wittgenstein allows that at times meaning refers in a rather direct manner to a given object, as we might say, "Please hand me that pencil." Because we sometimes use words to point but more often point to the use of words, the Wittgensteinian call is for a new sensitivity to the diffuseness of meaning, to how it operates without an edge or body, slipping by like quicksilver.

To defy this elusiveness, to hold meaning firmly in hand, we turn to the dictionary. It is as if we would protect ourselves from Wittgenstein by insisting that the meaning of a word is surely its definition in the dictionary. Each entry comprises a word and its definition, supported perhaps by a picture or an illustrative sentence. This suggests a logical relationship among the three, as the word signifies or stands for the definition, which is drawn from the illustrative material. The definition is the center; from it we know both the object as well as the word. That is, the layout of the dictionary entry suggests a sort of pyramid of regard that is perhaps best captured by C. K. Ogden and I. A. Richards's well-worked semiotic triangle in *The Meaning of Meaning* (1923, p. 11), published the year after the English edition of Wittgenstein's *Tractatus*.

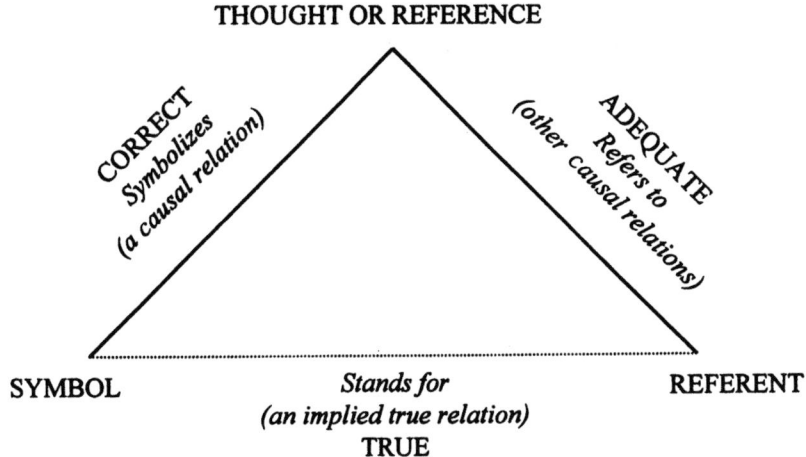

Figure 1. From *The Meaning of Meaning*

Without getting but halfway into the wonderful intricacy of this configuration, I ask you to note how well it captures the sensibility we bring to the dictionary and thus to our understanding of language. Ogden and Richards have little trouble placing thought at the pinnacle, a firm and fixed thing, like Colossus, spanning symbol and referent, word and object. As it is hard to imagine what form this symbol-less thought might take, the dictionary definition becomes a ready stand-in, a handmaiden to thought. According to this model, when we hear a word we are led through a causal relation to the appropriate thought, which directs, in turn, our attention to the referent; alternately, when we speak it is because a thought has been symbolized in the appropriate word.

The problem for Wittgenstein is this distance between symbol and thought. He can see no reason not to treat the symbol as a set of letters or phonetic sounds, as both word and thought, its use contributing greatly to its meaning or thoughtfulness. On those rare occasions when a perceptibly "thoughtful" statement simply pops out of my mouth or when it is worked up carefully, version after version, on the page, it makes as much sense to speak of my behavior as inspired and crafty work with language, as it does to regard it as the precise translation of my thoughts into words. If this extralinguistic thought hypothesis does little for our understanding of language, it then seems misleading to accept the dictionary as a model for how language works or how words come to meaning.[7] Turn not to thought or referent to know the language, he frankly recommends; "Let the use of words teach you their meaning" (1958b, §x). Such has certainly been the procedure for establishing most of our vocabulary, although at times we turn to the extra support of the dictionary as a quick guide to how words are used in a number of circumstances by what we trust is an authoritative sample of people. In either case, the word leads us into the world; thought, as we call it, follows willy-nilly, if at all. Or as Wittgenstein has it, "We talk, we utter words, and only *later* get a picture of their life" (§xi).

In yet another Wittgensteinian phrasing of the point, he undercuts the idea that we translate what we know into words: "Knowledge is not translated into words when it is expressed. The words are not a translation of something else that was there before they were" (1967, §191). Words have a greater life of their own. But where, one might ask, does that leave the world? As an advocate of Wittgenstein's social theory of knowledge, David Bloor reassures us that Wittgenstein is not denying a world outside of the word, but that "words are ultimately connected to the world by training, not by translation" (1983, p. 28). In his critique, Wittgenstein counts the dictionary as a model of the translation hypothesis: "A dictionary can be used to justify the translation of a word X by a word Y" (1958b, §265). Yet within the family of languages, this correspondence model breaks down. What was not so long ago a race to develop a computer program that could effectively translate texts from one language to another is now commonly regarded as among our unattainable technological fantasies. At a very basic level, translation machines and bilingual dictionaries work. But when it really matters, we dare not trust language to such mechanical notions. Because only a poet can translate a poem, and even then as only an approximation of the original, we retain a sense of how poems, not to mention legal contracts, remain tied to the nuances that arise from the use of the words, down to the sound of their consonants and vowels. What of the idea behind the poem, the universal sentiment it expresses? It counts for little, I'm afraid, outside the wondrous crafting of its particular expression, except perhaps in literature class.

One still wants to ask whether any word can be said to possess a specific set of distinct meanings. "Only in rare cases" is Wittgenstein's response. For the most part, it is otherwise: "We are unable to circumscribe the concepts we use; not because we don't know the real definition, but because there is no 'real' definition to them" (1958a, p. 25). He goes on to offer a critique of the precision-masters who would begin with a definition of terms:

> Philosophers very often talk about investigating, analyzing, the meaning of words. But let's not forget that a word hasn't got a meaning given to it, as it were, by a power independent of us, so that there could be a kind of scientific investigation into what the word really means. A word has the meaning someone has given to it. . . .
>
> There are words with several defined meanings. It is easy to tabulate these meanings. And there are words of which one might say: They are used in a thousand different ways which gradually merge into one another. No wonder that we can't tabulate strict rules for their use. (Pp. 27–28)

Note that in dividing words up between those with limited and those with unlimited meanings, Wittgenstein is himself slipping into a fixed and singular sense of *meaning*, one that can, on occasion, be captured in dictionary definitions. That is but one sense of how we use the polysemous word *meaning*. To suggest, as Wittgenstein does in this passage, that only certain terms are misrepresented when we speak of a word's limited number of meanings is only part of the story of the indeterminacy of meaning.

The definition is only an approximation of how a word is used, a blurred snapshot of a busy language in action. Given our metaphysical desire for something substantial that sits behind words, a sense that an apple sits behind the word *apple*, we want as much for concepts such as "meaning," no less than, say, "democracy" or "justice." Such concepts are treated as if they possess an extralinguistic essence that is the very thing itself. Yet when we look to all that is said and done in the name of democracy, we find not a singular sense nor a discrete series of meanings, but a myriad of uses that bear what Wittgenstein terms "family resemblances" (1958b, §67). Claims over what a word means cannot rest on an essential thread of meaning, genetic or genealogical, drawn from the registry of the dictionary. There is only the working of the word within a family of possibilities, as with the ongoing defining process of "democracy" among all of its competing aspects, from majority rule to representative government, from the Federal Bureau of Investigation to the American Civil Liberties Union. When Marshall McLuhan glibly observed that art was anything an artist could get away with, he was referring not simply to the decline of the modern aesthetic but to the process of naming, defining, and meaning within powerful language games and communities.

At one point in the *Blue Book*, Wittgenstein takes on the Socratic question "What is knowledge?" (1958a, p. 27). He situates the question within a classroom in which a pupil is asked for an exact definition of the word *knowledge*, returning us to the Dickensian realm of the proverbial Mr. Gradgrind, who demanded the definition of *horse* from girl number

22 in *Hard Times*. Wittgenstein interrupts the teacher's question to wonder, if we "don't know what it means . . . therefore, perhaps, we have no right to use it." Yet he finally advises that "we should reply: 'there is no one exact usage of the word "knowledge"; but we can make up several such usages, which will more or less agree with the ways the word is actually used'" (p. 27). The lexicographer takes this process a step further by turning those instances of usage into the parts of a definition. The definition is still at one remove from what lexicographers and Wittgenstein would agree is the meaning of the word, that is, one remove from the use of a word.

Let me try to be as clear about this crucial point as possible. If we accept that a word's meaning lies in its use, then the dictionary definition cannot be taken as the *meaning* of a word. The definition in the dictionary is, first, no more than a concerted effort to capture, to bring into other words, how a given word is used in a variety of common (published) situations; it is an abstraction drawn from a limited sampling. Second, the dictionary definition is itself a genre that gives a conventionalized shape to our understanding of meaning that is further removed from this sense of meaning as use.

In the classroom situation, Wittgenstein refers to the student's "right to use" the word *knowledge*. Backed by the dictionary, the school instructs the young in the authorization of language, in how the proper use of language is located in an institutional matrix of textbook and teacher, whether that knowledge is the meaning of a word or the significance of a river. One of the strongest forms this lexicographic lesson in knowledge and power takes is that right to undermine another's use of the language: "Why, that's not even written in what I would call English!" By this educational process, in Michel Foucault's terms, individuals become elements in "the articulation of power" (1980, p. 98).

The classroom is the domain of fixed definitions, many of them posted about the room above the blackboards. These definitions are memorized as a word's true meaning, so that it can be quite a surprise to students to discover years later that a word has a life of its own. The schooled representation of meaning sets language in the hands of those who hold the proper definitions. The Wittgensteinian equation is inverted by classroom and dictionary: defined meaning dictates use. Deliberate acts of definition are substituted for what is, before and after school, simply the rough-and-tumble conversation of growing up. In Wittgenstein's notes from his final years, collected in *On Certainty*, he reminds us that "a child learns by believing the adult. Doubt comes *after* belief" (1969, §160). He stresses at some length the importance of doubt, rather than belief, in the various ways in which we use the word *knowing*. But knowing still entails an element of belief, of having faith in what is learned in school and from the dictionary. Certainly, the dictionary leaves little room for appreciating the role that doubt plays in mature theories of knowledge and the role that indeterminacy plays in mature theories of meaning.

It is not that we teach the young only one meaning per word, although that happens often enough. James Murray was, I'm certain, duly proud of having ascertained 16 definitions in the *OED* for the word *knowledge*, dating back to the 14th century, although some are charmingly antiquated, such as the reference to a "knowledge-casket" as a "humorous name for the head." Yet to say there are 16 definitions for *knowledge* in the *OED* gives little to the indeterminacy of meaning. The dictionary certifies the forms of knowing that have currency, that count in classrooms and other venues. These senses of *knowledge* are culturally and, at times, legally warranted, as Socrates discovered in ancient Athens. Within the dictionary's descriptive function, with its careful show of fidelity to the language as she is published, knowledge retains that sense of earned rites of passage and certified propriety. Could it be otherwise in a book intended to define the language? My argument thus far has been that it might be enough if the tale of this power were told to students and users of the dictionary, as Plato told of Socrates' trial in the *Apology*. Or to be a little less dour about it, as Wittgenstein glibly notes in the *Investigations*: "My aim is: to teach you to pass from a piece of disguised nonsense to something that is patent nonsense" (1958b, §464). Off with the guises. Invest one's life in patent nonsense.

In my pursuit of Wittgenstein, I happened across a rather poignant, if not slanderous, treatment of this power to define meaning by the Austrian novelist Thomas Bernhard, which occurs in his *Wittgenstein's Nephew* (1988), a semifictional memoir of Paul Wittgenstein. I cite only part of the relevant section, asking that you note the repeated use of "so-called" as it challenges the right to designate, and the way Bernhard, amid his vituperation, realizes in the most vivid terms the power and fallacy of naming:

> The medical helplessness of the doctors and their sciences led time and again to the wildest designations for Paul's so-called mental disease, though naturally never to the correct one; all these designations for my friend's so-called mental disease repeatedly proved incorrect, not to say absurd, canceling one another out in the most depressing and disgraceful fashion. The so-called psychiatric specialists gave my friend's illness this name and then that, without having the courage to admit

> that there was no correct name for *this* disease, or indeed for any other, but only incorrect and misleading names; like all doctors, they made life easy for themselves—and in the end murderously easy—by continually giving incorrect names to diseases. (P. 7)

"There was no correct name for *this* disease, or indeed for any other." Every disease is so-called by the medical profession, and the naming is its great consolation, its handle on what ails us. The designation of a certain bundle of what are taken for symptoms and effects as a given "disease" also has that element of indeterminacy to it, especially as everyone suffers the disease slightly differently. Bernhard can betray the faith at times by allowing that there are inherently correct names for diseases. And certainly to name something is a form of claiming power over it, offering a measure of comfort, one hopes, for all concerned. For Wittgenstein, this amounts to a meaningful social skill: "To understand a sentence means to understand a language. To understand a language means to be a master of a technique" (1958b, §199). A word is not a unit of meaning in any simple sense.

The challenge this poses to the lexicographer has not gone unnoticed. Rufus Gouws accuses the meaning-as-use theory as "responsible for the common misconception that the different ways in which a word can be used should be accounted for as different meanings of that word" (1987, p. 88). He advises that, "ignoring the contextual evidence, the lexicographer should define a word in such a way that the same meaning or sense can apply to all the different usage applications of that word" (p. 89). He has little trouble speaking of how "a dictionary article has to accommodate both meaning and use" while insisting on a "lexical meaning" that is separate from "the different uses of a word" (pp. 88, 95). Wittgenstein fares little better in the hands of a more sophisticated student of dictionaries, such as Vincent Reagan, who attempts a Bakhtinian "dialogic perspective on lexicographical meaning": "While any word is mutable in its meaning as its applications change, perhaps only a lexicographical conversion to focusing on the thing, action, idea, or quality defined instead of the word itself will best elicit a word's natural polysemy" (1987, p. 80). The distinctions that lexicographers would make between word and meaning, between "lexical meaning versus contextual evidence," signal the need to have Wittgenstein's dictionary open before us to consult on how words earn their meaning.

In seeking what lexicographers make of meaning, we might also fairly consult the *OED*, where, in practice, some of that very indeterminacy is played out with a straight face in both definition and citation. Under *meaning*, we find both the intended and the expressed:

2. That which is intended to be or actually is expressed or indicated. (See also DOUBLE MEANING.)

This wavering (itself a doubling of sense) between what is thought to be intended, by the author presumably, and what indicates that oddly metaphysical state of the actual, neatly approaches the whole of literary theory's project. But this indeterminacy, as happens with the *OED*, is only heightened by the supporting citations from, among others, Francis Bacon—"Termes, so fixed, whereas the Meaning ought to gouern the Termes, the Termes in effect gouerneth the Meaning"—and John Milton—"That I [Satan] might learn in what degree or meaning thou art called The Son of God, which bears no single sense." Such is the *OED*'s virtue of citing what amounts to the counterevidence and, very specifically in this case, the undermining of meaning. Bacon decries the unnatural fixing of a "Terme," and Milton asserts that the assignation of meaning, as only Satan can know, is a rite of a holy power. Bacon and Milton here are as unsettling as Wittgenstein in regard to the determination of meaning by any force. And their 17th century, it is worth noting, was a time when vernacular dictionaries were just finding their feet.

Yet is there not, one might now ask, a demeaning of meaning in this Wittgensteinian analysis of language? Is Wittgenstein ignoring the force of language in poetry, in a postcard from a friend, or in the way in which a few innocent words from a child at bedtime can resound, we would surely say, with a meaningfulness that we will turn to many times again? "Can I not say: a cry, a laugh, are full of meaning?" Wittgenstein asks at one point, "And that means roughly: much can be gathered from them" (1958b, §543). The meaning of a cry or a laugh, in this sense, is sought in the words that it brings to mind, in how we name what has happened. Putting words to that event is itself an effort to pin down its meaning. "The kind of certainty," Wittgenstein points out, "is the kind of language game" (§xi). The dictionary is the rule book for this language game. It offers a certainty of meaning, which Wittgenstein made it his philosophical project to undercut. None of us may be prepared to give up on a belief in the distinct meaning of words, but for Wittgenstein this only points to our bewitchment by language, which must be checked against how language is "actually used." "Philosophy, as we use the word," Wittgenstein advised his class, "is a fight against the fascination which forms of expression exert upon us" (1958a, p. 27).

But if philosophy fights against this fascination, literature gives into it completely. In the literary tradition that feeds on the inexhaustibility of meaning, there is above all Marcel Proust, who, feeding on those "short, plump little cakes called 'petites madeleines'" from his childhood, tried to piece together the exquisite pleasure that invaded him from an earlier time: "Whence did it come?" he writes. "What did it signify? How could I seize upon and define it?" (1934, p. 34). The answer comes in the remaining pages of his seven-volume novel *Remembrance of Things Past* (1934).

Literature has long been the ally of the dictionary, although as Bacon and Milton revealed, its contribution is not always straightforward. Literature holds meaning within that wonderfully extended realm of conventions that move from metaphor to genre; it holds meaning, as well, to a realization of extremely singular sensibilities, as one might find by considering the canon that this chapter draws upon. Literature plays on, and plays out, the indeterminacy of meaning. It is, itself, a way of forestalling doubt.

This is not to say that Wittgenstein intended his mining of indeterminacy to be a license for vagueness in language. His notebooks demonstrate, entry by entry, that he was relentless in his efforts to clarify and delimit the meaning that can be drawn from the ways language is used. Yet there are two sides to the swath Wittgenstein cut through the question of meaning. On the one hand, his work is by no means as drenched in skepticism as the American philosopher Saul Kripke would have it, with his conclusion that, according to Wittgenstein, "there can be no such thing as meaning anything by any word" (1982. p. 55). Without pursuing the elaborate philosophical debates that have followed Wittgenstein's refutation of the possibility of a private language and the nature of following a rule in language, I hope it is apparent that Wittgenstein allows for precision in a word's use in a given context, without fixing the meaning of the word in any more general sense.[8] On the other hand, Wittgenstein's stance is by no means as clear-cut as Oxford dons G. P. Baker and P. M. S. Hacker suggest by scolding those who imagine Wittgenstein was supporting the idea that "language is vague" in his attack on the seeming "determinacy of sense" (1980, p. 226). Recall that Wittgenstein spoke of indistinctness as a quality that we often need with concepts (1958b, §71).[9]

One of the most persistent expressions of the desire for the determined quality of word meaning as suggested by the dictionary is found in the letters-to-the-editor sections of the respectable press. As I have established elsewhere (1988), major newspapers have become the lexicographer's source of choice. This suggests a symbiotic relationship between paper and dictionary, which John Campise captures rather well in this letter to the *Toronto Globe and Mail,* a letter I found over one breakfast while working on this chapter:

> How I wish somebody could declare an indefinite moratorium on the use of the word *icon*. The new (1989) edition of the *OED* recognizes, for general use only, the familiar meanings of *icon*: image, picture, representation, statue. . . . Common to all these meanings is the notion of visual resemblance.
>
> Recently, however, the word *icon* has come into vogue and is now used as a trendy substitute for any word the user imagines has a similar meaning. . . . The *Globe and Mail* uses *icon* with a range of meanings.
>
> The trouble is that all these intended new meanings have to be deduced from their contexts. Consequently, instead of understanding what the speakers and writers are saying from the meaning of the words they use, we have to figure out the meanings by guessing at what the users are trying to say.
>
> Everyone recognizes that a living language is bound to change. Sometimes it may be enriched in the process. But when being in vogue counts for more than exact expression, clarity and precision go by the board: the result is a poorer language. (1991)

It's all here in the most commonsensical fashion: use and context are opposed to meaning, and a range of meanings opposed to precision and clarity. Naturally, the authority underwriting the complaint is the current ruling body, the *OED*, which "recognizes, for general use only, the familiar meanings of *icon*." Campise's longing for someone who "could declare an indefinite moratorium on the use" of a word is an expression of a faith that meaning is the preserve of the language's rightful heirs. Although it may seem a terrible reduction of Wittgenstein to deploy him in a letters-to-the-editor squabble, such are language's public battlegrounds in this society. It can seem that the dictionary-wielding speaker feels absolutely compelled to deplore the lack of clarity in the speech of others in what often amounts to a reining-in of their language. This call for clarity, presented as a public service, is as much about language rights, as Wittgenstein suggested in his response to the question about knowledge.[10] If not for clarity and stability, are there no exceptions to the language games of use?

The test may be to apply the rules of the game to the philosopher's own reflections. There are times when he breaks with his insight that we do better to look at the way a word is used than to imagine that we are able to look through the word to the thing itself. Perhaps the most alarming instance of this is his reflections on the Jewish people, found in his notebooks of the early 1930s and later published as *Culture and Value* (1980). Wittgenstein clearly had no intention of publishing the notebooks, and in 1950, after years of storing them, originally in a fireproof safe that he kept in his rooms in Cambridge, he asked that a number of them be destroyed, a year before his death (1961a, p. v). Still it is difficult to deny the notebooks a place in his active corpus, and certainly they are used in the elucidation of his work. He had also acquired, I should note, British citizenship after the Germans annexed Austria in 1938, serving his new country diligently during the war as an orderly at Guy's Hospital in London and an assistant at a clinical research laboratory, apparently without letting on that he was a professor.

Wittgenstein spoke to others of being three-quarters Jewish while claiming to be German through and through (the genealogical facts are in some dispute, according to W. W. Bartley [1985, pp. 198-200]). Where he labels himself a Jew in his notebooks, it is in self-deprecating terms: "Among Jews 'genius' is found only in the holy man. Even the greatest of Jewish thinkers is no more than talented. (Myself for instance)" (1980, p. 18e). Note that here he has set aside philosophical concerns with how the word *Jew* is used, how a type is constructed by categorically setting "Jews" off from those who need not be named but are the very norm. It was a time in England, as well as in Austria, that needed another kind of analysis. Where he does critically treat the use of the term, he still fails to challenge the way the word is constructed around an essence that he cannot commend "by any means":

> It has sometimes been said that the Jews' secretive and cunning nature is a result of their persecution. This is certainly untrue; on the other hand it is certain that they continue to exist despite this persecution only because they have an inclination toward such secretiveness. As we may say that this or that animal has escaped extinction only because of its capacity or ability to conceal itself. Of course I do not mean that as a reason for commanding such a capacity, not by any means. (P. 22e)

In slipping into an anthropological search for culturally distinguishing behaviors, Wittgenstein contributes to the defining process, to a use of the term *Jew* that reinforces the difference, the otherness, of the term even as he tries to absolve the Jews of responsibility for what they were commonly charged with.[11] What I am asking is that we continue in Wittgenstein's pursuit of how use is meaning, and how this term's use in the press and in public, in homes and schools, needs to be seen as contributing to a demarcation, a fixing of meaning, that need not be accepted. The dire consequences of such usage need to be realized. Redefining how such concepts are used is a political act; ask the Israelis, the African Americans, the Native Americans—the list will not end in a world of contested meanings.

The point about whether one has the power to name oneself rather than be constantly named by others concerns what Wittgenstein terms "a form of life": "It is what human beings say that is true or false; and they agree in the language they use. That is not agreement in opinions but in the form of life" (1958b, §241). He goes on to add, "If language is to be a means of communication there must be agreement not only in definitions but also (queer as this must sound) in judgments" (§242). This extends the insight of the Renaissance scholar Giambattista Vico, who, in launching the new science of humanism, held that *verum factum*—the truth is something made (1968). Wittgenstein is offering a larger equation, beginning with the word. In his hands, the truth is a consequence of a language game. The game metaphor is meant not to trivialize the consequences of the word but to suggest how speakers enter into a normative universe with each game. We each live within the overlapping circle of many such games in the family, school, and shop. Wittgenstein adds to the weight of the language game by taking it a step further, arguing that ultimately the game becomes a form of life and, as such, bears a moral responsibility.[12] Yet it is a mistake, I have been arguing, to assume that the dictionary is language's rule book. It is far better to think of it as covering the game, providing snapshots of a certain kind of action, offering a guide to a certain level of play. The dictionary is a knowledgeable artifact, by all means, but it is neither the protector nor the enforcer of meaning.

> From word to game to life—in this process, Wittgenstein moves from semantics to the language of morality. In the second part of the Investigations, Wittgenstein draws from language the sense in which we define the human as more than a matter of opinion: "My attitude towards him is an attitude towards a soul. I am not of the opinion that he has a soul" (1958b, §iv). He finds in language a quality accorded all human beings. But the historical truth of the language games we play, along with their incumbent forms of life, is that such respectful regard for the other does not always exist. There are language games that make it their business to undermine others' claims to humanity. One lesson to be drawn from Wittgenstein, as we try to get a handle on agreements in judgment, is to attend to the way a word is used, to scrutinize the meaning in relation to the language game and form of life. My earlier point about how people are named and how they come to name themselves is that such uses of language matter not only to meaning but also to our form of life. As Allen Thiher concludes with regard to the later Wittgenstein, "Reality is in this view an unending process of articulation" (1984, p. 27).

Wittgenstein held that "philosophy may in no way interfere with the actual use of language; it can only describe" (1958b, §124). Although this quietism is generally taken as Wittgenstein's philosophical position, not surprisingly he can be found making other sorts of noises elsewhere in his work. In *Remarks on the Foundations of Mathematics*, for example, Wittgenstein uses a disease metaphor that calls for collective social action in the face of philosophical problems: "The sickness of a time is cured by an alteration in the mode of life of human beings, and the sickness of philosophical problems can be cured only through a changed mode of thought and of life, not through a medicine invented by an individual" (1956, §II-4). He illustrates this rather prophetically by pointing out that if the automobile is found to encourage certain illnesses, then we will have to abandon "the habit of driving" (ibid.). There are habits of language as well as of driving, which many are reconsidering in terms of the modes of thought and life in which they are implicated.

Although effecting such changes may be regarded as a form of extraphilosophical work, they can be guided by philosophical inquiry. The process of redefinition for women, for example, has found its form in literary expression and graffiti, art and politics, as well as in new editions of the dictionary. One sign of the success of this process, unfortunately, is an emerging backlash against what is perceived as pressure to be "politically correct" on a number of American campuses. Certainly, the conservative forces are right in thinking that they are now under pressure to eschew the language of sexism or to include more women authors in literature courses in a policing of the language and syllabi. Whether this inhibits the free expression of thought, as they contend, any more than do traditional forms of governance over language and education is another question. All of which is to say that words matter. The tension between respecting and challenging the way others work with language is a delicate moral issue. But it is also a political one. Language speaks of power and self-determination. One notable element of language's social basis, as Wittgenstein construes it, is that language doesn't so much reflect as sustain the social organization of meaning in all of its aspects. Language's limits are never merely philosophical.

In a comment on *The Golden Bough*, Sir James Frazer's scholarly study of myth and ritual in the development of religion, Wittgenstein noted that "indeed, the elimination of magic has here the character of magic itself" (cited by Thiher, 1984, p. 34). It should be obvious by this point that Wittgenstein's reasoning works a similar sort of magic for me. The slight help for the lexicographer that Russell disparagingly refers to in this chapter's epigraph might well be taken as a reduction in the dictionary's magical elements. It amounts to an ideal long in the making, a further turning of diction back to the people, as Wordsworth proposed in the radical poetics that he placed as a preface to the *Lyrical Ballads* (1815/

1968). It is Mary Wollstonecraft's call for "the simple unadorned truth" (1792/1975) during those earlier revolutionary and Romantic days. The dictionary's trick of turning its rough guide to the meaning of people's unadorned diction into a center of authority and certainty needs to be understood and appreciated. The dictionary needs to help people see how the magic and the meaning are still in the ineffable use of language.

When I speak of "Wittgenstein's dictionary," I refer to Wittgenstein's ability to lay out our desire for ordering and fixing the word. Like a trick birthday card that mirrors the face of the one who looks into it, it is a picture of us looking hard for a momentary stay against the uncertainty that lies as much in our words as in our silences. The *Tractatus*, after dividing up the world, arrives at this ominous advice: "What we cannot speak we must pass over in silence" (1961b, §7). This neat and tidy line between what we can speak and what we must pass over was to collapse for Wittgenstein. He found unspoken silences in our words. The later Wittgenstein, in his antidictionary, writing entries that do not divide up into discrete definitions and pose questions, does a better job of revealing the life of the language. By examining the indeterminacy of meaning, Wittgenstein's dictionary pulls together the greater sense of the world.

In turning to the actual dictionary on our shelves, it is time to concede that its pride and presumption, drawn from an earlier age and idea about language, are growing a bit threadbare. This is not a call to throw out this faithful companion of our reading lives, and I will continue to keep mine about me. The dictionary is a device of an earlier time, an earlier understanding of language, yet it remains, as we tend to regard antiquated machinery, remarkably endearing and enduring, as well as, for those who have grown accustomed to its ways, exceedingly useful. But after Wittgenstein, we need to look to the dictionary's representation of meaning as revealing a particular hold on the language, a hold especially precious for those who find literacy the defining feature of their command on the world, a hold that is implicated in the intersection of power and knowledge. This, too, is a form of knowing about language and ourselves. But as it takes shape in the anticolumns of a Wittgensteinian dictionary, it is a knowing that is formed out of doubt as much as belief. The world no longer divides itself neatly into facts, except as we work on it and find it worked on, in classrooms, dictionaries, newspapers, poetry, movies, and the words we share with each other.

References

Ackermann, R. J. (1988). *Wittgenstein's city.* Amherst: University of Massachusetts Press.

Ayer, A. J. (1985). *Ludwig Wittgenstein.* Harmondsworth, UK: Penguin.

Baker, G. P., & Hacker, P. M. S. (1980). *Wittgenstein, meaning, and understanding: Essays on the* Philosophical investigations (Vol. 1). Chicago: University of Chicago Press.

Baker, G. P., & Hacker, P. M. S. (1984). *Scepticism, rules, and language.* Oxford: Blackwell.

Baker, L. R. (1984). On the very idea of a form of life. *Inquiry, 27,* 277–289.

Bartley, W. W., III. (1985). *Wittgenstein.* London: Century Hutchinson.

Bernhard, T. (1988). *Wittgenstein's nephew* (D. McLintock, Trans.). Chicago: University of Chicago Press.

Bernstein, B. (1971). *Class, codes, and control: Theoretical studies towards a sociology of language* (Vol. 1). New York: Schocken.

Bloor, D. (1983). *Wittgenstein: A social theory of knowledge.* New York: Columbia University Press.

Burchfield, R. (1989). *Unlocking the English language.* London: Faber & Faber.

Campise, J. (1991, January 30). Confused language. *Toronto Globe and Mail,* p. A17.

Derrida, J. (1981). *Dissemination* (B. Johnson, Trans.). Chicago: University of Chicago Press.

Fodor, J. A. (1975). *The language of thought.* Cambridge: Cambridge University Press.

Foucault, M. (1980). *Power/knowledge: Selected interviews and other writings, 1972–1977* (C. Gordon, Ed. and Trans.). New York: Pantheon.

Gouws, R. H. (1987). Lexical evidence versus contextual evidence in dictionary articles. *Dictionary, 9,* 86–96.

Jackendoff, R. (1983). *Semantics and cognition*. Cambridge: Massachusetts Institute of Technology Press.

Janik, A., & Toulmin, S. (1973). *Wittgenstein's Vienna*. New York: Simon & Schuster.

Kripke, S. (1982). *Wittgenstein on rules and private language*. Oxford: Blackwell.

Lorca, F. G. (1989). *Four Lorca suites* (J. Rothenberg, Trans.). Los Angeles: Sun & Moon.

McGinn, C. (1984). *Wittgenstein on meaning: An interpretation and evaluation*. Oxford: Blackwell.

Marx, K. and F. Engels (1976). *The German ideology*. Moscow: Progress Publishers.

Monk, R. (1990). *Ludwig Wittgenstein: The duty of genius*. New York: Free Press.

Ogden, C. K., & Richards, I. A. (1923). *The meaning of meaning*. New York: Harcourt, Brace & World.

Pears, D. (1988). Wittgenstein's philosophy of language. In R. L. Gregory (Ed.), *The Oxford companion to the mind* (pp. 811–813). Oxford: Oxford University Press.

Proust, M. (1934). *Remembrance of things past* (Vols. 1–2; C. K. S. Moncrieff, Trans.). New York: Random House.

Reagan, V. (1987). A dialogic perspective on the variability of lexicographical meaning. *Dictionaries, 9*, 76–82.

Rizvi, F. (1988). Wittgenstein on grammar and analytical philosophy of education. *Educational Philosophy and Theory, 19*(2), 33–56.

Rossi-Lundi. F. (1983). *Language as work and trade: A semiotic homology for linguistics and economics*. South Hadley, MA: Bergin & Garvey.

Rubinstein, D. (1981). *Marx and Wittgenstein: Social praxis and social explanation*. London: Routledge & Kegan Paul.

Russell, B. (1959). *My philosophical development*. London: Allen & Unwin.

Thiher, A. (1984). *Words in reflection: Modern language theory and postmodern fiction.* Chicago: University of Chicago Press.

Vico, G. (1968). *The new science of Giambattista Vico* (Trans. T. Goddard Bergin and M. Harold Fisch, 3rd ed., original 1774). Ithaca, N.Y.: Cornell University Press.

Willinsky, J. (1988). Cutting English on the bias: Five lexicographers in pursuit of the new. *American Speech, 63*(1), 44–46.

Willinsky, J. (1994). *Empire of words: The reign of the OED.* Princeton, NJ: Princeton University Press.

Wittgenstein, L. (1956). *Remarks on the foundations of mathematics* (G. H. von Wright, R. Rhees, & G. E. M. Anscombe, Eds.; G. E. M. Anscombe, Trans.). Oxford: Blackwell.

Wittgenstein, L. (1958a). *The blue and brown books: Preliminary studies for the* Philosophical investigations. New York: Harper.

Wittgenstein, L. (1958b). *Philosophical investigations* (3d ed.; G. E. M. Anscombe, Trans.). New York: Macmillan.

Wittgenstein, L. (1961a). *Notebooks, 1914–16.* (G. E. M. Anscombe, Trans.). Oxford: Blackwell.

Wittgenstein, L. (1961b). *Tractatus logico-philosophicus* (D. F. Pears & B. F. McGuiness, Trans.). London: Routledge & Kegan Paul.

Wittgenstein, L. (1967). *Zettel* (G. E. M. Anscombe & G. H. von Wright, Eds.; G. E. M. Anscombe, Trans.). Berkeley: University of California Press.

Wittgenstein, L. (1969). *On certainty* (G. E. M. Anscombe & G. H. von Wright, Trans.). Oxford: Blackwell.

Wittgenstein, L. (1974). *Letters to Russell, Keynes, and Moore* (G. H. von Wright, Ed.). Oxford: Oxford University Press.

Wittgenstein, L. (1980). *Culture and value* (P. Winch, Trans.). Chicago: University of Chicago Press.

Wollstonecraft, M. (1975). *Vindication of the rights of woman.* (Ed. Miriam Brody). Harmondsworth, UK: Penguin. (Originally published 1792.)

Wordsworth, W. (1968). From the preface to the poems of 1815. In R. A. Foakes (Ed.), *Romantic Criticism, 1800–1850.* London: Arnold.

Notes

1. Derrida points out that writing is presented to the king in Plato's *Phaedrus* as a *pharmakon*, which is both a medicinal remedy and a poison. This idea becomes, in the hands of the great deconstructor, the source of a long "chain of significations" that plays, in its own way, with the indeterminacy of meaning: "When a word inscribes itself as the citation of another sense of the same word, when the textual center-stage of the word *pharmakon*, even while it means *remedy*, cites and re-cites, and makes legible that which *in the same word* signifies, in another spot and on a different level of the stage, *poison* (for example, since that is not the only other thing *pharmakon* means), the choice of only one of the renditions by the translator has as its first effect the neutralization of citational play, of the 'anagram,' and, in the end, quite simply, the very textuality of the translated text" (1981, p. 98).

2. Perhaps the strongest expounder of the continuity of the two Wittgensteins, Robert Ackermann, has argued that the later work "restricts the domain of validity of the *Tractatus*, retaining its analysis of certain kinds of factual assertion, and rejects only its pretension to have offered a complete analysis of clear meaning and language" (1988, p. xi). Wittgenstein may well appear to be making the break in his work out of modesty, but I think the significance of the timing of the break, in light of the entire tradition with which it breaks, must be kept in perspective. It was not "only" Wittgenstein's pretension that fell.

3. "The book's point is an ethical one," Wittgenstein wrote in a letter cited by Allan Janik and Stephen Toulmin as part of their argument that the "fundamental point" of the *Tractatus* "was to underline the ethical point that all questions about value lie outside the scope of such ordinary factual or descriptive language" (1973, p. 196).

4. One notable instance is Basil Bernstein's concept (1971) now largely discredited, of restricted and elaborated codes that were meant to explain differences in educational attainment among British students.

5. The relationship between Wittgenstein and Marx, as well as between the philosopher and Marxists at Cambridge in the 1930s (such as the famous economist Piero Saffra, who earned an acknowledgment in the preface to the *Investigations*), poses an interesting question for Wittgenstein's shift to a socialized notion of language and meaning. Consider, for the sake of a suggestive comparison, Marx's approach to language and mind in *The German Ideology:* "Language, like consciousness, only arises from the need, the necessity, of intercourse with other men. . . . Consciousness is, therefore, from the very beginning a social product, and remains so as long as men exist at all" (1976, pp. 50-51). There is also Wittgenstein's visit to the Soviet Union to consider, although his plans to move there did not materialize. For an extended treatment of the subject, see Rubinstein (1981). Notwithstanding this exploration, Rossi-Lundi has his virtues: "Do not seek a philosopher's *meaning*, seek his *use* in the culture" (1983, p. 1).

6   As it turns out, this prior-language assumption is precisely what philosopher Jerry Fodor, in *The Language of Thought* (1975), argues is the case in challenging Wittgenstein's denial of the possibility of a private language, an important element in Wittgensteinian philosophy which I have decided not to introduce into this already rather demanding chapter. Fodor holds that "one cannot learn a first language unless one already has a system capable of representing the predicates in that language *and their extensions*" (p. 64). Fodor's private "language of thought," shared by higher-order animals and governing nonlinguistic states that we also refer to in terms of thinking—"I thought of you when I saw that Fischl painting"—does not diminish the importance to my argument of the way in which natural languages, such as English, take their meaning not from private designations but from public acts of use. This language of thought is not the source of meanings for which the child finds the right words, as per the Augustinian, the early Wittgensteinian, and the lexicographical representational models.

7   There is a decidedly behaviorist tint to what Wittgenstein makes of meaning. He is certainly untrusting of cognitive suppositions. In the particularly apt words of his contemporary A. J. Ayer, Wittgenstein "effectively curtailed the empire of the mind" (1985, p. 133). But Wittgenstein's original position on the realm beyond behavior, dramatically set out in the final axiom of the *Tractatus*, remains a theme in his later work: "What we cannot speak of we must pass over in silence" (1961b, p. 7). This is not the talk of a pure behaviorist, and there are many who are quick to jump to the philosopher's defense on the question. David Pears, for example, allows only that it "may sound like behaviorism, but in fact there is no repudiation of mental events and processes" (1988, p. 813). Although there is indeed a repudiation of some such events and processes, Wittgenstein exposes those which do not make sense, given the way language is used.

8   At a glance, against Kripke's position on private languages and skepticism (1982), there have emerged Baker and Hacker (1984) and McGinn (1984), with Ayer (1985) doubting both sides of the argument.

9   There are further distinctions to be made on the point of vagueness. When linguist Ray Jackendoff, taking a leaf from Wittgenstein, insists that "the ubiquity of fuzziness in word meanings . . . must not be treated as a defect in language," he is making a category mistake (1983, p. 117). Fuzziness is in word meanings only to the degree that we compare the inadequacy of a word's definition to its use. The sense of fuzziness arises because of the static and highly focused quality suggested by the dictionary entry. Word meanings seem fuzzy for the same reason that people appear fuzzy in street-scene photographs from the 19th century but awfully sharp in studio photographs. But ask yourself, as Wittgenstein would, is the fuzziness in the lives of the people?

10 One might suspect that I am offering a veiled criticism of analytical philosophy here. Although that is so, I leave the more thorough treatment up to Fazal Rizvi (1988), who mounts a fourfold attack on the analytical philosophy of education's failure of Wittgenstein, despite its claims to owing a great debt to the philosopher.

11 Elsewhere, I have considered the anti-Semitic tone of citations that accompanied the definition of *Jew* in the *OED*, which then ran contrary to the ostensible neutrality of the definition offered (1994, pp. 140–141).

12 Lynne Rudder Baker (1984) provides one of the most thorough analyses of this key term, *form of life*, critiquing a number of major interpretations of it before arriving at a sense that little can be said about it: "The idea of a form of life emerges as the result of a kind of transcendent argument: We have a language that we use to communicate; we could have no such language if the locus of meaning were the individual or any facts concerning individuals; therefore meaning requires a community. 'Form of life' is Wittgenstein's way of designating what it is about a community that makes possible meaning. Given this role of the idea of a form of life, it is hardly surprising that little meaningful can be said about it" (p. 288). My stress is away from any sense of a singularity of community; the multiplicity that distinguishes the nature of language will hold as well for the forms of life within which we are subsumed.

PART FOUR
PERSONAL

Chapter 10

L'Essai d'Edgar Z. Friedenberg

> The prevalence of *ressentiment* seems to me to make it absurd and sentimental to suppose that liberty will ever be a popular cause in a modern industrialist society, whether that society be socialist or capitalist. Most citizens despise the very idea of idiosyncratic and personal self-expression as the very essence of privilege, and expect the bitter disciplines of adult life to stamp such tendencies out if the schools fail to do so. And, of course, they are right.
> —Edgar Z. Friedenberg, *The Disposal of Liberty and Other Industrial Wastes*

For over a quarter century beginning at the end of the 1950s, Edgar Z. Friedenberg proved himself a source of bracing, if not biting, social commentary. Although the academic discipline known as the sociology of education was his stock-in-trade, his avocation was the artful, literate defense of the individual at liberty among the rights of the many. In his earlier work, the schools appear as the persistent expression of a larger social malaise, a tension between rights and liberties that continues to pervade this society. Though he did go on to pursue the cause of liberty through a broad range of subjects, he continued to return to the nature of life in school as the test case for what we intend with our ideals and ideologies. Yet even in that returning, his concerns shifted, moving from a psychology of interrupted integrity to a politics of threatened liberty. The shift is marked by gains, constants, and losses. His work broadened considerably in scope, yet the forcefulness and sensitivity of his argument were relentlessly maintained. Still, in turning from the fate of the student to that of the world at large, he failed to reach as many or as deeply, even as he sought to speak to more.

This chapter explores one dimension in the particular meeting of avocation and vocation in Friedenberg's work; it proposes that his abiding intellectual fervor is the element that distinguishes his work as a writerly practice and sense of responsibility. In the three decades after the publication of *The Vanishing Adolescent,* Friedenberg's work developed beyond the school yard, which served as the original center for what he always tended to transcend; the same can be said for his fidelity to the scholarly methods of his academic training. Even as he participated in the production of systematic research in the study of education, his prose relentlessly escaped the predictable patterns of this mode of discourse. Though his concerns expanded, he maintained a certain constancy that was clever and caustic in its formulation of the educational dilemma. He altered usually, if not always, with the times, moving from a concern for the healthy development of the individual into a struggle for the political possibility of a distinct individuality. Still, questions remain: Where does this transcendental harping, this pursuit on behalf of the individual who would diverge and defy, lead after a long career of working it this way and that? What happens to the blend of art and science that animates the scholarship? What did it ask then and what does it ask now?

Friedenberg remained a writer who tended to thoroughly please or infuriate, as his argument runs strongly and on occasion falters. His rhetorical manner is marked in one distinct way: the discomforting metaphor worked to the point of hyperbole. His metaphorical explications, especially as they are brought to bear on the school, are rarely cheery or ingratiating. To great effect, he likened the school to the 19th-century Colonial Office, abdominal surgery, the minimum-security prison, and the very highway to hell. He suggested at one point that the school bears a striking resemblance to the waiting room of a terminal: "It combines the costly, well-appointed discomfort of the airport terminal with the atmosphere of the bus station."[1] On other occasions, the school can bring to mind an abattoir and in such a manner as to approach a metaphysical conceit. Consider this excerpt from Friedenberg's playing out of the abattoir metaphor before a needs-assessment conference sponsored by the Ontario Teachers' Federation:

> Our efforts to bring about education reform in order to eliminate the inequities we found in the schools seems to me, in retrospect, rather as if we had published the mortality rates among healthy cattle in an abattoir of Swift or Armour Canada Limited, of course and exclaimed in horror: "This place is a shambles." So it is; and management, had it been asked, would have admitted it with mild astonishment that anyone could have thought otherwise. I would not, I think, have defended the slaughterhouse as an institution designed to enhance, or even equalize, economic opportunity among the processed animals there. Yet it does, of course....
>
> Schools do not, of course, terminate the lives of their pupils. They are not as bloody as abattoirs; so one should, perhaps, be less sanguine about them.[2]

This hard sort of play with language and ideas is undeniably aggressive and, in part, self-congratulatory, just as it is intentionally offensive and sensational. But is it all of those things simply for effect? I tend to think so. Reporting the numerous statistical studies on the school's consistently dismal contribution to social mobility through the 20th century may have made the point more palatable or easier to swallow, but it would have turned few heads. Friedenberg's creative restatement of these findings conveys much the same information yet goes on to capture his mood of frustration with the smug intransigence of his fellow educators and, indeed, plays roughly with it. He might have been more polite about it in front of his kind hosts, but he could not have done as much to shake these teachers or he would not have been as honest with them.

In this manner, Friedenberg provides a social psychology of the school that, although it incorporates much from the scholarly literature of the field, still manages to realize a whole different form of validity and reliability through the literary device, a language and story that work from a much older authority than the recent human sciences. His argument for the possibilities of youth and human liberty was originally fashioned out of the instances of Sigmund Freud, Erich Fromm, and Henry Stack Sullivan in psychology, and out of Howard Becker, Christopher Jencks, and David Riesman in sociology. He later turned to Michael Apple and Paul Willis when a neo-Marxist sociology of education began to mount the most telling critique of the schools; but he also stuck by a great many lesser-known scholarly figures whose work he helped to disseminate. Yet his scholarly argument is also tightly made out of Homer, Dante, Oscar Wilde, and T. S. Eliot. He uses Shakespeare's *The Tempest* to illuminate the limitations of Fromm's psychology, and when he needs a simile to capture those long days in school, he turns to Rebecca West's reflections on the bookish shape of the good life. "If one's experience has no form," she states, "if the events do not come readily to mind and disclose their significance, we feel about ourselves as if we are reading a bad book." He finds in her words the acute measure of the high school: "I have found the life of the high school to be, in this respect, very often like a bad book; sentimental, extrinsically motivated, emotionally and intellectually dishonest."[3] In other instances, he builds subtlety and fine distinction into his reasoning by illuminating his argument with the lyrics of W. S. Gilbert, Bob Dylan, and Pink Floyd. But his work on the school, even as it dips into the arts, both classic and popular, also never loses sight of the *New York Times* and the evening news. Throughout his work one can find the lessons of Vietnam and Nicaragua, of Supreme Court decisions and legislative enactments, in his search for the school's place in things.

Friedenberg's study of education maintains a cultural sensitivity and a rhetorical finesse that bridge academic scholarship and the American essayist tradition of Emerson, though Friedenberg runs more toward Thoreau or, in more contemporary terms, toward Lionel Trilling and Paul Goodman in temperament. This rhetorical tradition might be described as blending its argument out of three elements: a certain critical authority (Emerson's clericalism, Friedenberg's sociology of education), along with an appeal to a shared cultural sensibility of common texts, which is then underwritten by the moral authority of crucial issues clearly perceived and felt. But even as the essay draws the reader in with these familiar tunes well played, even as it tugs deeper through this call to the cultural heights, this tradition is obliged to raise the overlooked and uncomfortable matters of a society moving hastily along, matters that, as often as not, entail elements of dignity, integrity, and other aspects of the good life. Friedenberg's work, in stepping out of and beyond the traditional formats of scholarly discourse, is unapologetic in its culturally enriched, morally indignant criticism of the school; it offers the force of an articulate sensibility moved with remarkable lucidity to bemusement, compassion, and outrage in turn.

One strength of the Friedenberg essay in its critical regard for the school, I would argue, is that it clearly grows out of the culture and language that it would preserve as part of its educational mission. That quality of literature which the school would defend, at least in principle, is the source and expression of the values that Friedenberg reveres in the student, though with ambivalence at times, and that he would protect from the school. He demonstrates what it means to be educated in something approaching a traditional, literate sense with all of its incumbent concerns for the individual's plight in a mass society, a sense that often eludes the state of free and compulsory education. From the top of the English class, one might say, he exhibits a much-desired, supple prose style, along with a strong, discriminating sense of the shoddy and the pretentious. What distinguishes his analysis from much of the critical work in educational research is that he speaks what seems to be the school's language, as if it were the center of this culture's educational enterprise. Seeming to share the language and the concern of public education, he is appalled by the forces within the school that deny what the school would ostensibly embrace and encourage along with him.

But for all of that, Friedenberg remained a man of two cultures, drawing on what might be distinguished as the literate and the academic. The breadth of his interest reminds us that a certain narrowness of vision, a certain adherence to the rigors of technique, can leave research into education separate from a genuine intellectual concern and isolated from the cultural milieu beyond the scope of the research instrument. Friedenberg's earlier research on the attitudes of high school and undergraduate students was conducted with all of the necessary rigors of subject selection and statistical measurement, using such techniques as the Sentence Completion Test and the Q-technique. When the results of these research technologies were worked into his books, however, they were immersed in the richness of Friedenberg's ability to make sense of what the young had managed to express in these various instruments. The question that might be asked is whether the hard findings of these measures were buried by the quickness of his apparently soft but always cutting commentary. Friedenberg told me once of how he was struck by the perceptive observation of a friend that in his book *Coming of Age in America,* based in part on students' sorting of statements (Q-technique), the research seems almost a superfluous accoutrement to the surrounding argument.

Although the original study was rigorously reported elsewhere,[4] in *Coming of Age* Friedenberg used its findings as a scaffold from which to build the tower of his apprehensions and hopes for the moral development of American youths. It might be added that his later work was neither so encumbered nor supported, but then, too, it was less often peopled with the likes of Thomas or Mr. D., the high school students whose forthright responses Friedenberg read with a great knowingness in the early books:

> Thomas regards his body as capital goods that had somehow come under his control. As a physical operation he is superb and knows it. His body earns him all the satisfactions he gets: status, victory, recognition, what he calls love. . . . It seems nearly all he possesses. He exploits it, he takes good care of it, but it does not seem to have occurred to him that he could live in it himself.[5]

One might suppose that in leaving behind the narrow, barren school corridors and conversations with students like Thomas, much might have been gained in return by the emerging breadth of vision in Friedenberg's work. But in taking up the case beyond the school, moving further into the realm of social criticism and political science, his urgent defense of civil liberties can be found to lack the same degree of embodiment. The illustrative examples he uses in this work are drawn from across the social scene, and indeed he makes the case that the threat is ubiquitous. But his focus of concern no longer has a singular and imaginative home in the life of a few individual adolescents who formed the core and contributed a great deal to the character of the earlier books. Yet he has not lost the rhetorical force of the telling instance in this shift to the governing institutions of the adult world and the courts:

> The best evidence I know of that heterodoxy of opinion or behavior is not really cherished in Canadian society is to be found in the statute forbidding the publication of material that would be offensive to the community standards of typical Canadians, the statute under which *The Body Politic* was prosecuted and acquitted, and prosecuted and acquitted, and prosecuted for publishing "Men Loving Boys Loving Men" .... It is against the law to tell Canadians anything they might really be shocked and offended by, no matter how important it may be or how true. Sex, as such, has nothing to do with the case.[6]

In the blend of literary and scholarly voices, Friedenberg stands apart from practitioners of the traditional academic forms of discourse, which tend to define and limit the voice and authority of the scholar in the educational community, as professors of education, for example, are notorious for failing to find a readership among those they would ostensibly move and serve. Of course, it would be difficult to establish to what degree Friedenberg's work, compared to traditional educational research, has reached educators. Still, he began from a different concept of service and did not as often propose a handy educational solution for those who cannot help themselves. He was also the first to realize that the adolescents he championed are those very ones who would not readily take their cue from college dons, and for his vigorous defense of their interest he was careful to ask nothing in return. To the school personnel whom he seemed so quick to admonish, he claims to offer no more than a certain accuracy of description, an evocative rendering of intention and ambience which, as the opening epigraph of this chapter suggests, he does not expect they will gratefully receive in every instance.[7]

Those teachers and academics who are made uncomfortable by Friedenberg's work most often take refuge in his seeming failure to proffer a solution, to outline the means of providing a new, improved form of schooling that might meet his scurrilous objections. In demanding of him a snappy program of improvement, educational advocates fail to realize both the profoundness of his objection to the nature of modern schooling and its fundamental simplicity: "Basically, I disapprove of compulsory school attendance in itself. I see no valid moral reasons to single out the young for this special legal encumbrance. The economic reasons are compelling enough; but they are likewise contemptible."[8] Though Friedenberg finds this compulsion lacking in moral purpose, he is not about to deny school its special function: "The development of an inauthentic response to the circumstances of one's life is the central function of compulsory schooling, central in the sense that the more concrete and familiar economic and political consequences of schooling are in fact expressions of this inauthenticity."[9] The moral vigor of Friedenberg as essayist is his ability to bring to bear the human consequence of institutional circumstance; it is to press our faces up against the implications of our own comforting constructions.

But would he allow for a form of schooling beyond this antithetical element of compulsion? In *Coming of Age in America,* Friedenberg does put forward a suggestion for restructuring education based on the premise of voluntary participation with something approaching a voucher system, but it is a system that would include, along with public and private schools, the addition of residential schools for those among the poor who are looking for an immersion course in a rather different way of life. Yet this relatively detailed proposal is an exception in his work, and, like Plato's *Republic,* one might say, it is far stronger in its explanatory power of the author's position and hopes than in its prescriptive promise as a blueprint for the future. The "highest function of education," Friedenberg ventures later in his book, is to help "people understand the meaning of their lives and become more sensitive to the meaning of other people's lives and relate to them more fully."[10] This educational motif of reflecting on the meaning of life also figures in his essay "Society and the Therapeutic Function," but this time as the primary function he foresees for psychotherapy.[11] Yet this progressive combination of a therapeutic and an empathetic hope for education, which figured in Friedenberg's work in the 1960s, does not appear to have survived the 1970s. His prescription of an educational ideal for students by the end of that decade was thoroughly realpolitik: "Best of all, perhaps, you stay right in the school and sit in with your teacher at board meetings in which policy is made: pupils are given a desk in the principal's office and listen to what goes on there when a parent tries to come in with a complaint; the school paper fearlessly exposes the fiscal manipulations that keep the school going, thus learning about political responses at first hand."[12]

If he was not always able to convince committed educators to share their office space with students, Friedenberg at times also ran into trouble with other critics who had taken up the issue of social justice in the schools. The weight of this educational critique in recent years has emerged from a reinvigorated left, whereas Friedenberg continued to develop his civil-libertarian critique. The distance, however, was not simply a matter of political philosophy. Even while supporting the insightfulness of his colleagues in the New Left, Friedenberg did not hesitate to thump them for their lack of his grace and lucidity. Consider his mixed review of Henry Giroux, from the rising new school of neo-Marxist sociology of education, and Giroux's book *Ideology, Culture, and the Process of Schooling:* "The very fact that nearly everything Giroux has to say in this book is both insightful and urgently significant makes his style infuriating; it seems a willful act of obscurantism and a betrayal of his own message."[13] The "betrayal" of message is very much the point for both Giroux and Friedenberg; they are striving equally for a language that is loyal to the spirit of their concerns. When on occasion Giroux has had to defend his turgid neo-Marxism from the attack of plain-speaking teachers, he has done so on the grounds that neo-Marxism is the necessary vehicle for establishing a new, uncorrupted expression of ideas that can escape the dominant ideology. Though Giroux and Friedenberg might be said to seek a greater liberty from debilitating rights, they are bringing to bear different traditions of discourse. If Giroux would bump us ahead to a new language for a new age, Friedenberg would seem to keep us looking back. "An aging romantic critic" is how he sets himself up in his review of Giroux, but he would look back in order to maintain a cultural connection with an artistic, if not an aristocratic, sensibility of individual dignity and integrity. Art was his vehicle, because art keeps an eye out for the past, even as it seems at times to rudely push too far ahead. It remains the wellspring for idiosyncratic and independent intelligence.

Still, it should be pointed out that Friedenberg, in rejecting the rhetoric of the New Left, did not turn his back on the social inequity that the school fosters rather than cures. But in his recognition of this problem, he did not base his case simply on a wronged working class. Again Friedenberg is remarkably lucid, if not blunt, about his interests: "I am not trying to be fair, or to identify and reward the most deserving, but to find educational means for sponsoring and nurturing more trustworthy and humane people than those among whom our lives now seem destined to be spent, and spent utterly."[14] In this pursuit, Friedenberg spoke out on behalf of a wide range of talents: "The gifted—intellectually, financially, spiritually, erotically; it does not matter—learn to expect no respect for their gifts; indeed to conceal them, except when they can be put to the service of the school's narrowly defined goals."[15] He also expressed a certain sympathy for such institutions of class privilege as the private school: "At best, they helped the adolescent to make himself into a strongly characterized human being; at worst, their impact made adolescence interminable and their victims permanently fixated 'oldboys.'"[16] Friedenberg, to some degree, must seem to have persisted in the chatter of the gentleman's club that, in fact, has sponsored a good deal of the inequity, even if he turned against much that it would hold dear. He also took up the wronging of the rich—the financially "gifted," as he put it—at the hands of the educators: "To paraphrase Oscar Wilde in *The Importance of Being Earnest,* it is evident that many schoolteachers find it is more than their duty to discredit the pretensions of the rich, it is their pleasure."[17] But then, too, in taking up, on occasion, the case of the wronged wealthy, he remained sensitive to those qualities that link the most distant of classes: "The rich and the poor, in short, can sometimes tolerate and even enjoy direct access to and expression of their feelings and senses in a way that the middle class consider disorderly."[18] His concern was to seek out the fate of that which he admired and found unduly threatened by the school as it remains an instrument of an anxious middle class. These special qualities, which we sometimes assume only the rich can afford, may not be as omnipresent in adolescence as Friedenberg suggests, although they might fairly be said to pervade the voice that emerges through his work:

> Adolescents often behave like members of an old-fashioned aristocracy. . . . Their virtues are courage and loyalty; while the necessity for even a moderate degree of compromise humiliates them greatly. They tend to be pugnacious and quarrelsome about what they believe to be their rights, but naive and reckless in defending them. They are shy, but not modest. If they become very anxious they are likely to behave eccentrically, to withdraw, or to attack with some brutality; they are less likely to blend themselves innocuously into an environment with an apologetic smile. They are honest on occasions when even a stupid adult would have better sense.[19]

Friedenberg was hardly the first to discover in those he wrote about that which he would cultivate in himself; but note as well that in this passage he is, perhaps, as tough on himself as he is on the adolescents. This does not mean that he was necessarily misled in seeking out the ill-fated fortunes of these qualities among high school students, nor was he beyond revising his conception of their virtues in the face of fresh evidence. A few years after making these observations, in *Coming of Age in America,* another study on the attitudes of high school students, he came to the conclusion that "fidelity and personal devotion are not what they value." These unsettling discoveries on his part were at least balanced on occasion by newfound virtues: "Their wretched taste in poetry was grounded in a refined and reliable poetic sensitivity."[20]

Over the course of his writing, Friedenberg also altered his conception of the relationship between the individual and the state; the shift is most clearly found in his view of what constitutes adolescence. Initially, in *The Vanishing Adolescent,* adolescence is described as having the marked psychological function of forming a "clear and stable self-identification." Similarly, in *Coming of Age in America,* he refers to adolescence as a "stage and a process of growth": "As such it should proceed by doing what comes naturally," which remains a realization of identity that in its later stages partakes of "dignity, self-confidence and the unquestioned assumption that the individual is significant in himself."[21] However, the human qualities he described as being at stake in schooling eventually developed in his work into less clinical matters than such things as a "stable self-identification." Rather than threatening what he had described as "real adolescence," he now suggested that more than a developmental stage was at risk. The schools were taking issue with certain behaviors and attitudes that he considered to be the right of people whatever their age, such as the urge among students and professors to ask awkward questions or to affect autonomous stances.

In this development Friedenberg seems to have grown less certain about what he at first presumed about the fixed nature of adolescence. After 20 years of considering this suspended state between childhood's end and maturity, he arrived at the conclusion that "adolescence is a political condition, not a biological one or psychological one; though, like all political conditions it has psychological concomitants; and like others it has biological roots."[22] It was as if Friedenberg realized that the organizational perpetuators of schools are the master carpenters of steps, stages, and (political) states, and that the elusive autonomy of the individual, to which Friedenberg was persistently drawn, is given to slip-sliding through such dangerous conceptual construction sites as the school, with a mark or two to show for it. If education is engaged in political work, then persistently trivial matters in the high school such as late slips and locked washrooms, which Friedenberg never let pass unnoticed, describe the nickel-and-dime assaults on the students' integrity as individuals. In playing down the importance of the school's contribution to the psychological formation of the student, he to some degree picked up the common notion among students that school is little more than small change.

Another important instance of this shift in Friedenberg's work is found in his choice of heuristic concepts for getting at the conflict underlying sites like the school. In *The Vanishing Adolescent,* one of the most interesting and daring points of discussion occurs in the chapter "Adult

Imagery and Feeling," a highly androcentric discussion in which he describes the role of homoeroticism in the adult's ill regard for youth, and which ranges widely over art, Prussian politics, and the *Iliad,* only to arrive at a description of the terror suffered by middle-class adults faced with a "subjective intensity, disciplined but non-repressed, [that] lies at the heart of integrity, of artistic creativity, and of adolescence."[23] This meeting of integrity, intensity, and art has always been one of the essential touchstones in Friedenberg's argument, especially when it is focused on their embattled state in the romance and promise of the young.

However, after the ensuing politicization of the school site in the 1960s and 1970s, Friedenberg began to employ the concept of "hegemony" as the most effective means of explaining the loss of self-realization in the schools. Hegemony also has its place in discussions of Prussian politics, but Friedenberg used it in the manner of Antonio Gramsci, to describe "the entire set of assumptions, conventions, values and categories of thought and feelings that are validated by a society and serve to legitimate and protect its dominant institutions and elites from being examined critically on terms other than their own."[24] With this shift, we have left the individual bodies and minds of the young behind for a political machination that processes the masses even as it channels their thoughts and feelings. In confronting the intransigence of the schools over two hectic decades, Friedenberg decided that the only thing left was to strip back the curtain, to unmask the educational struggle and expose the successful political campaign for the hearts and minds of the young. But notice, too, that in a politics of hegemony, he continued to cleverly dig with the metaphor: "We do all possess a degree of free will and autonomy and, like Archimedes, could move the earth if we had a place to stand, though this is not why his principle is taught in high school. But against the full weight of hegemony, major alternatives are unlikely to present themselves as possibilities. Rebellion itself is channeled and molded by hegemony."[25]

This hardening of the issue around a fundamental political principle of liberty as something that ranges far beyond the school yard may have occurred, for Friedenberg, as part of an earlier and troubling realization he made about the young. In a revealing piece of intellectual autobiography that forms the preface to his collection of early essays, *The Dignity of Youth and Other Atavisms,* he acknowledges that he may have been seeking an impossible combination of personal qualities in youth. Rather surprisingly, he gives the credit for this realization about human nature to the communication theories of Marshall McLuhan:

> But it took McLuhan in *Understanding Media* to finally get it through to me that the kind of person whose existence gave meaning to mine was already a product of a considerable degree of alienation simply because he was aware of his strength and pride and of his origins in a way that only people who stand aside from their experience and examine it in the light of various symbols can be.[26]

In courageously describing his own indignation at having devoted his life "to demanding that the young develop qualities that perhaps just don't go together," he employs the two characters who are friends in John Knowles's novel *A Separate Peace* to illustrate both what he once admired and where he might have gone wrong. He supposes that, in his work, whereas he once supported someone very much like Phineas, the "narcissistic and shallow but emotionally labile and responsive" character, he later came to realize that Finny's opposite, "Gene, who never makes a false move or wastes an ounce of energy, is really who I have been harboring all the time, that *he* is really the self-aware one, the boy who could define himself and who tells his own story knowing it to be the story of Cain."[27] Friedenberg gained a glimpse of a critical distance, a productive alienation, that facilitated rather than disturbed the possibility of an authentic response in students, even as it left that response unrealized: "The very source of their nobility is also, it seems, the instrument of their estrangement which saps their vitality."[28] Friedenberg was suddenly far more on his own in this endeavor; it put that much more stress on the alienated nature, the self-conscious integrity, of the intellectual who labors to find a metaphor and morality to stir that depleted vitality.

He goes on in this extended preface to reflect on how this conflict troubled him in his initial response to the free-speech movement; it was the preliminary to a decade of troubles that tested the mettle of a generation of students, teachers, and scholars. The piece represents a careful effort in accurately representing where these ideas lead and push in their human embodiment. Having found that what he was defending was more elusive than he had first realized, more given to being entangled in the fancy of psychological constructions of character, he seems to have looked away from the struggle of the adolescent in the school in order to draw a new line of defense. He recognized that he would have to rally around something more obviously fundamental to preserving the autonomy of the individual, something that had legal precedence and constitutional authority—the matter of civil liberties in an uncivil state. This matter of the individual's relation to the state, a singular ideal at the heart of the intellectual state of the country, increasingly pervaded Friedenberg's work after this collection of essays.

Such a critical and public self-examination is a necessary step in the pursuit of intellectual integrity. It goes on markedly in the preface to *The Dignity of Youth* but at other points in Friedenberg's work as well. It also bears a remarkable resemblance to the current academic enterprise of feminist scholarship, which seems worth noting. Sandra Gilbert, for example, has described this trend in the way in which "each participant inevitably begins her intellectual work with a careful study of the house of fiction(s) in which she has perhaps unwittingly dwelt all her life."[29] Remarkable, too, in its irony, is the fact that Friedenberg's work repeatedly suffered what he himself referred to as a sexual "astigmatism," though he used the term in reference to Paul Willis's work rather than his own.[30] This condition represents a failure of vision on both their parts, which has unwittingly made its own contribution to the marginalization of women in the study of education. But to criticize this lapse only serves to illustrate the breadth of the responsibility he seems to have taken on in bridging the intellectual concerns of the scholar and the social critic.

The responsibility of the intellectual as essayist, which I am suggesting sets this manner of writer apart from the academic, entails observing all the world as well as closely monitoring one's own complex responses as a check on the commonplace. In this way, Friedenberg made much of the politics of the person as he repeatedly explored the troubled play of liberties within a web of rights. His forthrightness amounts to a tough blend of art and politics; it serves to remind us of what is so often indelicately masked in the name of objective research. The best of that research lacks not conviction but just a subtle means of conveying the manner in which convictions are carried through the work. In reading about education and other social acts, we are too rarely treated to the force of a voice that stands up and apart and that takes its instances from art, scholarship, and the worst of the daily news; a voice which in this case is "sensitive and plucky, humorous and warm," to turn Friedenberg's characterization of Phineas from *A Separate Peace* on the man himself. But that voice, as Friedenberg demonstrated, is necessarily underwritten by a searching self-awareness and an unforgiving, acerbic wit. Without that, Edgar Z. Friedenberg could not so fearlessly have told his own story through the images of our times, though Cain has warned time and again that such troubling tales might not always be well received.

Notes

1 Edgar Z. Friedenberg, *Coming of Age in America: Growth and Acquiescence* (New York: Random House, 1963), 239.

2 Edgar Z. Friedenberg, "Children as Objects of Fear and Loathing," *Educational Studies* 10 (1979): 113.

3 Rebecca West, cited by Friedenberg, *Coming of Age*, 218.

4 Carl Nordstrom, Edgar Z. Friedenberg, and Hilary A. Gold, *Society's Children: A Study of Ressentiment in the Secondary School* (New York: Random House, 1967).

5 Edgar Z. Friedenberg, *The Vanishing Adolescent* (Boston: Beacon, 1959), 169.

6 Edgar Z. Friedenberg, "Law, Liberty, and Community Standards," *Canadian Journal of Sociology* 18 (1984): 210.

7 E.Z. Friedenberg, *The Disposal of Liberty and Other Industrial Wastes* (New York: Random House, 1975), xiv.

8 Friedenberg, *Coming of Age*, 249.

9 Friedenberg, "Children as Objects," 73.

10 Friedenberg, *Coming of Age*, 221.

11 "Society and the Therapeutic Function," in Edgar Z. Friedenberg, *The Dignity of Youth and Other Atavisms* (Boston: Beacon, 1965), 54.

12 Friedenberg, "Children as Objects," 71.

13 Edgar Z. Friedenberg, "Threading through an Intellectual Maze," *Review of Education* 8 (1982): 250.

14 Friedenberg, *Coming of Age*, 248.

15 Edgar Z. Friedenberg, "The Function of the School in Social Homeostasis," *Canadian Review of Sociology and Anthropology* 7 (1970): 14.

16 Friedenberg, *Vanishing Adolescent*, 23.

17 Friedenberg, *Coming of Age*, 199.

18 Ibid., 213.

19 Friedenberg, *Vanishing Adolescent*, 340.

20 Friedenberg, *Coming of Age*, 120, 116.

21 Ibid., 4.

22 Edgar Z. Friedenberg, "The Limits of Growth: Adolescence in Canada," *McGill Journal of Education* 15 (1980): 132.

23 Friedenberg, *Vanishing Adolescent*, 191.

24 Edgar Z. Friedenberg, "Hegemony and the Process of Schooling: A Second Look at the Hidden Curriculum," *Teacher Education* 17 (1982): 28.

25 Edgar Z. Friedenberg, "Deference to Authority: Education in Canada and the United States," in *Poverty, Power, and Authority in Education*, ed. Edgar B. Gumbert (Atlanta: Center for Cross-Cultural Education, College of Education, Georgia State University, 1981), 62.

26 Friedenberg, *Dignity of Youth*, 5.

27 Ibid., 6; original emphasis.

28 Ibid., 5.

29 Sandra Gilbert, "Feminist Criticism in the University: An Interview with Sandra Gilbert," interview by G. Graff, in *Criticism in the University*, ed. G. Graff and R. Gibbons (Evanston, IL: Northwestern University Press, 1985), 112.

30 Friedenberg, "Threading through an Intellectual Maze," 250.

Chapter 11

Up the Down Escalator

Reception

"So this excellent liquor of knowledge, whether it descend from divine inspiration, or spring from human sense, would soon perish and vanish to oblivion, if it were not preserved in . . . conferences." The words were beautifully inscribed on the invitation to the State University School of Education reception. They were attributed, Jay noticed with habitual attention to scholarly detail, to Francis Bacon, from his *Advancement of Learning*, 1605.

Along with the invitation, Jay was carrying a glassful of the reception's not-so-excellent liquor that she knew would cloud over whatever knowledge she'd garnered after a long day at the American Social Sciences in Education Association (ASSEA) conference. As she surveyed the shimmering curtains and glimmering chandeliers of the hotel's Grand Ballroom, she was hard-pressed to imagine what conferences Bacon managed to attend in the early 17th century. He didn't have a university to cover his expenses, after all. And hadn't the first association of scholars in England appeared only after Bacon died? Jay seemed to recall that the Royal Society had acknowledged his inspiration for—not least of all, perhaps—its conferences.[1]

Jay looked around to see that Jack Gianetto, one of her many conference nodding-acquaintances, was coming up to her, saying, as if they had already been well into a conversation, "It's really just another dead end." He looked rather dejected as he glanced around the hotel ballroom and took a sip of wine.

"You mean to say that you didn't like Cookman's presentation 'The New Capitalism and Education?'" Jay asked.

"Yeah, I saw you sitting ahead of me," Jack replied. "I mean, you've really got to wonder. Where do these sweeping critiques lead? Bang bang, capitalism takes a hit. Where can you go with it?" There was more than passing wonder and doubt in Jack's voice.

"Well, to conferences, certainly," she quipped, taking another forkful of the pesto-green tortellini and tomato-red fettuccine that she had just received from the chef who, decked out in a starchy white outfit complete with hat, was cooking over an open flame in a corner of the ballroom. The room was lightly peopled with just the sort of wine-glass-and-salad-plate groupings, like islands, that Jay and Jack formed.

"Sure, give the academic finger to the unnamed corporate suits with their backs turned," Jack said, eying her pasta, "but don't even ask where its going."

"What? You are not concerned with capitalism's impact on how teachers teach and students learn, and with our business of helping both do it all better?" Jay asked somewhat mockingly, as if the question had not been haunting her, not to mention quite a few of the 11,000 people attending the conference.

"But then tell me, how do you get out of this dead-end critique?" Jack asked a little distractedly, already looking about for another gathering to join, one that offered greater value than this meeting of relative equals.

"Well," Jay started, "you know you can always drive out of a cul-de-sac by just following the curve around and . . ."

"Hi there, Jack. What are you getting on about now?" Another wine-glass bearer had safely found himself an island, using Jack's nod of recognition as he walked by for his beachhead while giving the eye to Jay, whom he had just interrupted.

"Hi, Gary. We were just by to hear Cookman do New Capitalism. Gary, you know Jay?"

"Yeah, hi there, Jay. We met at the Michigan schmooze last year, I think. You were talking to Tim Goodly, that ol' book-a-year man," Gary said. Jay gave him a quizzical nod, indicating she was taking his word for it. The reference to Goodly's prolificacy reminded Jay of the publishers' displays at the conference, where once, in the early days, she'd been only too happy to place conference-discount orders on the likes of Goodly. Then there'd been the thrill of seeing her own first book on display there. And now, well, she mainly felt the weight of so many brand-new "relevant" titles popping up every year. But Gary was going on: "I was just meeting with the Fulbright people on overseas scholarships in a little sabbat-planning. So what's the problem this time, Jack?"

"Well, we're just saying . . ." Jack began.

"No, *you* were just saying, Jack, that the New Capitalism pitch, a.k.a. the Post-Fordism faddism, was just taking us down a street posted 'No Exit.' Right?" It was Jay's turn to repay the interruption.

"You had 'nough critique, Jack?"

"He may be losing his religion." Gary and Jay were suddenly on for a bit of tag-team two-on-one.

"Come on, you two. I'm just saying critique is too easy to do and walk away from." Jack was weakening and still doing room scans, watching for movement in the room like a hunter in a thicket. But then it was a room full of hunters and the wanna-be hunted. The exceptions sat at tables, presumably satisfied with their catches or exhausted with the hunt.

On glancing out over the crowd now swarming the ballroom, Jay couldn't help but be struck by how alive these faces were, compared to the tired, mildly interested ones that faced her during her sessions, flipping through their programs, a young one maybe making notes, another rising into a smile and a nod at her efforts at humor. Then there were the questions at the end of the talk, answered defensively but, eventually, gratefully absorbed. Perhaps a few would come up afterward, leaving their business cards so they might receive a copy of the paper, perhaps to cite or to use in class—and, on occasion, the real prize, an invitation to include the paper in an anthology. But still, it was all very subdued, compared to the buzzing energy of a ballroom of schmoozing, the gesturing and laughter, the hush-hush talk of deanships and endowed chairs, the hilarious anecdotes on grant competitions and book deals, the jockeying of self and students in some great horse race. Why, they were smoking, she realized, but without the irritation and intimacy of cigarettes.

"So, what was his case?" Gary posed, feeling pleased to be grouped and part of an obviously real discussion, having wandered around for the first few minutes without recognizing anyone at this reception.

"Well, the six sins of New Capitalism begin with 'possessive individualism,'" Jack said, glancing down at his notes on the back of the program, "which encourages a 'portable literacy,' an ability to pick up your reading skills and run to the next job. But doesn't that undermine all that capitalist talk of team building and community?"

"True enough," Gary chimed in.

"Yeah, and then," Jay took up the trail, "he denounced(how did he put it?('the commodification of work,'" dragging the phrase out to show the enormous burden it must carry. "He just doesn't like how we are forced to focus, not on the real value of what we do, but on its exchange value.

It can be so—how would Marx say?—*alienating*. Cookman's also feeling real grumpy about 'a narrowing of our future,' against, I don't know what, maybe young Marx's dream of being a fisherman in the morning, philosopher in the afternoon. Really, as if fishing all morning wasn't . . ."

"But what about how Cookman lashed into 'the domestication of critical thinking' and critical literacy?" Jack said, turning to his notes again. "There is only room for 'critique within the ends of the enterprise set on improving its stated goals.' And then, we must not forget the new obsession with technology, given over to shaving margins, improving work flow, global communications. There you have it; nothing new and still no way forward."

"You gotta admit that his swipe at postmodernism's obsession with 'the difference that doesn't make a difference' was clever enough to steal from him and use again and again," Jay said, only to see that Jack was setting sail, leaving with a slight wave of his hand and heading over to the cheese table, where his wandering eye had caught hold of someone of note, with whom he obviously wanted to catch up.

"But there's surely another angle to this," Jay said, turning to what was left of her island, Gary. "What Cookman named of New Capitalism is no less than what we are all about. It describes our work. Think about it for a minute. New Capitalism is no more than old public-sector meritocracy. The new knowledge economy began with us. Look around you, Gary: we're wearing our CVs on our sleeve; we're hunting out references for our next grant, our next move; we're trafficking in theories and studies."

"What are you on about?" Gary was obviously wondering if he shouldn't be making the leap to another group.

"Well, it just suddenly came to me, as we heard the seven—plus or minus one—sins of New-Cap: Those sins are no less than our own. It's the priest denouncing fornication with more than a little lip-smacking ardor. Start with an *easy* one, like the 'commodification' of an academic paper. It's strictly a matter of 'exchange' value. The paper's value depends on its being cited by another paper. Then that cite is exchanged, in turn, for career benefits, like promotions or research grants. But wait—it gets better, because the paper also establishes the currency of a certain portable literacy that can be shopped around, from job to job, grant to grant. It is surely as much a commodification of knowledge as any found in the knowledge business. The dead-endedness of critique shouldn't be troubling us as much as the deflection of our own sins onto others."

This was too much of a speech for a ballroom schmooze, and Jay knew it. She caught Gary peering over his wine glass and her shoulder, but she felt, too, that she may have turned this rant against Cookman into something. This was an idea, and she had come to this conference to gain ideas. Now, she wondered, a little tipsy with the chardonnay, what was she to do with it?

"Yeah," Gary said catching her eye again. "I heard Jack was looking at the sociology-of-ed posting at UCLA. Seems like he'd as soon traffic in the exchange value of your own domesticated literacy." Gary's citing of her phrase was enough to make Jay think that her speech wasn't going to waste, like the artfully arranged cheese drying out on the table in the center of the ballroom.

"Gee, I was thinking about that UCLA post myself, New-Cap sinner that I am." They were ready for disengagement, and Jay held up her empty plate for leverage.

"You given your paper yet?"

"Yeah, you missed it. I'll see you later, Gary."[2]

But at that moment, Jack was swinging back their way with Alice White in tow, the distinguished doyen who undoubtedly stood among the Famous Faces at this conference. She had made her name over three decades, championing the ever resilient powers of literature to help students find what is human and humane in us all.

"Have you met Jay before, Alice?" Jack asked, emphasizing his familiarity with Alice, Jay couldn't help feeling, without bothering to ask Jay if she knew Alice.

"Yes, I know Jay." Alice said, turning to Jay and looking at her from under a big black hat that shielded her age from the glare of the chandelier and fluorescent light. "You're famous, yes, of course. She is famous, you know," Alice said to Jack, catching everyone aback, as was Alice's way. Jay suddenly felt the flush of fame upon her. Alice smiled, showing her own pleasure at bestowing little gifts like this on people, gifts she knew were unlikely to be forgotten.

Yet as Jay fumbled in search of something to say, weakly offering, "And I've always appreciated your support, Alice," referring to the fellowship that Alice had openly backed her on some years ago. Jay noticed, however, that Alice was no longer looking at her but was turning to solicitous Jack and commenting that there really was so little going on this year at the conference. Jay realized, too, that this little was part of the little that goes on, even as she tried twice more to jump into the conversation that Alice was holding with Jack, before the two of them moved on to be received by another of the islands in the Grand Ballroom.

Breakfast

The next morning, halfway into her all-too-short stroll in the sunshine through the cityscape from her hotel to the conference center, Jay stopped for a bagel and coffee only to find herself, a stranger in a strange city, called by name by a couple of her colleagues from her university. She realized, as she sat down with them and peeled the lid back on her too-hot coffee, that she hadn't met with them, outside of the formal setting of departmental meetings, well, ever, at least until now.

"We're just gossiping about the Co-Vis project," Karen said, bringing Jay into the conversation. "You know it, Jay? Stands for 'Collaborative Visualization' in science education. It's all about science's visual representations of knowledge. You know, graphic science, hard-core, explicit science. A group at Northwestern got something like $20 million to help students in 50 schools do science with the sort of pictures that scientists use, and other nifty computer visualizations around weather and climate."

"Amazing money."

Karen just raised her eyebrows and nodded. "Yesterday, they did a great session, really, on the partnerships they formed with the schools, but you have to wonder, and not just at the buckets of money it takes to get something like this up and running. I wonder if anyone questions this educational ideal of getting kids to simulate on computers what a very small but privileged segment of the population does for a living."

"You know, Karen, it has occurred to me that you may not be the Great Friend of Science that you are supposed to be, given that you teach science teachers to teach science."

"The critic is the necessary friend," Karen responded with a knowing smile.

"You go to that Co-Vis session, Richard?" Jay asked. "You're the senior scholar here. You surely know just what it takes to make a difference."

"No, I didn't, and you know what's odd?" Richard asked in his thoughtful senior way. "I've ended up mainly going to our colleagues' sessions. That's me being collegial, right? Still, it seems a strange way (I mean, to fly across the country to a big hotel (to catch up on what someone down the hall is doing. The last one I saw, for example, was on Terry's running of the teacher-education doctoral seminar presented by our students, who did a great job, by the way."

"You're right. It's more than a little helpful in catching up with people otherwise always on the fly. In fact, I was going to ask you," Jay said to Ralph, who was working on his bagel, "if you're still doing the government's new school-to-work transition program."

"Sure am. We've got a government contract to evaluate it."

"Well, we're trying to get the government to consider our collaborative work-space Web site into that program. It just struck me sitting here that, hey, your name would be perfect to build into the proposal. You are on good terms with, say, John Gore and his team of happy 'crats at the Education Office?"

"I can't think why not. We deliver the good word on time, and they neatly shelve it on the good shelf of unread reports."

"Well, would you consider being cited as, say, a consultant to our project? We'd even carve out a research angle for you, if you'd like."

"Always tempting. But, no, save the angle. I got enough going on. But cite me, and maybe I could help in some way. E-mail me on it."

"All right. That pays for breakfast. Gotta run. But we've just got to find a coffee shop a little closer to our offices than this corner in Chicago. See you back on the farm, perhaps."

Keynote

The speaker walks to the podium and thanks Jay for her "warm introduction," which referred back to a time when they had both taught elementary school in the same province years ago, in a hasn't-at-least-one-of-us-come-a-long-way theme. The speaker then begins his address by half apologizing for his plan to "stay with his text," that is, to read to us "The Post-Psychologic: Catastrophic Cognitivism for Global Minds," rather than speak to us about it. Jay can't help but inwardly sigh at his comment, as so many of the talks at the conference open with perfunctory apologies for a reading of the paper. What is about to be read is not a story that begs for reading aloud, like *A Child's Christmas in Wales*, and the one at the podium is not a Dylan Thomas.

In the beginning was the word, Jay thinks to herself as the reading begins, and it was spoken, resoundingly, and then it was written down to keep a record of what had been said, and written down again until finally the spoken word was seen to take its weight from what had been written.[3] The conference is caught between the sociable and the professional, between the distributed authority of print and the amplified presence of speech. It brings together people who work out their research on paper to present in person. In this case, the presenters are educators who, having devoted their working lives to studying teaching, are often quick to condemn and seldom practice the lecture. Without much experience at fixing an audience with a dynamic lecture, they end up reading a "paper" to a roomful of readers for 20 minutes or, in the case of a keynote, 50 minutes.

In exchange, members of the audience are allowed a few minutes to ask questions, which is the moment when the spoken word holds the floor, as the reader deflects speakers' attempts to reform the failings of writer and text.

But as Jay listens, this speaker-reader is compelled to offer a second apology, this time for reading only a part of his paper. Tired habits offer telling moments, Jay realizes. The speaker-reader is reasserting the paper's ultimate authority as the natural and complete unit of knowledge. The transmission of knowledge will be incomplete, for the whole of this knowing work cannot be given in this forum. Yet is the whole essay, in its length at least, the result of what can be borne in a single reading? Jay wonders at how the form fits so many different sorts of knowledge so well, whether one is examining a particular reader's comprehension strategies or the comparative results of the International Mathematics and Science Assessment; whether one is considering the savagery of Caliban in *The Tempest* or a theory of special relativity, as the 26-year-old Albert Einstein did in 1905 with a paper that rewrote the book on physics, which he found time to compose while working in the Patent Office in Bern. Is the essay the codevelopment of the polished lecture and the studied journal article?[4]

Jay has had no time for speculating on the history of these forms, having been asked at the last minute to orchestrate a response to today's talk. Yet, on applying herself to the speaker's steady, slightly impassioned flow of words, she is finding it nearly impossible to make coherent notes, as she seeks to capture the citable phrase, wondering if she yet has the key idea of the work. This is not how she is used to responding critically to a work, and she is suddenly unsure how to anchor herself without a fixed text to stand upon.

Trying to catch the speaker's main points and hold them as they go haltingly by, Jay feels like a bear trying to snag great leaping salmon heading upstream. It's a day's work in paw-freezing water to grab and hold a good one. Jay writes down a few phrases on the invisibility of cognition, on bearing the consequences of cognition as eggheads, and on daring to choose against cognition, but she can see that she's out of practice as a note taker. Her mind drifts off, wondering whether more of the audience have had their interest in the speaker's work awakened or quenched. Why are they here? she wonders. Is it like attending a concert, feeling the exhilaration of those who create the music as it is meant to be heard? When this audience later picks up one of the speaker's many books, will that book read that much more easily, or make that much more sense, because of this familiarity?

The structure of the talk does gradually become clear to Jay, and the speaker does step out of the written text at one point, to say that "the search for a greater cognitive order is one of this talk's themes." At another point, the speaker looks up and says, "Let me summarize Appadurai's argument for you. Basically, what he says is . . ." Jay feels herself noticeably sit up at this heightened moment in the transfer of knowledge. Here the speaker is offering the condensed version, the pure idea, of another's work. He is doing for Appadurai what Jay was trying so hard to do for him, pulling out, with preapproval, the valuable idea. She finds herself making notes more often when the speaker is quoting others. She ends up seeing how his theme on globalization bridges with her own work, so she now has a place to stand in the paper's flow. She feels herself relax.

From where she is sitting, at the front of the room facing the audience with the speaker, Jay can see that people are earnestly listening. Although one man appeared to be snoozing, sitting with his eyes closed, it was only for a moment. Others have their heads slightly tilted toward the speaker like attentive dogs. One uses her hand to hold her head; another has his fingers to his lips. Arms are crossed. One or two make notes. But who can guess what thoughts they are lost in—the speaker's or their own—amid this river of words, delivered without pause in a near rush to completion, like a musical performance? The hotel ballroom has been transformed into a theater of the scholarly paper, the audience sitting as quietly as if they were together at the library reading their way through the same journal article. The speaker looks up again, and—in relation to what point, Jay cannot say—lets it be known that he has given this talk in Shanghai and Budapest. Perhaps he has sensed a flagging of attention, a momentary loss of this traveling theory's stature. Jay makes a mental note not to stop preparing fresh papers for each time she speaks.

Having figured out a line of response, she watches the delivery style of the speaker. It amounts to a regular sweeping of the hair from his forehead, a clinging to the tissue that keeps an unfortunately runny nose at bay, and a shifting from foot to foot. Certainly, he is able to provoke a ripple of laughter at times with a little deadpan sarcasm directed at the ideas of yesteryear, and he does hold the audience in the sway of his often alliterative running together of ideas along the lines of "the catastrophic confluence of the Cartesian *cogito*." Still, as theater, it lacks even the sentimental and cathartic resolution that many in this audience felt as the airplane movie ended on their way here. Nevertheless, it does add, more or less well than the movie did, to the audience's particular body of knowledge and their experience of the knowledgeable, and thus it may help them in their work as professors. Jay, worrying that her thoughts are running to an envious green, has to allow that the speaker's ideas might also help encourage or focus an audience member's research. Still, is it fair to ask how many in the room will make some specific *use* of what they have traveled so far to hear? At the very least, they have each had a glimpse of what it means to achieve a certain stature in one's work.

There are, after all, few spots in this massive conference that take advantage of the assembled audience to explore the language's grand oral tradition of ritual and theater. The spoken word, whether delivered from a podium, pulpit, stage, bench, altar, graveside, chair, or throne, has always had the resounding power to move the world, whether the word is read aloud, memorized, or made up on the spot. The conference, for all that is spoken in its name, is more often about something beyond the heralded performance of an artist before an audience. For it is everywhere the steady, if pedestrian, trafficking of ideas and careers, in a marketplace festival that offers much performance, if too little theater.

Escalator

"Hey there, Jay, how's the conference going?" It was Earl Decaffey, whom she seemed to run into just like this every year, riding down the escalator. They had taught together one summer at North Dakota, when they were both just starting in the business. Jay was standing at the base of the escalator that connected the ballrooms and meeting rooms, flipping through the conference program, in the great conference ritual constantly performed in hallways and during presentations. The escalator really captures, she'd been thinking, the conference's play in passing knowledge; one catches the name tags of the famous, as well as of forgotten friends, all riding up as one rides down. The conference was all about such ups and downs in the elevation and deflation of personal recognition and connection. Jay was trying to locate the room for what would be, for her, the final session of the conference.

As Earl got off the escalator and approached Jay, he introduced Doug, a colleague of Earl's, and Saroj, a graduate student, who were both following behind him.

"Well, Saroj, what about you? This is your first ASSEA. How're you finding it?" Jay asked.

"It's just so many people, really. But you know, after my talk, Michael Heuba came up to me and said he liked my paper (do you know him? He's done whole books on dyslexia (and he said that maybe we could collaborate together on something. That was like such a big moment for me. Right? Even the chair for my session came up to me after it was over and said others had praised my paper to him. I was awfully nervous, but it was worth it. You wanna bet I'm coming back."[5]

"That's what it should be all about, Saroj. That intensification of motive. I forget sometimes. How 'bout you, Earl?"

"Well," Earl offered the group, "I can say that I found the famous Stanley Bunker has finally gained a sense of humor, even if he hasn't changed his line in 17 years, and Michelle Rose's talk was very thoughtful. Although I'm not sure what to make of it, really, but I found her a fascinating presenter. Maybe, I'm just studying different manners of being famous, but for what, you may well wonder. I had this great breakfast meeting for three hours with Garavetz. It left me buzzing, I mean, the way he has of moving in on so many things."

"As for me," Doug jumped in, "it was a great chance to see what's going on in program evaluation. I've got this World Bank contract to do one in Thailand, and it's been years since I've done one, so I really wanted to, really needed to, get a general feel for where the field is going."

"That's handy, 'cause the best of those talks won't be published for a year, maybe more, at the rate most journals teeter along," Jay offered.

"As it turns out, the gurus that I had come to see all gathered in one place simply spoke off the top of their heads, but I guess that's as valuable as anything."

"Seeing them gathered or hearing them prate?" Jay couldn't resist asking.

"Now, now, there's something to hearing them simply speak out of their experience. And you never know when you'll be influenced by what I heard, or better yet, misheard from that illustrious panel. You take in so much, and then out of that rich, fetid compost comes . . ."

"You were in Smiley's session, Earl," Jay interrupted. "Did he say his scathing paper on declining support for research in education was available on the Web?"

"Yeah, wasn't it at www.no.time.to.be.com? Soon as he said that, I began drifting off, though it has stuff I need for my paper."

"Well, I'm off to see my editor at Hasties for my allotted dinner. Say, how's your latest book doing, Jay?"

"Gee, I couldn't do better than a power breakfast with my publisher. Looks like I'm doomed for the remainder bin already. I'd better head off to my final session."

"Remember, there's to be no "final sessions" in this business. The pursuit just goes on and on, luckily for us. See you 'round."

"Yeah, next year, probably. San Diego, isn't it?"

"Wherever..."

Notes

1 If elsewhere I have tried to plumb the architecture of knowledge in scriptorium and library, in *If Only We Knew* (New York: Routledge, 2000), here I dwell within the towering glitter of the architecturally indistinguishable chains of the Hilton, Hyatt, Sheraton, and Westin, each occupying their own city block in the core of the major metropolises. After all, there is no greater gathering point, no larger concentration of living knowledge in any one subject at any one time, than is to be found in any given week scattered throughout the lobbies, meeting rooms, ballrooms, hotel rooms, restaurants, bars, and washrooms of these megalithic hotels. For professionals in almost every field, the working holiday of the annual convention-hotel conference fits into the calendar with all of the seasonal weight of Christmas and Easter. They are modern-day pilgrimages, as David Lodge has it in his scurrilous novel *Small World: An Academic Romance* (New York: Macmillan, 1994, p. 1), on academic foibles and vanities: "When April with its sweet showers has pierced the drought of March to root . . . then, as poet Geoffrey Chaucer observed many years ago, folks long to go on pilgrimages. Only these days, professional people call them conferences." These chains of conference hotels have become as familiar to this generation of professionals as their grandmothers' homes were to them when they were growing up or as the library was to them when they were graduate students. The convention hotel constitutes a college life of upgraded dorms, complete with a library of live presentations and furnished with leather sofas and cozy bars, marbled washrooms and expense-account restaurants—the sheer perkiness of the intellectual high life. For those among the public who harbor doubts about the value of academic work, these conferences prove easy pickings. The press has more than once had a field day, during the slow-news Christmas season, with the Modern Language Association (MLA) conference, perhaps most famously around the incident of the masturbating-Jane-Austen paper of a few year ago. This conference has had its dare-to-be-scandalous titles, with such sessions as "Queer as Fuck? Queer Pedagogy, Educational Practice, and Lesbian and Gay Youth," but even then, the focus on "pedagogy" and "practice" in educating the young can give the outrageous presentation a relevance that distinguishes it from just getting on about a work of literature. The American Social Sciences in Education Association (ASSEA) conference, however, represents the hope of educational research, setting it apart from conferences devoted, say, to improving the study of literature. Such a massive gathering of educational researchers seems an encouraging event. Think of the combined brain power and accumulated wisdom passing through those hotel lobbies. Think of what it might mean if these people actually taught school, as many of them once did, knowing what they do of education now.

2 What the card catalog is to the library, in trying to bring order and access to users, the program guide is to the conference. The guide for the annual meeting of the ASSEA, which represents my professional interests in the social sciences, is the size of a phone book for a small city (as David Lodge notes for the MLA conference), with its listing in one case of "1,000 paper and symposia sessions, training

activities, invited presentations, state-of-the-art addresses, graduate student seminars, dialogues, poster sessions, roundtable discussions, networking opportunities, and receptions." Surely, you could build an entire world out of such a gathering of knowledge. How much did God know, after all, when he assembled the world in such a way that we are now able to house, feed, and water this many scholars in so few hotels? How could he not benefit from our tuning into this generation of knowledge? The conference papers run the gamut from the widescale analysis of SAT scores edging slightly upward to a solitary researcher's moment of doubt. The conference represents the best of the year's harvest, after a peer-review winnowing of two-page abstracts submitted nine months earlier. And for the presentation, the idea is to offer an overview of the paper while it is still in preparation, so that the audience can help further your formulation of the ideas. This is a harvest long before the final separating of the wheat from the chaff. Here you can catch the wave of new ideas months, if not years, before they find their way into publication. But there is still a lot of straw.

At any given time, there can be 75 sessions to chose from at a conference such as this, most of them made up of three to five loosely connected papers that are each allotted 15 to 25 minutes for presentation, which is enough time, perhaps, to deliver the highlights of what is typically a paper that would take 40 minutes to read aloud. Yet there is no doubting that each 90-minute slot seems to hold the answer to many pressing questions, as this 1997 program excerpt from an American Educational Research Association conference illustrates:

Evaluating Alternative Educational Programs (Division 21) 2:15–3:45—Sheraton, Columbus A, Level 3
CHAIR Steve Henry, Topeka Public Schools
1. *An Empirical Assessment of Self-Esteem Enhancement in A CHALLENGE Service-Learning Program.* Jianjun Wang, Betty Greathouse, CSU, Bakersfield; Veronica M. Falcinella, Delano USD
2. *Exploring Multidimensional Evaluation and Assessment Strategies for Service-Learning Programs.* Shelley H. Billig, Nancy P. Kraft, RMC Research Corporation
3. *Investigating the Effects of Participation in an Alternative Secondary School on At-Risk Students.* Karen E. Duhon, Stephanie L. Knight, Texas A&M University
Keeping Kids in High School: Do Alternative High School Programs Help? Mark R. Dynarski, Philip Gleason, Ann Rangarajan, Robert Wood, Mathematica Policy Research
4. *At-Risk Students Attending Second-Chance School Choice Programs: Measuring Performance in Desired Outcome Domains.* Cheryl Lange, Camilla Lehr, University of Minnesota
DISCUSSANT George Olson, Appalachian State University.

Given the number of concurrent sessions much like this one, sandwiched from 8:00 in the morning to 8:00 at night, how does one best swim the torrent? What exactly is the economy of scale here? You can pursue one of the seven conference themes, or choose among the 100 special-interest groups, from "Accelerated Schools" and "Action Research" to "Wholistic Education" and "Writing." Or you can turn to the index of the program guide and find 50 sessions on collaboration,

65 on teachers' professional development, and 125 on school reform. How do these papers, this work, these people relate? What can one afford not to be interested in? A common approach is to attend sessions with paper titles that sound like those you might have written yourself; another is to attend sessions with the best-known names to see what the fuss is about. Rushing between sessions and across hotels, one has to wonder how so many educational problems manage to survive such concentrated attention only to appear on the program of scourges addressed the following year. Yet the waves of scholars moving between sessions are acting out a ballet of information explosion and fragmentation.

3 When Walter Ong reflects on how the movement from oral to literate culture amounts to a "technologizing of the word," he speaks of the danger and hope for that development: "Fortunately, literacy, though it consumes its own antecedents and, unless it is carefully monitored, even destroys their memory, is also infinitely adaptable. It can restore their memory, too." *Orality and Literacy: The Technologizing of the Word* (London: Methuen, 1982), 15. He holds that "oral cultures indeed produce powerful and beautiful verbal performances of high artistic and human worth, which are no longer even possible once writing has taken possession of the psyche" (14). I'm tempted to counter with Dylan Thomas's recorded performance of *A Child's Christmas in Wales*. Reading the text in his inexpert way not only affirms what Foucault describes as the "absolute privilege on the part of writing" that began in the Renaissance but also ensures that no one mistakes the fact that "the sounds made by voices provide no more than a transitory and precarious translation" of the written word. Michel Foucault, *The Order of Things: An Archeology of the Human Sciences* (New York: Vintage, 1970), 38.

4 The journal article was initially a form of correspondence among scholarly types, an extension of the common letter for distribution among subscribers of learned societies, filled with self-contained works addressed to no one, except through passing reference to pervious works. The first learned journal, the vastly interdisciplinary *Journal des sçavans,* appeared in 1665 in France, followed by the *Philosophical Transactions* in Britain. The editor of the French journal sought to create a structure for the flow of correspondence within what he saw as a republic of letters. See J. C. Guédon, "Electronic Academic Journals: From Disciplines to Seminars," in *Computer Networking and Scholarly Communication in the 21st Century,* ed. Teresa M. Harrison and Timothy Stephen (Albany: State University of New York Press, 1996), 335–350.

5 Richard Wunderli writes, in *Peasant Fires: The Drummer of Nicklashausen* (Bloomington: Indiana University Press, 1992), 60: "Pilgrimage sites indeed were holy places, and they all had one thing in common: they were the site of a past miracle which could recur at any moment. At a pilgrimage shrine a breach had opened in the veil that separates heaven and earth, a tear in the fabric that would not be closed. It was as if a heavenly ray—here we must imagine, with medieval artists, a ray breaking through clouds—were shining from heaven on a specific earthly location. Anybody who entered the holy spotlight partook directly of the miraculous, for the light was filled with the unseen presence of a saint, or Christ, or the Virgin."

Chapter 12

The Parker Vacumatic and the Diaspora

Having struck up a friendship in Calgary a few years before, Peter Chin and I met up again in Vancouver where I was teaching and he had come to do his doctorate. We soon found our talk turning to race in a way it hadn't before. It had struck me, for example, that Vancouver's vibrant yet sometimes troubled cosmopolitanism, perched as it is on the West Coast's dissolving boundary between East and West, might be a test site for the supranational and racial identities of a Pacific future. Peter was grappling with the far more personal question of how this city seemed intent on teaching him his own placelessness, his lack of the city's sense of his coming-from-China. Here, he was Chinese again, in a way he had not been growing up in the prairie city of Calgary. Nationality and race were confounded in what seemed even the most innocent of conversations in this city, which left us wondering if this racial awareness represented an effort by whites to restake their claim to this country.

Our discussions set me to thinking about my own roots, and I was left wondering how it was that only a generation ago, Jews had also constituted an alien race for this nation, no less than for most of the rest of the world, a racial status that has now all but evaporated. It became clear that Peter and I were at decidedly different points in a global process of diaspora. Between the two of us, it has proved simpler for me to go first in writing out a version of the displacements that differentiate and link our histories in what, for our ancestors, was to have been the New World. This piece is a temporary measure against the otherwise numbing uncertainty of histories that can only be approximated and geographies shaped by the imagination. The artifacts that I have assembled here—the friendship, a Parker pen, the names, journeys, and texts—are read for their themes of identity that extend beyond our own stories, themes of identity that we have come to realize go largely unspoken in the schools with which we work, although students there are immersed in living out similar histories, another generation along.

Among the many forms identity themes can take, Anthony Walton gives a particularly eloquent expression to how race figures in the ambivalence of assimilation for African Americans: "I have, for most of my adult life, wondered what, exactly, is the stain we black Americans carry, what is it about our mere presence, our mere existence that can inflame such passion, embroil the nation in such histrionics for so long a time?" (1993, p. 255). This is not, of course, just an adult's question. It is something the young also wonder about, beginning with that first innocence-shattering moment when they realize the stain is theirs to carry. It is thus a question that educators owe it to the young to at least begin addressing as part of their schooling. For Walton, the answer lies in teaching black history, as it can help students understand "what, exactly, it means to be black, to occupy this mythological space in the nation's imagination" (p. 259). For such a profound question, the answers are going to come in many shapes, and none of them will guarantee an end to the passion and histrionics.

Nonetheless, the question needs to be faced, I would argue, as part of a responsible education. At this point, the schools are finding answers through initiatives in multicultural and non-Eurocentric curriculums, through feminist perspectives and antiracist programs. Yet multicultural programs, for example, have at times made a mystery of "race" by using it as if it were a natural, God-given category. Even as they teach about other cultures, they do little to assist the young, and the not-so-young, in answering the question of why race continues to play such a large role in the formation of identity. My contribution to these measures is to argue for a new reckoning of "race," "nation," and "culture" that challenges the certainties of meaning typically attributed to these categories. I have sought to retrace with teachers and students the steps that have been taken, above all in the academic disciplines, to build up and fill out these pervasive ideas of who we are (J. Willinsky, 1998).

Rethinking what the schools have invested in and have meant by these concepts has been the work of a larger project, of which this chapter is but one rather odd part. The utopian imperative that lies at the core of every curriculum is, in this case, driven by a desire to comprehend not any particular representation of humankind but how the divisions have been constituted, especially through the noble contribution of the arts and sciences over the last few centuries, which educators would seem to have a special responsibility in critically scrutinizing. This imperative seeks to create a more open space in the classroom for the increasingly common sense of feeling out of place in this nation, as a means of rethinking the place of national identity. It asks that we hold up a mirror to the humanist gaze, the making strange, that can set off another—or oneself—as Other. The call for a reflexive curriculum means having students learn to carefully attend to the school's own history of dividing the world.

This chapter's approach to the enigma is rather different. It is more of an experiment in identity work, a demonstration of how naming the parallels between otherwise distinct lives can lead to an extended curriculum vitae. It toys with the always-present challenge of what is worth learning and teaching at this point in the world, by trying to find the meeting of personal and public lives, the connecting of self and Other. The specific instance that I want to run with here, against the learned distancing of the oriental in the West, is the identities represented in the lives of two friends, as I am a Jew and Peter is a Chinese or, in our sometimes ill-tempered language, a "Chinaman" (a designation that in the 20th century was glossed as "John Chinaman" [Ward, 1990]). The lessons here, then, are about naming and being named, about the processes of identification as particular acts of power.

The parallels between Peter's and my histories, around ways of naming, actually opened for me through a Parker Vacumatic fountain pen that Peter gave to me as a gift from the assortment that his father had brought with him to Canada from Hong Kong a quarter century ago and had handed on to Peter. After using the pen that he had given me for some time, as these identity themes played around in my head, I began to realize how, in more than one of its features, the pen signified the parallel journeys of displacement and diaspora that brought us to Vancouver. The pen appeared capable, with a little imaginative coaxing, of tracing out the well-marked trails across the map of modern history, filling in the intersecting paths where they might not otherwise appear to exist.

Our histories are radically different, at one level, given the centuries-old placelessness enjoyed and suffered by the Jewish people and the immense historical locality of the walled-in Chinese dynasties, which occupied the middle kingdom in an expanding but, compared to other empires, contained and insular universe. Our two histories are neither of the colonizers nor of the colonized in the great age of European imperialism. Yet the Chinese and the Jews have suffered no less the scourge of racism that has so often accompanied imperialist expansion. Even if, as Peter was coming to consider his race again in Vancouver, I was thinking about how race had almost disappeared for Jews only a few decades before, it is nevertheless true that Jews have been repeatedly named an alien race by a good number of nations. Now, it seems that the Jewish people have come to whiteness, with our ethnicity an option, like wearing a yarmulke in public.

This theme of cast-off and found races—in how we are identified in the construction and deconstruction of difference—is part of finding the Other in oneself or, as Julia Kristeva names it in *Nations without Nationalism,* "among the foreigners that we all are (within ourselves and in relation to others)" (1993, p. 47). This return to how we are all variously constituted across our different histories, without a fixed center or with a series of centers and points of identification, seems a proper project for these transnational times. It becomes a way of rereading the great stories of civilizations and peoples, nations and races that are so often told with an emphasis on essential differences. It offers a way to take hold of the threads that link human lives across such boundaries, as one means of unraveling the telling of these histories and other curricula that simply do not serve everyone equally well.

I should also say at the outset that in addressing race through Jewish and Chinese turns, I can feel myself skirting the heart of the issue, standing apart from the point where it is most sorely felt on this continent, between whites and blacks. But the lives of Jews and, more recently, those of Asian descent are caught up in that larger question. It is a time to talk about race, even as a genuine sense of discouragement has entered African American discussions of race. So we find, among many others, John Hope Franklin, the distinguished historian of the American Civil War and Reconstruction, speaking of how current race relations in the United States have reached an abysmal level as a result of neoconservative measures that have done little but deepen "the color line" (1993). That deepening of the line was felt through the 1990s, from the Crown Heights conflagration between Jews and African Americans to the Los Angeles riots involving Asians, Jews, and African Americans. In 1993, pointing to the Los Angeles uprising as an instance, Phoebe Eng, publisher of *A. Magazine,* noted how the Asian ascription of a "model minority" is used to further divide: "Asians are, as the Jewish population was, . . . pitted against other minority groups" (cited by Lee, 1993). Education's special challenge is to provide an understanding of how that line has come to be drawn—how races have come to be named and how those names are used—as well as to encourage forms of life that begin to obviate those lines.

I have also been made conscious, as part of this racial history, that I am writing this piece at a university that occupies Musqueam land, land which this First Nations people has yet to cede to the Canadian government through treaty. Indeed, various branches of that government have fought against recognizing those sovereign rights in the courts. The diaspora often entails this doubling up, this displacement of yet another people.

It is through these localized senses of race and diaspora that I want to follow my friendship with Peter Chin, knowing that it is a privileged and marked instance of how race has been defined, refined, and redefined through the traumatic struggles of the last few centuries, just as a river changes its course most radically after the big storms, the torrential downpours. It is a search, in this deliberately postcolonial way, for what counts as "here" and "there," who "we" are and who "they" are, after the cold war, after the ages of discovery and empire, and into the age of transnationals, multinationals, and other worldly economic interests. It seems possible to pause over how the globe has come to be so effectively underwritten by differences of race, culture, and nation. The first step is to examine how these differentiating gazes were constituted in the first place, as the Chinese people were placed, in the white imagination, at the ends of the earth and the Jews were said to be its rootless interlopers. The story of these displacements can be told through my modest Parker Vacumatic pen as easily as through any other artifact, in representing a prevailing geography of the imagination that is in the process of being redrawn.

If I begin with the question of how I am situated in this world, I find that China is often part of the answer. China is, I learned long ago, the other side of the world. In the geography of the Western imagination, "the Chinese" are placed as far as earthly possible from the center (of the curriculum), even when those I think of as Chinese are here, living beside me. The Chinese have been cast in the West as the other side of humanity's coin. This is what the graffiti means here on newspaper boxes when it cruelly reads, "Chinks go home." This place could not be "their" home, as it is "ours." They need to "go" because they are clearly so far from their home. Even this helps me know that my place, as non-Chinese, is on this side of the coin—heads I win.

Peter must have learned these lessons too, growing up in Calgary, and it is hard to imagine unlearning them and ever being able to see China in some other way. To know the devices of such distancing is to know in an additional sense what "Chinese" means. It is this imagined and projected distance between peoples which I have sought to understand (1998), insofar as it has been produced not by virulent racists but by the intellectual arm of the Western imperium that has for centuries defined distances, staked out borders, and mapped the natural and human boundaries that are seen to separate peoples, cultures, and races, all in ways implicated at times in our work as educators.

This chapter's pursuit of the connections that come of the Parker pen are intended to make these projected distances less daunting. Jewish contact with the Chinese reaches far into history, as does the presence of Chinese Jews (underscoring that we need to learn how our categories are fragile conveniences). One of the early sources on this confluence is the legendary and perhaps mythical Marco Polo, who has held the honor of being, along with Christopher Columbus, among the most exciting of schoolbook explorers for young students. Polo carried us to the wonders of the East, personifying the European gaze, filled with a sense of adventure, wonder, and opportunity as he peered out at the rest of the world. In this, Polo was an explorer of Otherness. For him, as for much of Europe, the Jews were the original source of a human difference, which his Mongolian experience simply extended. So I try to imagine his surprise, or surprising lack of it, in the 13th century on coming across Jews in the court of Kublai Khan. Presumably these were not metaphorical Jews (as in the saying "the Irish are the Jews of Europe") but literal ones who, by their own accounts, had reached "Chin," as Polo first identified the land. Polo noted the Jews' presence in a minor aside about the accomplished Mongolian emperor of China:

> And after the Great Kaan had conquered Nayan, as you have heard, it came to pass that the different kinds of people who were present, Saracens and Idolaters and Jews, and many others that believed not in God, did gibe those that were Christian because of the cross that Nayan had borne on his standard, and that so grievously that there was no bearing it. (Yule, 1871, p. 307)

The 19th-century editor of Polo's journals, Col. Henry Yule, notes that although this is "the [work's] only allusions to Jews in China," there is a "Chinese-Jewish Inscription" from 1511 that refers to Judaism entering China during the Han Dynasty (200 B.C.E. to 226 C.E.), with perhaps the first synagogue built in 1164 C.E. at Pien (p. 309).

The Jews first reached China through the long journey of the Diaspora, following King Nebuchadrezzar's destruction of the Temple in 586 B.C.E. Pockets of Jews found their way into different parts of Europe, Asia, and Africa in a global sense of dispersion, not in acts of exploring, trading, or touring but in exile, with no aim other than finding a place to be, as if they had discovered that without a homeland there was no longer a land that was foreign to them. Yet they were, by definition, different, not one or indigenous with the land in which they resided. Daniel Boyarin and Jonathan Boyarin, whose thesis on the Jewish Diaspora I want to return to later, note how in medieval Europe "the place of difference increasingly becomes the Jewish place, and the Jews become the very sign of discord and disorder in the Christian polity" (1993, p. 697). The difference would gradually become codified by Western science as race, growing out of the19th-century early anthropology of racial differences. In his analysis of the Jewish body as a racial source of color, disease, and ugliness in that era, Sander Gilman reports that "the general consensus of the ethnological literature . . . was that the Jews were 'black' or, at least, 'swarthy'" (1991, p. 171). The Jew was an internal source of difference for the West, a difference close at hand, whereas China, when Marco Polo first opened it up, represented a new, fascinating source of colored Otherness, safely exoticized and operating outside any internal threats of discord and disease. The Jews and the Chinese, then, even in their bodies of difference, were at opposite ends of this colored spectrum. They were worlds apart, yet together in that apartness.

So it happened that during the Second World War, 18,000 Jews were able to flee Austria, Germany, and Poland by heading east, thanks in large measure to the visas issued by Feng Shan Ho, a Chinese consul in Vienna. The diaspora again led to China, if this time on the promise of emigration to America. Here their desperate journey came to a temporary end, as visas for America and Canada were not forthcoming. (The Americans feared, it seems, that these Jewish refugees were Communists. Certainly some had relatives in the Soviet Union.) China proved a home of convenience, a refuge and unexpected sanctuary. A number of Eastern European rabbis and their students managed to reestablish the vanquished yeshivas in the cities along the coast of the China Sea. They and Jewish organizations in both the United States and Canada petitioned the Canadian government for visas. In a rare instance of successful lobbying and application, it was announced that two seminaries, with some 300 members, would be accepted. Yet the final release of the forms was so deferred that half the complement, staying back to celebrate the High Holy Days in 1941, was stranded in the port of Shanghai by the outbreak of war with Japan.

The makeshift yeshivas assembled in Shanghai by the hapless rabbis and their bewildered students who then found themselves detained there exemplified the always unsettling instability of the diaspora. Is there nowhere in the world for us now? they must have thought as Japanese soldiers secured the gates of the detention camps. Has this centuries-old diaspora finally exhausted the entirety of the globe? It was a better fate by far than that faced by Jews who remained in Poland, yet a fate still linked to racial definitions in Canada at the highest levels.

In their devastating history of Jewish immigration to Canada between 1933 and 1948, *None Is Too Many*, Irving Abella and Harold Troper mount a discouragingly convincing case that this country had one of the worst records among "refugee-receiving states" (1986, p. xxii). Policies common to the Allies seriously compounded the fate of European Jewry. Abella and Troper make it clear that, given the policies and practices of this country at the time, the number of Jewish refugees who were rescued was pitifully small, when all that stood between the Nazi death camps and a new life in Canada was a visa. When I asked my mother about this chapter in our family's history in Canada, she was quick to tell me the names of the two Jewish refugees from Germany who were all that the Council of Jewish Women in Toronto, largely through her mother's efforts, had been able to bring to Canada.

In the period between the wars, Canada vigorously enforced a standard of racial immigration that, beginning in the 1920s, relegated Jews, Asians, and blacks to a "non-preferred immigrant" status (Abella & Troper, 1986, p. 5). For the Chinese attempting to come to Canada, the 1923 changes to the Immigration Act virtually closed down the country, except to a very restricted class of diplomats and students, although these changes also ended the humiliating head tax that had been imposed on the Chinese alone in 1885, after the completion of the railway. Canada's West Coast media were not above raising the specter of a "yellow peril," and the period was marked by the formation of such organizations as the Vancouver Asiatic Exclusion League and the White Canada Association (Ward, 1990, pp. 128–136). The nativist resurgence, as Ward terms it, culminated in 1942, when the government interned people of Japanese descent who were living in British Columbia. This country's immigration policy of racial restriction, even if it avoided the racial quotas used in the United States, meant, in effect, a deliberate splitting and isolation of families for both Jews and Chinese that continued for decades. Advocates of the policy spoke openly and proudly of the need to preserve and protect the nation as it was "rightly" constituted—a British colony with a French legacy.

Frederick Blair, Canada's director of the Immigration Branch from 1935 until 1943, warned various government officials of the threat posed by the constant pressure to allow refugees into Canada. "Jewish people are usually the first on the move, and, therefore, nearest the door when the door is open," he is quoted as reporting to a member of the Canadian Parliament. "This characteristic [had] its origin in the many migrations of the Hebrew people" (cited by Abella & Troper, 1986, p. 145). The government of Canada, following the lead of the mother country, explained to the critics of its policies that increased immigration might further stir up feelings of anti-Semitism among the general public. It used this line, and a dozen other ploys, from the 1930s up to 1948 to avoid disturbing the racial complexion of the nation. In 1947, Jewish workers were refused admission to Canada after vigilant officials struck out the identification "white" that had been written in under the category of race, replacing it with the correction "Hebrew" (Abella & Troper, p. 254). The theme of the Jews coming to whiteness in the course of a generation haunts the inquiry, between Peter and myself, into linked fates of race lost and found. In addressing the prime minister's cabinet, Blair's successor, A. L. Jolliffe, insisted that the "prohibiting of entry of immigrants of non-assimilable races is necessary" (cited by Abella & Troper, 1986, p. 199).

Blair was simply rehearsing values that had long been used to restrict immigration from China, Japan, and India. In 1922, for example, British Columbia's attorney general and minister of labor reassured the Retail Merchants Association that "the Oriental is not possible for a permanent citizen in British Columbia," drawing his warrant from the natural sciences by adding that "ethnologically they cannot assimilate with our Anglo-Saxon race" (cited by Ward, 1990, p. 131). A decade later, the White Canada Association proclaimed that "we must remember we are trying to evolve a Canadian race as well as a Canadian nation" (cited by Ward, 1990, p. 137). The denial of a place in this society was upheld through the denial of the franchise to those of Chinese, Japanese, or Indian descent (as well as to First Nations peoples) until after the Second World War.

The theme of "non-assimilable races" also survived the war and the devastating knowledge of what racial identification had come to mean among the civilized peoples of Europe. A telling, if damnable, phrase, it appears to crystallize what was most urgent, not only for those deeply concerned to maintain the racial integrity of the Canadian nation but also for those who sought, through changes in name, closet, refrigerator, and a thousand other ways, to prove "non-assimilable" a mistaken concept, at least in their case. We Jews could prove our Canadianness only by assimilation, by assuming a mask thoroughly fixed in place, without a forelock showing, even as we lost our ability to understand, outside of a few phrases, our (grand)mother's Yiddish tongue. Canada is founded, we were to hear repeatedly, on two great races, and that, we were to suppose, was race enough.

The rest, from outside those two founding races, knew what they had to do, given the privilege of entering this well-founded land of rights and liberties after leaving the European ghettos and shtetls, where the sense that one might stop being the Other was not even to be imagined. Many Jewish families kept kosher and wore the marks of their Judaism as signs upon their doorposts, around their necks, and on their heads. But that was not the choice made by me or my family, apart from a period when I wore a mezuzah around my neck during the fervent period of my bar mitzvah. We sought to move what had been insisted upon as our race into simply our denomination. The men sought to be known by their professions, as in the many jokes on "my son, the doctor." This, too, is part of the gentle art of renaming a people, the act of denomination.

If the Jewish question was at the forefront of restrictive immigration practices around the Second World War, the link between the Chinese and the Jews continued to serve as a reference point for the nation. In 1946, the chairman of the Pacific Regional Advisory Board did not shy from alluding to the Kublai Khan connection suggested by Marco Polo: "I do not object to Jews as such, but do not believe that the Mongol type of Jew from Poland and Russia is very readily assimilated in Canada" (cited by Abella & Troper, 1986, p. 235). In the aftermath of the war, with Europe filled with camps of "displaced persons," Canada's prime minister, Mackenzie King, noted in his diary that "there should be no exclusion of any particular race," mentally testing the principle with the instance of Chinese immigration to Canada and concluding that "that [categorical racial exclusion] I think has really been wiped out"—a conclusion that seems less than thoroughly reassuring (cited in Abella & Troper, 1986, p. 241). His point, however, was to reaffirm that "a country should have the right to determine what strains of blood it wishes to have in its population," a sentiment that had guided and continued to guide the immigration policies of a government that was determined to contain both Jewish and Chinese access to what the English and French had made of their stolen land. King feared, finally, that "there is going to be a great danger of the U.N. refusing the idea of justifiable rights of selected immigration with race and other discriminations" (cited in Abella & Troper, 1986, p. 241). It is in finding unlikely links among peoples that the process of undermining such divisions works. In this, the Jews and the Chinese share a sense of Otherness, matched by the extremes of proximity (with the indwelling of the ghettoized Jews among the Europeans) and distance (with a China that was not to be colonized, aside from a few trading ports).

I have not forgotten the fountain pen that Peter gave me. The Parker Vacumatic was purchased by his father in the British colony of Hong Kong in the early 1950s, after the return of the colony to British control and the Communist revolution in China. The pen reveals the industrial craft of that era. The barrel and top are cut, turned, and polished from dark translucent and shimmering green layers of plastic. Rather than going for the Chinese-lacquer effect typically found in pens of polished black, red or blue, this one imitates the effect of a precious jade, with its echo of Hsün-Tzu's *Odes*: "Gracious and splendid, / Like a jade scepter, a jade baton" (1963, p. 148). For all of its gracious and splendid jade effects that respond to the play of light, even as it reveals how much ink remains, the barrel announces itself as a Parker Vacumatic, made in the USA. The name sounds more suitable for a Hoover vacuum cleaner from the techno-age of hyphenated wonders that first introduced automation into the home. This pen's availabilty in Hong Kong marks the growing American economic presence and sensibility in the Pacific over the course of the 20th century, a long-established cultural exchange of technologies and aesthetics, and each country's incorporation of the other's ways in the perpetual quest for market development, manifested in a Vacumatic jade baton.

The Chin name is engraved on all of the pens that Peter's father, Yuen Lung Chin, handed over to Peter, the most elaborate of which reads, "Dear Mr. Chin, Good Luck & Health, H. S. Ting." Peter's father explained to Peter that Mr. Ting had given it to him as a gift on leaving Hong Kong for Canada. But once here, Peter's father put away his set of fountain pens, finding disposable ballpoint pens better suited to this land's form-filling habits.

The barrel of the pen Peter gave me is engraved with two names, Y. L. CHEN and, half a twist a way and further along the barrel, Y. L. CHIN. This intriguing inscription begs an explanation. At first, I thought it might have been a case of the name originally being misunderstood by the engraver, and that may well have been what happened. But the typefaces used to engrave the names are slightly different, suggesting that the engravings were done at different times or places.

In discussing the issue with Zhengwei Lu, a student in one of my classes, he explained to me how China has gone through a series of movements to bring a phonetic transcription system to the Chinese language, most using the roman alphabet, in an effort to bring a written form of Chinese within the reach of more people. He thought it could be the case that Peter's family name was originally transcribed "Chen" in the romanization of the language instigated by the National Party while he was growing up in the Republic of China, only to have it rendered "Chin" in Hong Kong under the influence of the Wade-Giles method that was developed in the 19th century by an English military diplomat and a scholar. (Had Peter's father remained in China, his name would have been transcribed "Jin" in the pinyin system instituted by the People's Republic.) It could well be that the Chin name was transformed at the border between the two Chinas by officials trained in the Wade-Giles method. The transliteration of the name into English transforms it twice, by changing a single letter, and here lies the odd connection between us, Chin and Willinsky, set by this pen. The transliterated name is a moment of identity misplaced and renamed forever on this momento that itself writes and transliterates from one entire manner of constituting a written language to another, bridging a linguistic gorge that we imagine as one of the last great historical barriers, that between the ideogram and the alphabet (Hansen, 1993). In the finely cut inscription of the names Chen and Chin, both approximations of the real name, lies a pattern of naming and misnaming that needs filling out in the broad brush strokes that normally mark the artful calligraphy of the Chinese language.

Peter's father entered Hong Kong after crossing the immense imaginative gulf between the Chinese and British worlds. He entered a China that was not China's, while leaving a China that seemed in the hands of ideas that were not Chinese. With the Communist takeover in 1949, the China that he knew was suddenly nowhere. The home is always an imaginary dwelling, he might well have thought, even when it is built upon foundations that, although crumbling, still run many centuries deep. Peter's father and mother were exiles in their own land as they journeyed down from Shanghai to Hong Kong. That their names were transformed by this political relocation might seem the smallest of points, but it is the naming in such realms that constitutes the reality of affiliations as surely as the barbwire boundary fences they had to skirt around and the officials they had to bribe in the loosely secured colony. This oddly set city-colony had been wrested from China in 1842 by the British under threat of military action. In establishing a trading center in Canton, the British found the "Chinese assumption of superiority" to be "vexing and humiliating," as G. B. Endacott puts it in his history of the colony (1964, p. 8). British merchants could not enter the walled city of Canton, live where they wanted, possess firearms, study Chinese, hire sedan chairs, or employ Chinese servants. In addition, the Chinese dared to interfere with the British trade in opium. The remarkable irony suggested by this discriminating reversal—as we might imagine how Chinese merchants would have been treated in London—no less than the presumption that it was reasonable for the British to ask for a colony with which to carry on its business, goes unnoted by Endacott.

Rey Chow, in describing the Hong Kong in which she grew up before coming to America, speaks of it as a juncture between diaspora and homeland, reminding us that spaces are distinguished not so much by geography but by the desires of those who occupy them: "Perhaps more than anyone else, those who live in Hong Kong realize the opportunistic role they need to play in order, not to 'preserve,' but to negotiate their 'cultural identity.'" Chow makes it clear that her own diasporic project is "to *unlearn* that submission to one's ethnicity such as 'Chineseness' as the ultimate signified" (1993, p. 25). She identifies herself unmistakably as both part of and removed from this sense of Otherness: "Even though my 'personal' history is written in many forms of otherness, such otherness, when combined with the background of my [British-colonial and American] education, is not that of a victim but of a specific kind of social power, which enables me to speak and write by wielding the tools of the enemy" (p. 22). The question, in talking up these literate tools, is whether this act, in itself, plays into the hands of those who would write one as other. One can only write one's way out of such dilemmas by reshaping how the language is used.

Peter Chin's father, Yuen Lung Chin, took the first name Allen when he set up shop as a tailor in Hong Kong, knowing that in selling suits to the English and other westerners, it would be good to give them an easy, familiar name. This name is more than a bridge, more than a point of access, as it reflects a very specific deferral to the other's power of naming, an apology for the difficulties posed by one's "exotic" being (from the Greek for "outside," in this case, outside the realm of the readily imaginable, the pronounceable). Upon later entering Canada, Allen became an official part of Yuen Lung Chin's moniker. His wife, Wai Man Chin, however, uses the name Mary with English speakers but leaves it off of any official forms.

When Peter was born, six months before their departure from Hong Kong for Canada in 1964, his parents made this pattern official, giving him an English and a Chinese name, Peter Man Keung Chin. Upon their arrival in Calgary, the local paper ran a photograph of Allen Chin and the woman who had sponsored the family's immigration to Canada. This woman became the grandmother of Peter and his three brothers, picking up the boys each week to go to the Baptist church, where they also joined the Boy Scouts. They did not go to Chinese classes after school with the other children whose parents had emigrated from China. They grew up without a mother tongue, their mother's tongue, except as a kind of music, a form of anger, when she spoke to them directly in her own words.

From the other side of this naming process, among the Jewish immigrants who came to America from Eastern Europe, "Willinsky" is more often found, when at all, spelled "Willensky" or "Welensky" or "Wolensky." Here seems to be the same form of phonetic slippage that "Chin" experienced in the transposition of vowels, as if the ear could find its match either way, as if we were being first orally named and only then recorded, given letters to hold the name constant across accents and slurs. When I asked a friend who knows the Polish language very well about these surname transcriptions, she assured me that "Willinsky" was more likely "Wilinski" or "Wilenski" in Polish (the first syllable pronounced VEE). It is a name associated with the city of Vilna and was assumed by—or assigned to, perhaps—Jews who in the 19th-century spirit of emancipation had moved there from the shtetls, which operated with their own legal system, economies, and language. For Aleksander Hertz (1988), the shtetls reflected a caste system, but they might more effectively be described as an exercise in race and apartheid. The caste system was better represented by the court Jews who found postings all over Europe providing financial advice and support to governments and kings, in yet another form of nationlessness. "The Jews," Hannah Arendt offers in her famous inquiry into the origins of totalitarianism, "very clearly were the only inter-European element in nationalized Europe" (1968, p. 40). This stormy and stateless history of Jewish displacement, which ended in the Holocaust and the founding of Israel, created a people who were used to living within the spaces provided by others invested in the land of borders and boundaries.

In my grandfather A. I. Willinsky's memoirs, he records how his mother had married the youngest of two brothers who had moved to Kansas City while the rest of their family remained in Europe. Each brother had a slightly different spelling of his last name, my grandfather remembered: "The name is very elusive, for [my uncle] Michael spelled it Welensky, as we learned many years afterward" (1960, p. 3). My grandfather—the Willinsky, as it were—offered a short paragraph of explanation, as if to smooth over what provokes in me a sense of marvel and wonder:

> ... Welensky or Willinsky? But both are phonetic spellings. The Jewish family of eastern Europe is known by a "given" name. His family name is properly constructed with "ben" (son of)—Maimonides's name, for example, is Moses ben Maimon. Such names confuse government officials, who solve the difficulty by dealing out surnames better suited to their records—an understandable measure, though it had the effect of cutting a family off from its earlier history. (p. 4)

On one level, this passage simply confuses the issue, as we are led to believe that "Willinsky" and "Welensky" are phonetic transcriptions, but from what language, and how was the name "given" if not by the state? Is my grandfather suggesting that there was a Hebrew name, like "ben Maimon," that is now lost? His book is full of the Greek and Latin etymologies that give medicine its learned vocabulary, as if this had been his native tongue as a born professional man. On another level, this passage on naming exudes an evenhanded reasonableness that makes the dealing out of surnames an eminently sensible act. However, it cut "a" family off from its past, as my grandfather put it, using the impersonal and scholarly tones that he sought in his autobiography, which was ghosted by an "amanuensis," as he proudly called the poet Margaret Avison (p. vii).

Being cut off is the diasporic state, not being able to look out over a landscape or into a town and somehow know or feel deeply that it carries some living part of who you are, to see yourself in the trees that sheltered your parents' parents, to use a name that fits the land so well that you do not have to continually spell it out as if it cannot be understood as spoken. Are we to imagine that all this goes missing, as one lives instead according to the conveniences of government officials? This passage from my grandfather's memoirs leaves me with only a greater sense of the loss.

The two brothers living together in Kansas City did not arrive with quite the same surname and appear to have thought little of bringing their names into brotherly alignment. It does seem likely that they came across at different times, with one brother sending for the other, as happened with the other side of my grandfather's family. Each faced an American immigration officer at the end of a long, bedraggled line at Ellis Island, within eyesight of the promised land, smelling of the kerosene used to delouse the immigrants and standing in mortal fear of being deported. Each may have received, in turn, a paper with "Willinsky" and "Welensky," respectively, scrawled in the space marked "Name." And so those admittance papers fixed and set who they now were, even after they had ridden the train for days into what was still something of a Wild West. ("My father used to boast about the time he met Frank James as a customer in his store," my grandfather writes in a story that thrilled me as a youngster trying to envision outlaw gangs shopping for, say, eyeglasses [p. 3].) Not unwillingly did they suffer these transliterations, and I do not want to exaggerate the loss, even in nostalgic reflection. Had the brothers stayed in Poland, holding to their true Yiddish name(s), after all, what then?

My point is, rather, to see the act of being named—Welensky or Willinsky, Chen or Chin—as another ordering of space, another part of placement and identification through which we find ourselves. The act of naming is, at heart, a patriarchal power, reenacted by the government, that marks the genealogy of authority through the male line. It is the men of the family who are constituted by tradition and law to hold inviolable identities. Thus, I recognize that these concerns over misnomers have a particularly masculinist ring to them, although the right to a name has more recently become an issue for both genders. For the point has always been not just the significance of a name but the power to name:

> And out of the ground the Lord God formed every beast of the field, and every fowl of the air; and brought them unto Adam to see what he would call them: and whatsoever Adam called every living creature, that was the name thereof. (Gen. 2:19, King James Version)

The colonial renaming of immigrants has its rougher echo in those who came to America in slave ships and in the children they bore in slavery. An African American spiritual goes, "I told Jesus it would be all right / If he changed my name," invoking a sense of both master and husband but with the clearly asserted privilege of voluntarily being bound by name. Sojourner Truth, one of the 19th century's most highly regarded African American women, on freeing herself after 30 years of bondage, took it upon herself, as part of a revelation, to rename herself, thereby moving beyond the naming of the Dutch and English who had enslaved her. In her dictated *Narrative*, Truth explains how the naming of a slave worked at the time:

> A slave's surname is ever the same as his master; that is, if he is allowed to have any other name than Tom, Jack, or Guffin. Slaves have sometimes been severely punished for adding their master's name to their own. But when they have no particular title to it, it is not a particular offense. (1993, p. 30)

My intention here, as elsewhere, is not to suggest a moral equivalence between struggles, that is, in this case, between an emancipated slave and a Jewish doctor. But I think the value of pulling these stories together is a way of drawing us into the intersecting and parallel histories that can be seen both to distinguish and to connect the lives we are living today.

Maxine Hong Kingston, in her "memoirs of a girlhood among ghosts," treats these themes of identification in terms of the secrecy with which her parents' generation, in moving to America, protected their Chinese names, strangely echoing the naming I have described: "The Chinese I know hide their name; sojourners take new names when lives change and guard real names with silence" (1976, p. 5). Some hide their names, some dispose of them, some rechristen themselves, some lose their names, cut off from the very language and life in which these names were mother-tongue sounds.

For the epigraph to the final chapter of his book, my grandfather selected a passage from Confucius's *Analects* that might well serve as the theme for this entire meditation: "To be able from one's self to draw a parallel for the treatment of others, that may be called true philanthropy." I have drawn parallels here for gaining a sense of how our lives take on patterns that can be read for their connections, as a way of double-crossing the distances that have been imagined through the arts and sciences. Yet I also know that the quotation from the *Analects* serves my grandfather's book just as I fear that Peter's story may be serving my tale—as an ornament on the order of a Ming vase copy, set on the mantel of his work to attest to his worldly and well-traveled cosmopolitanism, accompanied by his favoring of the medical wisdom of Maimonides.

As it was, my grandfather developed a great interest in travel photography. He recorded the journeys he made in conjunction with his medical conferences, and he began showing them to others in churches and schools, accompanied by a commentary of dry wit, my family tells me, that was meant to entertain, even as it educated, his audiences. The films portrayed, for the most part, as I recall, endless shots of the sleepy, dusty streets of Spain. The diaspora of a wandering people became a minor "edutainment" outlet for this professor of travel. One of my grandfather's great disappointments in life was not to hold a university position, and he spoke of his "old heart-soreness" over this aspect alone of the anti-Semitism he experienced. That my brother now holds a medical position at the University of Toronto, down the street from our grandfather's (now our) home, gives an odd truth to our grandfather's opening epigraph, from Proverbs: "A good man leaveth an inheritance to his children's children" (13:22, King James Version). That inheritance, if not secured by my grandfather's name, lies buried in the aspirations and efforts marked by his journey, by how he was identified and how he tried to identify himself.

In the *Analects*, when Confucius speaks of the proprieties of naming, he emphasizes an accord between names and the truth of things:

> If names be not correct, language is not in accordance with the truth of things. If language be not in accordance with the truth of things, affairs cannot be carried on to success. (Cited by Chow, 1993, pp. 104–105)

It may be that we can no longer trust the accord between the names of things and the truth of things without questioning that naming. If the affairs of the world are to be carried on with any measure of success, there has always to be that questioning of how things have been named, how that assumed accord has been struck. The instability of our designations, suggesting the tenuousness of the accord, is some part of what Peter and I have inherited in our signatures, as they each inscribe their own record of movement over water and land, borders and languages.

Some sense of that movement, as an evolving identification, is found in David Yen-ho Wu's description of Chinese identity. He holds the West responsible, for example, for introducing the ingredients of race and nation into the naming of the Chinese: "In order to create a modern identity to cope with conditions created by China's confrontation with the Western world, the Chinese were obliged to deal with foreign concepts, including that of nation, state, sovereignty, citizenship, and race; more recently with cultural and ethnic identity" (1991, p. 159). I would work it the other way as well, proposing that the West's conflagration with the Orient helped it define those "foreign concepts" as a form of intellectual technology to muster—along with gunpowder, paper, and the compass, among other transformed appropriations from the Chinese—in extending its global dominion. Wu points out how, beginning in the early Republic of China, the terms *Hua*, *Xia*, and *Han* took on an interchangeable sense of China as nation-state, as race or tribe, and as geographic location (p. 161). In a similar shift, Bernard Lewis describes how the Arabic term *watan* was expanded from "place of birth" to "fatherland" under the influence of Western nationalism (1988).

For the Chinese, this geo-poli-racial centeredness, in the very naming of themselves, comes out of contact with Western concepts of identification. Yet the Chinese sense of centeredness, this "cultural and historical fulfillment," which for Wu typifies the Chinese identity, is very close to what Peter cannot claim or even pretend to know, as he realizes that, to those who are not Chinese, he cannot be other than Chinese. He cannot know or guard his real name. He can only meet the idea of it with silence. His is the other shape of modern identity, the one without a fixed center. It is the diasporic identity, not rootless but distributed in its rooting, like the runners of a strawberry plant. As people find themselves displaced by the changing history of nations, they seek their history elsewhere, looking for advantages for themselves and their families through migration. In these re-placements, they become candidates for the sort of supranational identity—attuned to concepts of interdependence, normative universalism, global challenges, and world order—that Furio Cerutti has recently described as "thinkable and necessary" (1993, p. 158). At the very least, it becomes necessary to rethink the inclusiveness of identity in the nation and to consider alternative conceptions of the state. It means thinking about a curriculum as a way of learning about the world that does not root identity in the coinciding of nation, race, or culture.

An interesting variation on this supranational stance is pursued by Daniel Boyarin and Jonathan Boyarin when they argue that the Jewish Diaspora provides the very grounds of Jewish identity. It is nothing less than "the most important contribution that Judaism has to make to the world" (1993, p. 723). They point out how, through the state of Diaspora, "the Jews discovered their well-being was absolutely dependent on principles of respect for difference," which formed the basis of a nationless morality free of the "deadly discourse" of "race and space" (pp. 721, 714). The Diaspora represents "a theoretical and historical model to replace national self-determination," an idea they freely concede is inspired by utopian ideals of Jews living free from persecution and "yet constituted by strong identity" (p. 711). If such conditions seem rarely met in the world that we know, the Boyarins are still prepared to reject the alternative of Zionism, as Israel finds itself forced, in effect, to engage in acts of political hegemony and other abuses of power. Theirs is clearly a welcomed and voluntary diaspora, driven by the choice to live apart from power. The goal is "to renounce any possibility of domination over Others by being perpetually out of power" (p. 722). They make an eloquent case for the disengaged and disruptive quality of this particular diasporic identity: "Jewishness disrupts the very categories of identity because it is not national, not genealogical, not religious, but all of these in dialectical tension with the other" (p. 721). The point also appears in Stuart Hall's claims for a "new ethnicity," which, if it is not able to offer "a powerless perfect universe," is also not "framed by those extremities of power and aggression, violence and mobilization, as older forms of nationalism" (1987, p. 46).

There is a undeniable attractiveness to this state of absolution from the corrupting influences of power, at least in the form of nationhood. However, neither the Boyarins' call for a strong (Jewish) ethnic identity nor their desire to leave the workings of power up to others presents a viable alternative for Peter or me. Neither of us is rooted in ethnic identity, even though we are both professional educators working, in some sense, in the service of a national educational system. The two of us want to revisit the historical moments of disruption and displacement, not so much in a hope of recovering a robust Jewish or Chinese identity but because we have come to understand the disengaged qualities that mark the path our families followed to be a reading of the past that is still present in us. Equally so, we do not imagine ourselves free to renounce "temporal power," which the Boyarins hold as the Diaspora's saving grace (1993, p. 723).

It is in the nature of our work, and thus our culture and identity, to pick up a pen and sign this or that form, minting ourselves as, in effect, a new schoolteacher, a new professor of education. We thereby authorize the workings of an institutional apparatus that continues to certify and exclude on grounds that we are also seeking to challenge and reform. We look to the past to gain some feeling for how what are now obviously abuses of power become normal operating procedures. Hall, for example, offers one focal point, with his call for "countering to the old discourses of nationalism or national identity" (1987, p. 46). We are all migrants or "recently migrated," in Hall's sense of the postmodern condition. If we can begin to grasp that sense of human flux, then the celebration of ethnicity ceases to be the only hope for living beyond the bounds of the nation and what it would make of us.

What this means is that the nation's role as a source of primary identification, in the study of self and other, of who "we" are and who "they" are, should now itself become a subject of study. Students can examine how we are placed by name and nation, with all of their racial implications, while our perspective becomes more global and polyglot, our identifications more fluid and thoughtful. The complexities of this postmodern and migrant identity are closely set by Joan Scott as she considers how, in light of the current politics of multiculturalism, we need to teach students and ourselves that "subjects are produced through multiple identifications, some of which become politically salient for a time in certain contexts, and that the project of history is not to reify identity but to understand its production as an ongoing process of differentiation, relentless in its repetition, but also—and this seems to me the important political point—subject to redefinition, resistance, and change" (1992, p. 19). The need is to work with our own histories and the larger histories of nation and race, to understand these productions, whether whimsically drawn from such unlikely sources as a Parker pen and its engraved misnomer or from any of a thousand threads. There is considerable hope in learning how to distinguish the many identifying signatures that become apparent in asking how it is that we have arrived "here."

In a certain light, like the sort of light that it takes to catch the engraved names on the Parker pen, there emerges a common thread between Peter and me that carries some part of how we were determined, how each of us has been named and how much of us has been renamed. Yet just as I began to suspect that I was making too much of my jade green pen, I came across another Parker pen that helped Claude Lévi-Strauss make sense of life in New York City, where, as a refugee, he worked during the Second World War. Looking back from 1977, Lévi-Strauss uses the pen, as I do, to inscribe incongruities. In his case, they include the meeting of cultures writ large in that great American city, with the ever-present Chinese signifying the cultural depths of time and distance. Lévi-Strauss includes the Chinese opera and the Parker pen in his grab-bag collection of telling artifacts and events that take on their meaning within the time machine that is anthropology:

> We watch for hours at the Chinese opera under the first arch of the Brooklyn Bridge, where a company that had come long ago from China had a large following. Every day, from midafternoon until past midnight, it would perpetuate the traditions of classical Chinese opera. I felt myself going back in time no less when I went to work every morning in the American room of the New York Public Library. There, under its neo-classical arcades and between walls paneled with old oak, I sat near an Indian in a feather headdress and a beaded buckskin jacket— who was taking notes with a Parker pen. (1985, p. 266)

In that final line, like a comedian continually seeking to throw his audience off stride, Lévi-Strauss offers the absurd scene of a feather headdress in one of the most civilized public rooms of New York City, the classic colonial image of the savage at court, only to pause before delivering his real punch line, with a pointed dash, that this fellow was taking notes with a Parker pen. Is it the fountain pen amid the feathers or, more likely, the native informant doing his own research that proves surprising? Was Lévi-Strauss, as James Clifford suggests in making his own big deal of "the feathered Indian with a Parker Pen," going back to the future with this image, to a time in the years ahead when Native Americans would successfully mount their own court cases and anthropological studies (Clifford, 1988, pp. 236)?

The pen appears to anchor this bedazzling, oak-paneled scene in reality. It is the instrument of incongruity, the signifier that signs for itself. The pen is contrasted with the headdress as anthropologist is merged with informant. It may signal the end of an era, not least of all for Lévi-Strauss, as the 20th century's last great anthropologist-as-hero. When he goes on to write how he "sensed that all these relics were being assaulted by a mass culture," you can hear his defense of cultural artifacts against "mass"-produced objects, of what can be properly identified (named) as art and fact, versus what goes nameless (1985, pp. 266–267). The Parker pen is a crossover point, an industrial craft and culture preserver that is worth naming. It has been in just that spirit, tinged with something of the domesticated nostalgia evoked by Lévi-Strauss's use of the Native American, that I have used the image of the Parker pen. However, evoking a sense of cultural loss that infuses the anthropologist's work is clearly not my purpose. In fact, Lévi-Strauss concludes his essay with the rather dismal judgment that the absorption in seemingly out-of-place "cultural" activities amounts to "the thousand and one tricks offered, for a few brief moments, by the illusion that one has the power to escape." And what is to be escaped, for Lévi-Strauss, now writing in the Paris of 1977, is "a society becoming each day ever more oppressive and inhuman" (1985, p. 267). It seems odd to reach such a conclusion, comparing the world in 1977 to life in 1941, when the Nazis were in Paris and the French Jews were soon to be rounded up. That horrible time is past, we might say with some relief, if it were not for the elements of a fiery turmoil in Europe today that include neo-Nazi activities. We are still struggling to understand the making of a cultural order that continues to hold people within the grip of identities, naming them by nation and race, and we need to ask, against Lévi-Strauss, might this understanding alone hold open for us the momentary power of escape? Or is it only a trick?

Although the specter of racism and loss have played a large part in what I have spun out of the Parker pen that Peter has given me, I do not mean for such despair to be the principal lesson passed on to the young through the exercise of tracing historical parallels. In a sense, the same point is being debated today in Israel, where educational questions are being asked about "dwelling" on the Holocaust. The Israeli educator Yehuda Elkana asks, "What are children to do with such memories?" and his fear is that "blind hatred" will be the result (cited by Elon, 1993, p. 5). Elkana warns that "the past must not be allowed to become the dominant element determining the future of society and the destiny of a people" (cited by Elon, 1993, p. 5). In light of his very real concerns, my plea is for going into that past as a check against this very sense that destinies belong to peoples, for calling into question not only the place of injustice in the past but also the impossibility of determining precisely where that injustice is situated, the impossibility of finally naming it in accord with some greater truth of things, greater than the sense of injustice. As part of a continuing education, we return to these events through so many different configurations that we begin to appreciate—with some outside guidance, perhaps—that the arts (and sciences) of naming need to be as carefully attended to as those objects which they appear to identify. Whether this is still too much for children I am not yet certain, but I like to think it should at least be part of a teacher's education and a challenge in educating others.

References

Abella, I., & Troper, H. (1986). *None is too many: Canada and the Jews of Europe, 1933–1948.* Toronto: Lester.

Arendt, H. (1968). *The origins of totalitarianism: Part 1. Anti-Semitism.* San Diego: Harcourt Brace Jovanovich.

Boyarin, D., & Boyarin, J. (1993). Diaspora: Generation and the ground of Jewish identity. *Critical Inquiry, 19*(4), 693–725.

Cerutti, F. (1993). Can there be a supranational identity? *Philosophy and Social Criticism, 18*(2), 147–162.

Chow, R. (1993). *Writing diaspora: Tactics of intervention in contemporary cultural studies.* Bloomington: Indiana University Press.

Clifford, J. (1988). *The predicament of culture: 20th-century ethnography, literature, and art.* Berkeley: University of California Press.

Elon, A. (1993). The politics of memory. *New York Review of Books, 40*(16), 3–5.

Endacott, G. B. (1964). *Government and people in Hong Kong, 1841–1962.* Westport, CT. Greenwood.

Franklin, J. H. (1993). *The color line: Legacy for the 21st century.* Columbia: University of Missouri Press.

Gilman, S. (1991). *The Jew's body.* New York: Routledge.

Hall, S. (1987). Minimal selves. In L. Appignanesi (Ed.), *The real me: Postmodernism and the question of identity* (pp. 44–46). London: Institute of Contemporary Arts Documents.

Hansen, C. (1993). Chinese ideographs and Western ideas. *Journal of Asian Studies, 52*(2), 373–399.

Hertz, A. (1988). *The Jews in Polish culture* (R. Lourie, Trans., L. Dobroszycki, Ed.). Evanston, IL: Northwestern University Press.

Hsün-Tzu. (1963). *Basic writings* (B. Watson, Trans.). New York: Columbia University Press. (Original work published ca. 264 B.C.E.).

Kingston, M. H. (1976). *The woman warrior: Memoirs of a girlhood among ghosts.* New York: Vintage.

Kristeva, J. (1993). *Nations without nationalism* (L. S. Roudiez, Trans.). New York: Columbia University Press.

Lee, F. R. (1993, October 19). An editor sees Asian-American identity as a work in progress. *New York Times,* p. E7.

Lewis, B. (1988). *The political language of Islam.* Chicago: University of Chicago Press.

Lévi-Strauss, C. (1985). New York in 1941. In *The view from afar* (pp. 258–267). (J. Neugroschel & P. Hoss, Trans). New York: Basic Books.

Scott, J. W. (1992). Multiculturalism and the politics of identity. *October, 61,* 12–19.

Truth, S. (1993). *Narrative of Sojourner Truth* (M. Washington, Ed.). New York: Vintage. (Original work published 1850).

Walton, A. (1993). Patriots. In G. Early (Ed.), *Lure and loathing: Essays on race, identity, and the ambivalence of assimilation* (pp. 245–263). New York: Penguin.

Ward, W. P. (1990). *White Canada forever: Popular attitudes and public policy toward Orientals in British Columbia.* Montreal: McGill-Queen's University Press.

Willinsky, A. I. (1960). *A doctor's memoirs.* Toronto: Macmillan.

Willinsky, J. (1998). *Learning to divide the world: Education at empire's end.* Minneapolis: University of Minnesota Press.

Wu, D. Y. (1991). The construction of Chinese and non-Chinese identities. *Dædalus, 120*(2), 159–179.

Yule, H. (Trans. & Ed.). (1871). *The book of Marco Polo, the Venetian, concerning the kingdoms and marvels of the East* (Vol. 1). London: John Murray.

Chapter 13

Why Allan Isn't My Friend Anymore

This book about forms of literacy that come after literacy, I realized in an indulgent moment, might have been entitled *Why Allan Isn't My Friend Anymore*. Allan and I had had a friendship, after all, that had everything do with literacy, books, and libraries. The collapse of this friendship after 32 years was over an argument about the forms of literacy that come after literacy. This personal aside, then, seems a fine way to close this collection, as it conveys the ambivalence I sometimes feel over where I have traveled, after literacy. I include it, as well, to keep our thinking about what we would have of literacy from slipping too far into philosophical abstraction. We do seem on the brink of yet another literacy. And to understand what to make of literacy's new machines, we have only to think back through what we have already made, and have always wanted to make, of this way with words.

It has always seemed to me that the histories of literacy that I have explored over the years, from medieval scriptoria to postmodern libraries, arose of my friendship with Allan. This work has always been about what books and libraries, writers and readers made of knowledge. And while my current work may be with what distributed database algorithms and hyperlinked indexes might mean for public knowledge, I am still playing with little more than variations on the book in the library. It is still working with ideas like an engineer building a bridge by playing on the simple strength of triangles.

The particular variation, represented by this friendship with Allan, could be said to hinge on an evening's chess game during my undergraduate days in Toronto. Allan had unexpectedly turned up at my door, after having hitchhiked his way back and forth across the country in those years when the young came of age by taking to the road, with outstretched thumbs and Kerouac in their pack. His arrival brought to that warm September evening the drama of a completed odyssey. We had been friends all through our teenage years, and here he was again, after his first great journey out into the world. Six months earlier, he had quit university and taken to the road. He had now returned, road weary and wise. He had barely sat down at the table in the communal kitchen of the old Admiral Road rooming house I lived in before he had me convinced that this was an occasion in need of marking. In his flair for the dramatic, if not the histrionic, he proposed that we immediately play chess for something of great personal consequence. In a strange variation on the odyssey theme, we decided to stake our youthful beards and our libraries on the outcome of the match.

That I achieved such a concentrated grip on the game and eventually wrested checkmate from him, when I recall rarely winning in previous matches between us, reflected just how much of a hold our paperback collections had on me. That I then watched him shave off his beard and that I eventually (and foolishly) took charge of his books, however, is not the important thing here. I'm beardless now, and both of our libraries have grown manyfold since then, suffering less dramatic but just as large losses along the way. Though it introduced some strain at the time, the consequences of that chess game did not put an end to our friendship, which sailed on for another two decades.

The important thing about the chess game was, of course, the standing of books with us. They were as close to us as the beards of our countercultural days. We were unhesitatingly certain about what those libraries could hold, certain about how the world was written in a way that we could take in hand. This faith may have taken root during our high school days, but it was a literature that was constantly set against institutions of knowing and aimed at the self-sufficiency of the book. It was all about, I realize now, the quirky, defiant, proud, and accomplished powers of autodidacticism, the writer amid his books.

This sense of a literature against education came through wonderfully in our high school days, with Allan's ostentatious boycotting of those English classes that would presume to teach him about his favorite poets. Such classes were inimical to whatever was poetic and profound in Dylan Thomas or John Donne. The school could have its science labs and gym classes, and even the inevitable football pass to the side of the head, but it posed a serious threat to poetry. I lacked the courage of such conviction and took my "Fern Hill" and "A Valediction: Forbidding Mourning" verse by verse, in gruesome guessing games over metaphorical allusions and other literary devices that were played out in class after class.

Allan managed to stake out his own intellectual and aesthetic refuge in the small northern Ontario steel town in which we lived. It was to be found in the book section of Edward's Paint and Wallpaper on Queen Street. Apart from the local drugstore paperback racks, we had only Mr. Edward's two diminutive aunts, who shared a passion for reading and were allowed to stock along one wall and on a few extra shelves what seemed to us a very wide range of books indeed for a paint and wallpaper shop. Allan and I saved up our allowances for whatever titles received serious paperback treatment, from Darwin to French cheeses, but we were mad over Joyce and Yeats, Faulkner and O'Connor, Turgenev and Dostoyevsky, for the way they could write with such intensity about the crushing drama of adult life that seemed absent from any adult life we knew, and certainly from our own approximation.

We were stirred to a real excitement by the store's annual book sale, as we gradually transferred its stock to our respective bedroom libraries. We also haunted the town's old Carnegie library for serious literature and literary lives, and we worked for the distempered, bibliophilic high school librarian, George Whalen, if only to gain for ourselves the right of first refusal on new books coming into the library. I still remember unpacking the beautiful volumes of Proust's *Remembrance of Things Past*, hearing for the first time of its legendary literary accomplishment—a single novel running to seven volumes—from Mr. Whalen, who quickly told me that, of course, he had ordered such a masterpiece for himself. He set up a listening corner where we used headphones for the first time, to hear the slow, measured tones of T. S. Eliot and the lilt of Dylan Thomas as they read their poetry, and we began to read the *New York Times Book Review*, where each week's new array of books seemed to matter.

During those years, we'd meet up for coffee and butter tarts at the Small Fry Restaurant, which sat on the edge of the highway that headed off to the south. I can recall racing over one evening to meet him filled with enthusiasm for James Agee's *Let Us Now Praise Famous Men*. I'd been tipped off to the book's wonders by the *Saturday Review*'s series on overlooked classics. Agee offered a fervent and poetic, metaphysical and Marxist polemic against injustice woven out of the tired and true lives of a few sharecropper families during the Depression. Set off by Walker Evans's stark photographs, the book was the meeting of an art and a caring that could well be said to have determined my life in the social sciences. (On looking back now, I realize that I did not really follow in its heartfelt, thoroughly artful, yearning footsteps, given over as I was to scholarly pursuits and comforts. Nor did I feel that I held its like in my hands again—not because no one could write as well but because writing like that works best by far on one's first discovering that it can even be done.)

I remember well how Agee spoke so eloquently of the great unknowingness of a lamp shining against the darkness. He seemed able to write inspiringly against what was both wrong and unfathomable. I feared, though, that Allan found the book somewhat overwritten and perhaps overcommitted to something that lay beyond the accomplishment of the art. For his part, he handed out to his friends a remaindered cache of Halldór Laxness's *Independent People*, the Icelandic Nobel Prize winner's novel of bleak, historic rootedness in a barren land.

Books were our sure purchase on the world, mapping what it held for us and what we knew of it, as it was mapped for other young people by school teams, report cards, hot cars, and hot steadies. As life could at best imitate art, we were not to be caught without a book in hand. We traveled with books as our guides, and we made bookshops the destination of our travels. We also carried pocket-size black notebooks, knowing that in taking in so much literature it was surely bound to flow back out of us, and we'd be ready. Looking back now, the only phrase I can recall from all of my poem-filled notebooks is "smokestack sunset," because Allan had suggested that the phrase warranted its own poem, which didn't say much about what surrounded it. But then for me, Allan was the real writer.

Not long after high school I entered into a happy marriage with Pam (who should not go unnamed in this story), with whom I had book-raised if not quite book-loving sons, Paul, David, and Aaron. I shuffled through my days as a schoolteacher that, by slow degrees, led to university professing. Each step of the way was always with an eye to the books with which I continued to build my bridge into the world. I worked hard, as I saw it, to bring the spirit of those books, the life of the reader and writer, into my classroom with its library of cast-off classics and its publishing workshops.[1] Later, my studies as an educational researcher amounted to an inquiry into why others were not quite as inspired as I was in their pursuit of such knowing libraries. I was making a profession of my books, even as I seemed to pursue research that led through the great used bookstores of the English-speaking world in my search for the educational implications of literacy, dictionaries, literary criticism, and imperialism.

Although Allan and I more than once lost touch with each other over the years, as we lived in different cities and occasionally grew into indifferent correspondents, our libraries remained connected, as I'd find myself in a bookshop wondering whether Allan could possibly have found as good a used set of Woolf's essays as I just had. Still, over the years and the hundreds of letters, I grew convinced (and remain so) that Allan was as talented a writer as I would ever know. The sensation of a relentless Joycean poetics carried me along page after page of blue airmail paper. When each letter came to an end, I would hold it at arm's length, amazed at how such an undrafted orchestration of literary tricks had been pulled off with nothing but a fountain pen or an Olivetti portable. He wrote as he played the piano, with an intensity that honored the art of playing alone, without seeming to mind the serving or pleasing of another soul. As with his reading, his writing was an end in itself, yet there were times when he keenly sought to share that end, as he pursued over a number of years and with a number of organizations elaborate plans for an all-literature shortwave radio station.

Allan tended to treat the jobs he held over the years—with literary-press shops, newspapers, and headhunting firms—as imaginative exercises played hard against each job's limits and theme. The breakthroughs he achieved often left his bosses, I sensed, unable to fathom the heart and heat he poured into making something more of his work. Although I pushed and cajoled him more than once to pursue a literary career, he steadfastly refused, for much the same reason, I now suppose, that he stayed away from those poetry classes in high school: he did not want the world to ruin or tamper with what he loved most.

And then, four years ago, when Allan had begun living part of every year in Vancouver, where I was then and still am working, we met in an all-night café for another sort of chess game, late into the evening. At that point, we were the only two chessmen on the board of our respective lives. It developed into a match over literature that I may well have lost by winning, the culmination of what had been eating away at our game and my life-in-the-library for some time. I may not yet have a clear perspective on the whole of it, but my work with technology in the schools had drawn me into a high-tech start-up company, and the hold of books on me was slipping, as I found myself struggling at times to recall what the sense of telling stories was.[2]

My self-defeating checkmate against Allan that evening came while I was fuming over his disappointment that my life and reading were slipping into these technology ventures. I had admitted to him early in the evening that I felt as if I'd left the garden of the library, having tasted from the wrong tree, one that led me to ask after the knowledge of good and evil, or rather the good and indifference of knowledge. My work on the educational relationship between imperialism and Western culture, and my growing investment, both intellectually and professionally, in what was to be had of new technologies of knowledge, led toward an increasingly instrumental approach to ideas, to a cost-benefit analysis of how knowledge can really serve the benefit of humankind.

I could sense how such thinking appalled Allan, draining him of respect for me, and in the heat of that moment I foolishly turned on him, adamantly demanding that he explain just how much better a human being *he* had become, how much more *he* was, for having so thoroughly pickled his life in literary brine. Tell me again, I demanded, why we had devoted our lives to these books. What good came of this self-cultivation, this endless self-improvement, that we so relentlessly sought to absorb and did so little to repay? I knew immediately that I had gone too far, that I was asking him to bear the burden of what had really broken in my own life. He rose and walked out to his car without a further word, and I walked glumly home. That was five years ago. We have not spoken since.

Life imitating Russian literature, perhaps. But set aside the café pathos for a moment. We had built a friendship around the particular epistemology of the library, and it was coming undone for me, as I found myself at the time overwhelmed by shelves of endless journals spilling over into abstract-clogged databases, all written in the name of humanity's benefit yet signifying little, if not nothing. My error may have been dragging my friendship with Allan into my professional crisis of the spirit, asking of him what I was clearly asking of myself and my work. And, of course, it was more than a professional crisis of confidence that I was passing through.

Allan's error was, perhaps, to expect me to sustain two faiths. Literature makes a different promise from the social sciences, just as they repay what we devote to them differently. I had played my social-science research around literary themes, but I was feeling a combined inadequacy. The world is written in both cases—written out of caring, out of a desire to make others share in that caring, and perhaps out of the wonder of that caring. Were the social sciences more responsive to immediate needs, without the pretenses of art? Or did they offer less than literature's rendering of life's pulse, in presuming that they could deal directly with the scope and the troubles of this world?

An answer cannot be simply stated, if at all. But it can at least be said that literature offered Allan, as it had once offered me, an identification with the artfulness of which the world was capable. It brought clarity to the form of our lives. It brought the feel and sense of other lives sharply into focus. The indisputable good of that art and feeling, which I had glimpsed coming together with the interests of the social sciences in James

Agee, had been lost to me that evening with Allan and elsewhere, as I wandered the aisles of the social-sciences division of the library.

My work since then has been on how the social sciences might realize more of their promise.[3] I have returned to the hopes of the library, to the way it houses our knowing aspirations across forms of writing. What I am seeking to reestablish is the architecture of common knowledge, a shared and ancient urge to assemble what can be known, to make a library of knowledge and to understand knowledge as no more than the whole of the diffuse library. This is about recovering the continuities between library and information technologies, as the one is an extension and not a betrayal of the other. It is about the library as both the metaphorical and literal house of knowledge.

In the 19th century, Victor Hugo used this architectural motif to portray the profound challenge that print technology first posed to the Christian world of the 15th century. For him, the Notre Dame cathedral was a fully realized body of Christian knowledge, a memory-storage device of breathtaking capacity, sustained by flying buttresses and fearsome gargoyles. But such towering and intricately inscribed temples of wisdom were soundly shaken by the portable and personal houses of knowledge first mass-produced with typefaces cast by the goldsmith Johannes Gutenberg. The introduction of this new technology led the archdeacon in Hugo's *Notre Dame of Paris* to flatly declare, "This will kill that. The book will kill the building. That is to say, Printing will kill Architecture."[4] This may be to claim too much. Printing did kill one magnificent architectural form, although the Gothic came back in other ways (not least of all with the Collegiate Gothic style, which makes many high schools the outstanding architectural feature of their small towns). The books that flowed from the printing press, while undermining the church as the principal architectural form of knowledge, surely gave rise to that many more ways of building (for that many more people) a knowledge of our lives and faiths.

Where once the cathedral stood at the center of the community, drawing people's eyes heavenward with its aspiring and encompassing knowledge of this world and the next, we now want to hold the whole of what can be known in the palm of our hand. And when the *New York Times* announced IBM's historic crossing of the 10-billion-bits-of-data-per-square-inch barrier for the hard drive not long ago, it explained that the laptop computer would now be able to hold 725,000 double-spaced pages, "which would make a stack taller than an 18-story building."[5] The silicon cathedral is now that much closer than Notre Dame to heaven.

"This will kill that" may well have been what Allan was saying to me about the impact of my technology interests on our libraries. It may be, but I have kept the library at the center of my project in reflecting on what we would have of knowledge and on the tension between completeness and comprehensibility, between wanting to know everything and wanting it all to make sense. And my recent work on what has and will be made of the library draws inspiration and substance from the pocket selection of Leibniz's works that I won from Allan in that chess game many September evenings ago. Leibniz was the great philosopher-librarian, concerned with finding the order of knowledge among the endless shelves of books, and his proposals for a calculus of ideas has long been a model for cybernetics.[6]

I continue to be guided by library and book, then, in thinking about what we are likely to make of new technologies of the word, so that the power of this literate engagement continues to expand and inspire our knowing. The literacy that we seek for ourselves and for the young in school is still about a reading of the world. It is about how our own histories with the word are but starting points for the yet unwritten and for what is so obviously in need of writing and rewriting. The dictionary and E-mail that I discussed earlier in this book are a small enough part of it all, the play of identity and culture somewhat more, but the limits of the known world and the limits of each of our worlds need to be endlessly spelled out and pushed, as if it lay within our power to write, word by word, the world anew.

Notes

1. See my *The New Literacy: Redefining Reading and Writing in the Schools* (New York: Routledge, 1990).

2. On the business, see Vivian Forssman and John Willinsky, "A Tale of Two Cultures and a Technology: A Musical Politics of Curriculum in Four Acts," in *Curriculum Politics, Policy, Practice: Cases in Comparative Context,* ed. Catherine Cornbleth (Albany: State University of New York Press, 2000).

3. See my *Technologies of Knowing: A Proposal for the Human Sciences* (Boston: Beacon, 1999); and *If Only We Knew: Increasing the Public Value of Social Science Research* (New York: Routledge, 2000).

4. Victor Hugo, *Notre Dame of Paris* trans. J. Sturrock (Harmondsworth, Middlesex: Penguin Books, 1978), pp. 188-189. Ivan Illich notes that "the construction of twelfth-century cathedrals can be understood as a public creation of a symbolic universe of *memoria*: the solemnly celebrated reminiscence of *historia.*" *In the Vineyard of the Text: A Commentary to Hugh's "Didascalicon"* (Chicago: University of Chicago Press, 1993), 38 n. 30.

5. Lawrence M. Fisher, "I.B.M. Plans to Announce Leap in Disk-Drive Capacity," *New York Times*, 30 December 1997, C2. Fisher cites Currie Munce, director of storage systems and technology at IBM: "Demand for storage is essentially insatiable. . . . As we get more mobile, and expect information at our fingertips, we're going to be more focused on our data, where it's stored and how we get access to it."

6. See my *If Only We Knew*, pp. 65-72.

Index

Abella, Irving, 260
aberration in electronic communication, 41, 43, 47–51
Académie française, 171x
ACT UP, 24
adolescence, 232–35
Advancement of Learning (Bacon), 239
advertising, 30–31, 35n. 13
Agee, James, 281–82
AIDS, 24
Akiba, Rabbi, 71–72, 78n. 7
aliteracy, 15–16
alphabets, 62, 65–66
American Heritage Dictionary, 150, 176
American Social Sciences in Education (ASSEA) conference, 239–52
Analects (Confucius), 269–70
Anatomy of Human Bodies Epitomized (Gibson), 178
anthropology, 86–91
Antiracism and Ethnocultural Equity in School Boards (Ministry of Education and Training, Ontario), 130
anti-Semitism, 121–23, 210, 219n. 11, 255–75
architecture, postmodern, 26
Arnold, Matthew, 96
Atlantic, the, 152
Avis, Walter, 161–62
Augustine, 198, 199

Bacon, Francis, 207, 239
Baltimore Sun, 158
Balzac, Honore de, 18–19, 22
Banks, James, 131
Barthes, Roland, 18–19, 22, 33–34n. 5
Baudrillard, Jean, 31
Beauvoir, Simone de, 121
Berger, John, 179
Bernhard, Thomas, 205
Berube, Margery S., 151
Bhangara dancing, 132
Bishop, Elizabeth, 164
Bissoondath, Neil, 133, 136, 139n. 9
Blair, Frederick, 260–61
Bloom, Harold, 73
Bloor, David, 202
Blue and Brown Books (Wittgenstein), 194, 203–204
Boas, Franz, 6, 84–93, 100, 103, 105–106, 108–109n. 10
book, people of the, 72–73
books, love of, 279–87
Bosker, Baruch, 70–71
Boston Globe, 152
Boyarin, Daniel and Jonathan, 259, 271–72
Bread Loaf School of English, 42
British Museum, 128
Burchfield, Robert, 189, 146–47, 157–59, 164, 168n. 7
business/school partnership, 41–54

cabala tradition, 73
Campise, John, 208–209
Canadian Broadcasting Corporation (CBC), 162
Canadian Multiculturalism Act of 1987, 129–34
canon, literary, 7–8, 25–26
Carmichael, Stokely, 93–94
categories, creation of, 106, 122–40
Chase, Stuart, 91
Chaucer, multicultural translation of, 7–8
Chin, Peter, 253–75
Chin, Wai Man, 265–66
Chin, Yuen Lung, 263–66
Chinese language, phonetic transcription of, 263–64
Chow, Rey, 265
Christian Science Monitor, 149
citation practice, 64–67
civil rights movement, 92
"civilization," 95–96
class, social, 60–78, 230–31
classroom: critical thinking in, 74–75, 106; English in, 181, 280–81; mainstream, 60–66; projects in, 7–8, 23–24, 41–54
Clifford, James, 88
Cole, Michael, 59–60
collecting as pedagogical practice, 86
Columbus, Cristopher, 86, 258
Coming of Age in America (Friedenberg), 227–32
commerce and state, intersection of, 22–23
compulsory school attendance, 228–29
computer-mediated communication (CMC) project, 41–54
Condit, Celeste, 106
conferences, academic, 239–52
Confessions (Augustine), 198, 199
Confucius, 269–70
Congressional Record, 151
copying of texts, 19–20
coyotes, 17–18, 20, 32
Createch, Inc., 42–54

Createch Pacific News, 43, 51, 53–54
Crèvecoeur, J. Hector St. John de, 134, 139n. 11
culture: comparative study of, 127–28; diaspora in, 253–75; and globalization, 103–105, 111–12n. 30; history of concept, 83–106, 107nn. 1, 3; and imperialism, 85–91, 103; literate/oral divisions in, 59–78; loss of, 93; and nation, 97–106, 111nn. 25–29, 129; and race, 7–8, 84–97; and schools, 83, 85

definitional process, 174–82, 184n. 1, 195–206, 213, 217n. 1
Delany, Martin, 93
Derrida, Jacques, 16–17, 29–30, 33n. 2, 33–34n. 5, 66, 190
Derrida at the Little Big Horn (Ulmer), 30
Dialog online database, 159
diasporic culture, 253–75
dictionaries: authority of, 165–66, 168n. 8; commercial editing of, 145–68; computerization of, 158; and gender, 171–82; limitations of, 145–46; and meaning, 190; philosophical impossibility of, 188–213; publishers of, 172–82; sources for, 147; Wittgenstein and, 187–88
difference: in gender, 85, 108nn. 7–8, 131; in language, 171–82; political history of, 131–32
Dignity of Youth and Other Atavisms, The (Friedenberg), 233–35
Dirlik, Arif, 105
Disuniting of America, The (Schlesinger), 134–35
Dreyfus Affair, 122–23
Dryden, John, 164
Du Bois, W. E. B., 131
Dylan, Bob, 63

education: business partnership in, 41–54; and categories, 106, 122–40; and collecting practice, 87; conferences on, 239–52; Friedenberg on, 224–35; and globalization, 101–105, 111–12n. 30, 112nn. 33–34; and identity politics, 121–40; and imperialism, 282–84; and Internet, 41–54; postmodern opportunity in, 31–32; and race, 94–95, 109–10n. 17, 130–32, 256; writing on, 224–25
Einstein, Albert, 246
Elazer, Rabbi, 67, 69–70, 72
Eleazer, Rabbi, 72
electronic communication, student-adult, 41–54
Eliezer, Rabbi, 72
Eliot, T. S., 281
e-mail, classroom use of, 41–54, 286
Endacott, G. B., 264–65
essayist tradition: American, 226–35; British, 62–67, 226–35
ethnocentrism, 62, 67, 102
eugenics movement, 90–91
Evans, Walker, 281–82
expression, clarity of, 48–49

Fairclough, Norman, 6–7, 12n. 8
feminism, 125, 171–82, 254
Feminist Dictionary, A (Kramarae/Treichler), 166, 179–80
Finnegan, Ruth, 59
First Nations people, 96–97, 110n. 18, 257
Fish, Stanley, 74–75
FitzGerald, Edward, 50
"flaming," 42
Flexner, Suart Berg, 154–56
Foucault, Michel, 84, 121
Frege, Gottlob, 187–88, 191
Friedenberg, Edgar Z., 6, 223–35
"From Utterance to Text: The Bias of Language in Speech and Writing" (Olson), 60–66

Gage Canadian Dictionary, 160–62
Gage Educational Publishing Company, 146, 160–66
Gage Senior Dictionary, 160–62
Gap clothing company, 30–31, 35n. 14
gender difference, 85, 108nn. 7–8, 171–82
Gershuny, H. Lee, 172–73, 181
Gibson, Gordon, 97
Gibson, Thomas, 178
Gingrich, Newt, 100
Giroux, Henry, 14, 230
Gladstone, Donna and William, 96
Glas (Derrida), 17
global-education model, 101–102
globalization, 103–105, 111–12n. 30, 271
Gómez-Peña, Guillermo, 105
Gove, Philip, 145–46, 150, 152, 153, 164
Gouws, Rufus, 206
Graff, Harvey, 63
grammar, 47–48, 66
grammatology, 29–30
Gramsci, Antonio, 233
"grand narratives," 24–25
"great divide" theory, 59
Greek phonetic alphabet, 62, 65–66, 77n. 3
Gregg, R. J., 161
Gutenberg, Johannes, 285

Haggadah, the, 5, 61, 66–78, 77nn. 5–6
Han Dynasty, 258
Heath, Shirley Brice, 59, 75
Hebrew language, 68–76
Heiltsuk Nation, 96–97
Hendrie, Tim, 160–62
Herbert, Christopher, 86
Heritage Language programs, 129–30
hip-hop, 21
Ho, Feng Shan, 259
Holocaust, the, 259–60, 266, 274–75
Holzer, Jenny, 27–28
homoeroticism, 233

homographs, 65–66
honor, concept of, 123–25, 132
hooks, bell, 25
Houghton Mifflin, 146, 149–52, 163–66
Hugo, Victor, 285
Hutcheon, Linda, 14–15

IBM, 285, 287n. 5
identity: and diaspora, 254–75; and naming, 269–70; politics of, 121–40
Ideology, Culture, and the Process of Schooling (Giroux), 230
"If You Lived Here" (Rosler), 26
illiteracy, 4–5
"image commodities," 105
"Image World," 15–16
immediacy in electronic communication, 41, 43–47
Immigration Act of 1923, Canada, 260–61
Immortality (Kundera), 14
imperialism, European, 85–91, 98, 103, 106, 108n. 6, 255–75, 282–84
Independent People (Laxness), 282
intellectual property, 21, 34n. 8
Internet, 41–54
Interpersonal Computing and Technology, 42
interpretation, 62–76, 78n. 9, 86
interviewing skills, 43–47
Israel Haggagah for Passover, An, 71

Jameson, Frederic, 21, 34n. 10
Jew as term, 210, 219n. 11
Jews: in China, 258–59; diasporic culture of, 253–75; identity of, 271–72; racial status of, 253, 261
Joan of Arc, 123
Johnson, Samuel, 148, 164, 167n. 3, 178, 190–91
Jose, Rabbi, 72
Judaism, 67–76, 78n. 8, 262, 271–72

Kaplan, E. Ann, 14
Kedourie, Elie, 98–99
Kermode, Frank, 75
Kersey, John, 178
Khayyam, Omar, 50
Khomeini, Ayatollah, 22
Kimball, Roger, 95–96
King, Mackenzie, 262
Knight, Phil, 104
knowledge: good of, 283–86; and power, 204; social theory of, 202–204; as term, 204–205
Knowledge Is Power Program (KIPP), 4–5
Kramarae, Cheris, 166, 179–80
Kristeva, Julia, 136–37
Kublai Kahn, 258
Kundera, Milan, 14

language: acquisition of, 198–200, 218n. 6; difference in, 171–82; as framing world, 3–4; habits of, 212; inadequacy of, 66; laws of, 100, 129–30; and logic, 191–92; vs. mathematics, 187–88; oral vs. written, 75–76, 77n. 1, 151, 156, 159, 164, 167–68n. 5, 252n. 3; philosophy of, 187–213; and race/culture, 7–8; words in, 196–201
language games, 199, 203, 207, 211–12
law as oral practice, 64–65
Laxness, Halldór, 282
Let Us Now Praise Famous Men (Agee), 281–82
Letters from an American Farmer (Crèvecoeur), 134
Lévi-Strauss, Claude, 16, 273–74
lexicography: commercial practices in, 145–68; and philosophy, 187–213; and schools, 172–82
Lexis-Nexis, 156, 159

libraries, love of, 281–86
literacy: critical, 6, 8–9; cultural, 25; and democracy, 7–10; as ending illiteracy, 4–5; vs. orality, 59–78, 252n. 3; postmodern, 13–32; range of topics in, 3–4; researchers in, 62–63; and self-presentation, 46; students of, 15; as term, 4; visual, 13–18
literature: anthologies of, 181; canons in, 7–8, 25–26; deconstructing, 13–15; and meaning, 207–208; vs. social sciences, 284–85
Locke, John, 62, 67
Loewen, James W., 97–98
Los Angeles riots, 256
Los Angeles Times, 151
Lu, Zhengwei, 263–64
Lucaites, John, 106
Luke, Allan, 6–8
Luther, Martin, 62, 66–67, 71
Lyotard, Jean-François, 24–25

magazine-publishing project, 23–24
Malcolm X, 94
Malinowski, Bronislaw, 89–91, 109n. 14
marginal interjection practice, 63–64
McLuhan, Marshall, 233–34
Mead, Margaret, 88–89, 91
meaning: circulation of, 21–22; and dictionaries, 190–213; as term, 206–207; theories of, 201–209; webs of, 32; and word usage, 200–201, 204, 206, 218n. 9
Meaning of Meaning, The (Ogden/Richards), 200–201
Merriam-Webster, 146, 147, 150, 152–53, 163–66, 167nn. 2, 5
Michaels, Walter Benn, 93
Miller, Kelly, 131
Milton, John, 207

Ministry of Education, British Columbia, 102–103, 130
Ministry of Education and Training, Ontario, 130
"miscegenation," 90–91, 109n. 14
Mish, Frederick, 152–53
Moore, G. E., 191
multiculturalism, 83, 85, 94–96, 100–101, 107nn. 2, 4, 110n. 23, 124–29, 254, 272
Murray, Elizabeth, 157
Murray, James, 147, 157–60, 164, 178, 190, 193, 205
museum artifact display practice, 92
Muslims, French, 124–25

naming, power of, 203–206, 210–11, 269–70, 274–75
Nation of Islam, 94
National Council of Teachers of English conference, 173–74
National Geographic, 92
nationalism: and culture, 97–106, 111nn. 25–29; and identity, 121–25, 135–36; and race, 136, 253
Nature, 153
Nebuchadrezzar, King, 258
Need for Roots, The (Weil), 121–22
neo-Marxism, 230
neo-Nazis, 274
New Capitalism, 239–43
New England Journal of Education, 4
New Oxford English Dictionary, 150, 157
New York Times, 146, 149, 151, 152, 154, 155, 156, 163
New York Times Book Review, 281
New Yorker, the, 146, 153, 159, 163
Nike shoe company, 104, 112n. 32
"non-assimilable races," 261–62
None Is Too Many (Abella/Troper), 260–61
Notre Dame of Paris (Hugo), 285

Ogden, C. K., 200–201

Olson, David R., 60–66, 70–71, 73–74, 76
"one drop" rule, 122
on-line databases, 148, 156, 159–60, 162, 165–66
oral culture, 59–78, 151, 156, 159, 164, 167–68n. 5, 252n. 3
Orientalism (Said), 122
Oxford Centre for Computing in the Humanities, 159
Oxford English Dictionary (OED), 146–47, 157–60, 167–68n. 5, 178–82, 184n. 2, 190, 193, 196, 205–207, 209
Oxford English Dictionary, Supplement to, 146–47, 157–59, 189
Oxford University Press, 146–47, 157–60, 163–66

Pacific Regional Advisory Board, 262
Pacific Rim Education Initiative, 102–103
papers, academic, readings of, 245–46, 251–53n. 2
Parker Vacumatic pen, 255, 258, 263, 273–75
Passover service, 5, 61, 66–78
pasticheur role, 19–20
pedagogy in electronic communication, 41, 43, 51–53
Phaedrus (Plato), 66, 190, 217n. 1
Philosophical Investigations (Wittgenstein), 194, 196, 198, 205
phonics, 4–5
Plato, 66, 190, 205, 217n. 1, 229
Pollock, Jackson, 27
Polo, Marco, 258–59
postmodernism, 13–35
power: and identity, 271–72; and naming, 203–206, 210–11, 269–70; packaging of, 27–28; and self-presentation, 46
Principia Mathematica (Russell/Whitehead), 187–88
print, invention of, 285
Proper Study of Mankind, The (Chase), 91

Proust, Marcel, 207–208, 281

Q-technique, 227

race: construction of, 131–32; and culture, 84–97, 110nn. 20–22, 129; and diaspora, 253–75; and identity, 121–23; and language, 7–8, 129–30; and nationalism, 97–99, 105–106, 129–30, 134, 136, 253
racism: anti-Chinese, 253–75; and culture, 84, 107n. 5, 255–75; and education, 105, 130–32, 256; undoing, 31
Random House, 146, 154–56, 163–66
Random House Dictionary, 156, 172
Ravitch, Diane, 6
reading: goal of, 5–6; teaching of, 4–5
Reagan, Vincent, 206
recognition, 125–29, 138n. 4
Remembering Postmodernism (Hutcheon), 14–15
Remembrance of Things Past (Proust), 207–208, 281
Retail Merchants Association, 261
Rhodes, Cecil, 103
Richards, I. A., 200–201
rock videos, 13–14
Roderick, Rick, 104
Romanticism, 98–99
Rosler, Martha, 26
Rubáiyát, The (Khayyam), 50
Rushdie, Salman, 22
Russell, Bertrand, 187–88, 191–92, 194, 197–98

Said, Edward, 122
samizdat, 24
Sarrasine (Balzac), 18–19, 22
Sartre, Jean-Paul, 121–22
Scargill, Matthew, 161
Schlesinger, Arthur, 134–35
schools: business partnership with, 41–54; compulsory attendance, 228–29; and culture, 83, 85; dictionary in, 171–82; and

nationalism, 97–104;
politicization of, 233–35;
private, 230–31; social
psychology of, 225–35;
technology in, 41–54, 283,
285–86
School Dictionary, 175, 176
Scribner, Sylvia, 59
self-presentation, 46
*Selling Illusions: The Cult of
Multiculturalism in Canada*
(Bissoondath), 133
Sentence Completion Test, 227
Serra, Richard, 29
Sex and Temperament (Mead), 91
Shakespeare, William, 164
Simon and Schuster, 174
Smith, Anthony, 99
Smith, Dorothy, 18
social studies curriculum, 97–104,
106
Socrates, 66, 205
Soukhanov, Anne, 149–52
speech sounds, 65–66
state and individual, 232–35
Stoler, Ann Laura, 90–91
Sto:lo Nation, 96–97
Street, Brian, 62–64
Supreme Court of Canada, 96–97
Survival Series (Holzer), 27–28
symbol systems, extralinguistic, 66
S/Z (Barthes), 18, 22

Taylor, Charles, 125–29, 133, 136
technology, new, 41–54, 148, 156,
158–60, 162, 165–66, 283–
86
Television Delivers People (Serra), 29
text: and authority, 165–66, 171–72;
copying of, 19–20; as
defining world, 18–19;
interpretation of, 62–78; oral
basis of, 61, 66–78; sacred,
70–71; social, 31; vs.
utterance, 60–66, 164
Thomas, Dylan, 280–81
Time, 154, 163
Torah, the, 68, 73

Tractatus Logico-Philosophicus
(Wittgenstein), 188–89, 192–
94, 197, 213, 217n. 3
transliteration, 263–64, 266–68
Treichler, Paula, 166, 179–80
Tristes tropiques (Lévi-Strauss), 16
Troper, Harold, 260
Truth, Sojourner, 268
truth as language game, 211–12
TV Guide, 153
Tye, Barbara Benham and Kenneth A.,
101–102
typography, 70

Ulmer, Gregory, 21, 29–30
Updike, John, 153
utterance vs. text, 60–66, 164

Vai, the, 59–60
Van der Peet, Dorothy Marie, 96
Vanishing Adolescent, The
(Friedenberg), 223, 232–33
video, 13–14, 29–30
visual literacy, 13–18

Wade-Giles method
Wall Street Journal, 149, 163
Ways of Seeing (Berger), 179
Ways with Words (Heath), 59
Webster, Noah, 178
Webster's High School Dictionary, 175
Webster's New World Dictionary,
174, 176
*Webster's Third International
Dictionary*, 150
Weil, Simone, 6, 121–25, 129, 137
Whalen, George, 281
White Canada Association, 260–61
whole-language method, 4–5, 23
Williams, Raymond, 21–23
Willinsky, A. I., 266–68
Wittgenstein, Ludwig, 6, 66, 180,
187–219
Wittgenstein's Nephew (Bernhard),
205–206
women: as category, 126–27, 138n. 2;
language and, 171–82;
objectification of, 179–80

"Word Watch" (Soukhanov), 151–52
World Reporter online database, 159
World War I, 192
World War II, 259–60
Wright, William, 42
Writers in Electronic Residence Program, 42
writing: as constituting reality, 17–21; on education, 224–35; essayist tradition in, 62–67, 226, 235; goal of, 5–6; history of, 63; and Internet, 41–54; plain style in, 62; rhetoric vs. logic in, 67
Wu, David Yen-Ho, 270

"yellow peril," 260–61
Yiddish language, 262, 268
Yoshimoto, Mitsuhiro, 105

Studies in the Postmodern Theory of Education

General Editors
Joe L. Kincheloe & Shirley R. Steinberg

Counterpoints publishes the most compelling and imaginative books being written in education today. Grounded on the theoretical advances in criticism, feminism, and postmodernism in the last two decades of the twentieth century, Counterpoints engages the meaning of these innovations in various forms of educational expression. Committed to the proposition that theoretical literature should be accessible to a variety of audiences, the series insists that its authors avoid esoteric and jargonistic languages that transform educational scholarship into an elite discourse for the initiated. Scholarly work matters only to the degree it affects consciousness and practice at multiple sites. Counterpoints' editorial policy is based on these principles and the ability of scholars to break new ground, to open new conversations, to go where educators have never gone before.

For additional information about this series or for the submission of manuscripts, please contact:
        Joe L. Kincheloe & Shirley R. Steinberg
        c/o Peter Lang Publishing, Inc.
        275 Seventh Avenue, 28th floor
        New York, New York 10001

To order other books in this series, please contact our Customer Service Department:
        (800) 770-LANG (within the U.S.)
        (212) 647-7706 (outside the U.S.)
        (212) 647-7707 FAX

Or browse online by series:
        www.peterlangusa.com